The Trend of Corporate Social Responsibility in the EU

Editor

Li-Jiuan Chen-Rabich

Tamkang University Press

The Trend of Corporate Social Responsibility in the EU
Editor
Li-Jiuan Chen-Rabich

ISBN: 978-986-96071-3-1

Published in Taiwan by
Tamkang University Press
151, Yingzhuan Rd., Tamsui Dist., New Taipei City 25137, R.O.C.
Tel: 886-2-8631-8661; Fax: 886-2-8631-8660
http://www.tkupress.tku.edu.tw/
E-mail: tkupress@www2.tku.edu.tw

CONTENTS

Preface

It is an honor to take place the third-year Jean Monnet Chair conference at Tamkang University in Taipei.

The Corporate Social Responsibility (CSR) has a comprehensive content. CSR has become a widespread topic in business and public discussion. CSR covers interests of companies, consumers and stakeholders. Responsibility aspects have already been integrated into the strategic management in many companies.

First of all, thanks to the EU's cofounding for this international conference. CSR is currently a global issue. The EU has actively engaged in the CSR since 1995 not only through its reform of the company law and financial market law, but also through raising awareness and understanding of CSR among stakeholders and the general public.

CSR has become a more important issue after the global financial crisis in 2008. The EU published a new policy on CSR in 2011. Enterprises have to behave themselves to integrate social, environmental, ethical and human rights concerns into their business operations and core strategy in close collaboration with their stakeholders in order to fully meet their social responsibility.

The German legal system is a model of the continental legal system and has a great influence in Japan, Korea and Taiwan. The interaction between the EU and Germany is increasingly close due to the Germany's membership and the loyalty to the EU. The EU's CSR has an indirect influence on the three countries by the linkage with the German legal system.

It is a great pleasure and honorable to have the opportunity of sharing the CSR practices from Japan, Korea and Taiwan. There are seven papers related to the CSR practice in Japan, Korea and Taiwan under aspects of corporation law, labor protection and consumer protection.

The EU plays a global actor for a long time. Trade is an important instrument for global governance and implementing the European value. The EU has an exclusive competence for the common trade policy. The EU has recently concluded comprehensive free trade agreements with most trade partners. This type of free trade agreement is so-called new generation trade agreement. The new generation trade agreement also includes CSR value. Another five papers will be presented CSR under the aspect of the global governance.

Li-Jiuan Chen-Rabich
Jean Monnet Chair on European Trade Law
Director of Center for EU Studies, Tamkang University

CSR in the EU's Financial Market Law

Prof. Dr. Li-Jiuan Chen-Rabich

Jean Monnet Chair on European Trade Law

Director of Graduate Institute of European Studies

Director of Center for EU Studies

I. The development of the CSR in the EU

With the globalization and internationalization, the Corporate Social Responsibility (CSR) has increasing become an important issue, especially after the global financial crisis in 2008. The international community has paid more and more attention to the CSR in the multinational undertakings. The EU has taken a series of reform measures to enhance the CSR awareness and to promote the stable growth of the international economy.

The OECD proposed the Principles of Corporate Governance highlighting the close relation between the CSR and the good corporate governance.[1] The CSR program has a positive influence on the behavior of consumer. Shareholder and stakeholder recently have more and more concerned about the CSR.

The CSR is an instrument of the management, which enhances social concerns in the internal and external environment of corporation.[2] As a result, the corporate organization needs to be changed. The

---

[1] Yasemin Zengin Karaibrahimoğlu, "Corporate social responsibility in times of financial crisis," *African Journal of Business Management* Vol. 4 (4) 2010, p. 382.

[2] Activities of the European Commission on Corporate Social Responsibility, http.// ec.europa/eu/employment_social/speeches/2004/09090204_en.pdf (accessed 10 December 2010).

corporate takes its social responsibility for each stakeholder. The business objective of corporate has to create the economic and social value. The role of corporate is very important to balance the mutual interest and expectation for each stakeholder. It is also very crucial to the society and business environment.[3]

With the global change of the international trade and economy, every corporate has confronted more and more challenges of the multinational norms and regulations. The CSR includes lots of business activities with various economic, social and eco interests.[4] Each country has its own legal system and industrial structure. Therefore, some multinational undertakings have taken advantage of these international legal loopholes. Some undertakings use the difference of the wage levels and the protection regulation under the labor law. They have relocated their production plants to those countries with lower wage level and insufficient labor protection. Recently, many multinational undertakings have taken into account their international image and reputation. Therefore, they gradually have voluntarily complied the CSR.

The CSR has not only become the theory of the economic and business ethics but also the legislative action to obligate undertakings to fulfill their social responsibility.[5] The explanation of corporate governance according to the German Corporate Governance Code is a good example.

The CSR has gradually become a very important issue since 1980s. The EU underlines the meanings of the CSR, which contributes to the sustainable development and strengthening the competitiveness. The European Council in 2000 in Lisbon required all member states to enhance the CSR awareness. The CSR Green Paper has been published

---

[3] Yasemin Zengin Karaibrahimoğlu, op.cit., p. 382.

[4] Axel Birk, Corporate Responsibility, unternehmerische Selbstverpflichtungen und unlauterer Wettbewerb, GRUR 2011, S.196.

[5] Gerhard Karl Homann/Franz Blome-Drees, Wirtschafts- und Unternehmensethik, 1992 Göttingen: Vandenhoeck & Ruprecht, Kap.2.1.3.

in 2001.[6] The European Commission proposed a CSR Communication[7] in 2002 and established a CSR Forum, which consists of business representatives, trade unions and civil representatives. The CSR Forum reached a consensus of the CSR concept. A social dialogue has been introduced at different levels that efficiently contributed to the CSR. The role of employee, representative of employee and trade unions must be enhanced. In addition, NGO, consumer and investor and so on must play a more important role for achieving the CSR. All of these concrete actions were an important milestone for creating the EU as an excellent model of CSR in the world.[8]

The CSR contributes to the sustainable development and enhancing the European innovative potential and competitiveness. The promotion of the CSR becomes the core of the growth and jobs.[9] The promotion of the CSR aims to perform sustainable development. The CSR reflects the core value of the EU. The European Commission expects that all member states, undertakings and all stakeholders build a close partnership to make the EU as an excellent model of the CSR.

II. The concrete measures of the CSR after the global financial crisis

The European Commission reiterated the EU strategy to promote the CSR. The CSR is a key element to ensure the labor protection and the confidence of consumer. The CSR is one of the goals of the Europe 2020 Strategy. The CSR can assist to recover the business confidence, especially against the emerging economic recession after the global

---

[6] COM (2001) 366 final.

[7] COM (2002) 347 final.

[8] COM (2006) 136 final., p. 5.

[9] COM (2006) 136 final.

financial crisis.[10]

The business confidence is an important basis for the stable social market economy in the EU. The European Commission highlighted that the CSR is the right way for the recovery from the financial crisis. The CSR is advantageous for the society, environment and business.

Facilitating CSR has recently become one of the priority policies of the EU. The CSR has been promoted by the European Alliance for Corporate Social Responsibility. The dialogue of the European Multistakeholder Forum on Corporate Social Responsibility has been promoted.

The CSR is a necessary value for building a new economic and social system. The European Commission proposed "A renewed of the EU Strategy 2011-2014 for Corporate Social Responsibility" on 25. October 2011.[11] The CSR is a core of the Integrated Industrial Policy for the Globalization Era[12] within the Europe 2020 Strategy.

The global financial crisis led to the economic recession and social impact. The consumers' trust and confidence in business have been distorted to certain degree. Consumer paid more attention to the CSR and ethic behavior of corporations. Hence, the European Commission realized that it was necessary to review the CSR in order to create sustainable growth, responsible social behavior of corporations and continuingly create good conditions for jobs.[13]

The European Commission appealed large undertakings to comply international acknowledged CSR principles and guidelines such as OECD Guidelines for Multinational Enterprises, UN Global Compact,

---

[10] European Commission, Enterprise and Industry, E & I online magazine on 29.07.2010, p. 2.

[11] COM (2011) 681 final.

[12] COM (2010) 614 final.

[13] COM (2011) 681 final., p. 4.

ISO 26000 Guidance Standard on Social Responsibility, ILO Tripartie Declaration of Principles Concerning Multinational Enterprises and Social Policy, UN Guiding Principles on Business and Human Rights. These international acknowledged principles and guidelines have established the global framework of the CSR. The EU has followed the global framework to set up own CSR policy.[14]

The CSR includes eight core values according to the above mentioned international acknowledged principles and guidelines as followings: human right, practice of labor and jobs, environmental issues, prevention against corruption and bribe, integration of the disabled, consumers' interest, promoting social and environmental responsibility by the supply chain, disclosure of non-financial information.[15]

The main contents of the Action Agenda from 2011 to 2014 by the European Commission included:[16]

1. Enhancing the visibility of the CSR and promoting good practice.
2. Improving and tracking standards of business confidence.
3. Improving the procedure of self-discipline and common regulation.
4. Enhancing the market rewards for the CSR.
5. Improving the disclosure of the CSR and environmental information.
6. Integrating the CSR concept into the education, training and research.
7. Emphasizing the CSR policy in the member states.
8. Furthermore combining the European and global CSR research approach.

---

[14] COM (2011) 681 final., pp. 6-7.

[15] COM (2011) 681 final., p. 7.

[16] COM (2011) 681 final., pp. 8-13.

All member states must develop or upgrade their own program or priority plan to promote and support the CSR within the Europe 2020 Strategy. All member states, undertakings and all stakeholders have to work together to comply international principles and guidelines.[17]

The European Commission has proposed many regulations to react against the financial crisis after the global financial crisis in order to ensure more responsible and more transparent financial system. The investor can efficiently allocate their capital and achieve long-term investment through adequate related non-financial information. The disclosure of social and environmental information is one of the priorities to strengthen complying the CSR. The EU has enacted No. 95 Directive of Non-Financial Information in 2014.[18] Large enterprises with more than 500 employees have to disclose policy, risk, environmental affairs, social and labor interests, human respects, anti-bribe and anti-corruption, diversity of directors in their management report according to this Directive. The management report has to provide a comprehensive business performance landscape for investors and stakeholders.

III. Conclusion

To sum up, the EU has actively developed the CSR since 2000. The CSR has become an important instrument to achieve the smart, sustainable and inclusive growth of the Europe 2020 Strategy. The CSR is not only a core of the European Platform against Poverty and Social Exclusion but also of the Single European Market Act.

---

[17] COM (2011) 681 final., p. 13.

[18] http://ec.europa.eu/internal_market/accounting/non-financial_reporting/index_en.htm.

Toward Open Shareholders' Meetings

Prof. Maki Saito

Faculty of Law, Kyoto University

I. Traditional business ethics in Japan and CSR concept

1. Serving the public as raison d'être

The harmonization of commercial profit and social values has long been one of the core principles in traditional Japanese business ethics, before the CSR concept penetrated the international business community. The ethics shared among business persons and the general public suggest that corporations can and should serve society and actually in many ways as mentioned below.

First, the core business of successful corporations usually meets the demands of society. Corporations are successful because they offer goods and services to consumers who need and can afford them. This aspect tends to be forgotten when we speak of CSR, where adverse effects of profit-pursuing are often emphasized. "Companies are public institutions of society." These are the words of Matsushita Konosuke, the founder of Panasonic, a Japanese electric company. Matsushita successfully disseminated electric products to poor rural areas and firmly believed that corporate prosperity should be aligned with the prosperity of the society in which it found itself.

Second, corporations revitalize regional economies through commercial transactions and employment during the course of their business activities. In this process, some profits from the business are returned to the local residents. One of the family precepts of Omi shonin, is called sanpo yoshi (benefit for all three sides). Omi shonin is the business people in the Omi area near Osaka, who engaged in wholesale sales from the early modern to the modern period. Sanpo means three sides: vendors, buyers, and society. Since yoshi means to go well, sanpo yoshi means benefits for vendors, buyers, and society. Many Japanese retailers and trading companies originate from these people, Itochu, for example. During famine and recession, they restored their shops or temples or did other public works to revitalize the local economies instead of simply distributing money to the poor, which is known as otasukebushin (charity public works).

Third, corporations can indirectly serve society by conducting business without harming society or nature in the areas where they are active. The Sumitomo Group, which managed a copper mine on Shikoku Island since the late 17th century, increased its mining production during the Japanese industrial revolution in the Meiji period, which began in 1868, causing sulfurous acid gas pollution in the local neighborhoods. According to a study describing the history of the Sumitomo group[1], Sumitomo imposed itself the production limitation until it finds a way of fully removing harmful gas, besides promising to pay damages, although merely paying damages to neighbors would have been much cheaper. After struggling for over 30 years, they finally mastered technologies that did not emit any harmful gas with the support of a German engineer, Hugo Petersen.

This attitude of the traditional business ethics that encourages business people to serve the public is partly influenced by samurai behavior standards[2]. One example is Ishida Baigan (1685-1744), an

---

[1] Sumitomo Shiryokan (ed.), *Sumitomo No Rekishi* (Shibunkaku, 2014), pp. 186-192.

[2] Katsuragi Takao, *Jihi to Shojiki No Kokyo Tetsugaku* (Keio University Press, 2014), pp. 131-164.

Edo era philosopher, who influenced business people around Kyoto and Osaka. He opened a private school in 1729 when Japan's monetary economy developed into one from which merchants became rich. He advocated honesty, diligence, and thrift and defined a merchant's profit as identical as the samurai's reward in the sense that merchants deserve it because they are serving society. This idea helped justify the accumulation of merchant wealth almost 200 years before Max Weber's *The Protestant Ethic and the Spirit of Capitalism* and simultaneously linked wealth and the public interest.

The famous Berle-Dodd debate in America triggered by Adolf A. Berle's article in 1931, *Corporate Power as Powers in Trust*[3], which addressed whether corporations should serve society or shareholders, also gained traction in Japanese academic circles and legal studies from the 1950s to the 1970s, especially after air and water pollution became social problems[4]. But the discussion did not deepen in Japan at that time for a couple of reasons. The idea that corporations are socially responsible did not sound novel in Japan. Furthermore, at that time Japanese legal circles lacked scholars who emphasized that the only purpose of corporations is to make profit for their shareholders, so little energy was devoted to this discussion.

2. *Increased interest in CSR concept*

Since the beginning of the 21st century, the concept of corporate social responsibility (CSR) has gradually spread throughout the Japanese

---

[3] A. A. Berle, "Corporate Power as Powers in Trust," *Harvard Law Review* 44 (1931): p. 1049.

[4] Tanaka Seiji, "Kabushiki Kaisha No Shakaiteki Sekinin Ni Tsuite No Shohojo N Ri'poronteki Kosatsu," in *Shojiho Kenkyu* (3) (Chikura Shobo, 1977), p. 81; Kawamoto Ichiro, "Kigyo No Shakaiteki Sekinin," *Jurisuto* no. 578 (1977): p. 106; Morita Akira, *Gendai Kigyo No Shakaiteki Sekinin* (Shojihomukenkyukai, 1978).

business community[5]. One trigger might have been the publication of the Green Papers on the Corporate Social Responsibility by the European Commission. Its impact was rather indirect, however. Such a policy debate in EU attracted the attention of Japanese policy makers, including the Ministry of Economy, Trade and Industry (METI), and social-conscious CEOs of leading companies, but it had limited influence on Japanese business practices in general without any regulations or other enforcement mechanisms. A more decisive event was the UN Global Compact initiative, which started in 2000. This initiative promulgated the word sustainability among the members of the Japanese business community. Currently literature in the field of management often links the CSR concept with this initiative.

Other factors have fueled the recent increased interest in the CSR concept in Japan. The first factor is the globalization of Japanese business activities. Spurred awareness of social responsibility among business leaders reflects not only the fact that due to the globalization of corporate activities, more people will be affected by corporate activities. Japanese companies were exposed to more social-conscious consumers, especially in Europe, and international NGOs that are keen on social sustainability since they are more active in western countries through branch offices and subsidiaries. Moreover, the extraterritorial application of such foreign laws as US foreign anti-corrupt law and the UK Modern Slavery Act encouraged Japanese businesspersons to understand the policies that support such international movements. In other words, the interest in the CSR discussion increased among business leaders as they were more aware of the importance of global risk management[6].

---

[5] For the historic overview, *see* Nomura Shuya, "Kigyo No Shakaiteki Sekinin," in *Kaishaho No Soten*, ed. Hamada Michiyo and Iwahara Shinsaku (Yuhikaku, 2009), p. 6.

[6] Kawamura Kanji, "Naibutosei to Risuku Manejimento (3)," *JCA Journal* 62, no. 6 (2015): p. 80; Kawamura Kanji, "Naibutosei to Risuku Manejimento (4)," *JCA Journal* 62, no. 7 (2015): p. 71.

Second, due to the privatization of some important public utilities, such as the postal office and the national railway service (a move that started in the mid-1980s), the compatibility between the promotion of public interests and the pursuit of profit in private enterprise has been recognized as a critical issue[7]. This idea is especially true for the management in such business areas, which must justify continuing activities that are relatively less profitable but still needed by the local residents. During the Great East Japan Earthquake in 2011, the Japan Freight Railway company, which was part of the former national railway service, successfully delivered gasoline quickly to the disaster areas, overcoming many difficulties. Since the track on the Pacific side was unusable due to the damage caused by the earthquake, gasoline was delivered through a railway on the side of the Sea of Japan[8]. The railroad company had to achieve the following steps to deliver gasoline: secured diesel locomotives to pass through areas without electricity; located engineers who could drive such old locomotives; repaired the railroad tracks damaged by the earthquake; and confirmed the safety of these new routes. Although quickly accomplishing these tasks was expensive, time-consuming, and unprofitable in the short-term, the management and the company employees were all aware of their social mission.

Third, as Japanese citizens have been more and more exposed to information about what is happening in the world[9], they have become more aware of the social values promoted in the international society, and entrepreneurs are identifying opportunities to promote social values (not in non-profit organizations) in corporate forms. These people are called social entrepreneurs. Motherhouse, a handbag producer founded in 2006,

---

[7] Symposium, "Ima Naze CSR nanoka," *Horitsujiho* 76, no. 12 (2004): pp. 4-5.

[8] Kibayashi Norihiko, "Solutions for JR Freight Affected by the Great East Japan Earthquake," *Butsuryu Mondai Kenkyu* 57 (2011): p. 7.

[9] Ogino Aiichi, "Kigyo No Shakaiteki Sekinin," *National Diet Library Issue Brief* 476 (2005): pp. 1-3.

which is one of the most successful examples among social enterprises in Japan, established a factory in Bangladesh.

3. How CSR concept distinguishes itself from traditional Japanese business ethics

It is difficult to determine whether traditional business ethics lead companies in the same direction as the corporate social responsibility provoked by the European Commission or the Global Compact. However, it might be useful to cite some aspects that traditional Japanese business ethics do not cover but that are emphasized by the present international movements.

First, international initiatives require corporations to focus on people and nature whenever their activities will directly or indirectly reach the end of their supply chain, for example. Traditional business ethics encourages corporations to consider the interests of society, but society here means the local society in which these corporations are located. Therefore, both Japanese companies and consumers are often indifferent to the negative effects of the activities of Japanese business on foreign society and nature.

Second, in Japan, it is traditionally regarded as a virtue, not only in business but also in general to secretly do good works without letting them become public. But an important aspect of the CSR concept is the requirement that corporations report their efforts to promote social values to let the public evaluate their activities.

Third, the European CSR initiative stressed the unemployment problem. In contrast, in Japan unemployment has not been an urgent issue, since Japan enjoyed a low unemployment rate due to its lifetime employment practice and labor shortages during the postwar economic growth, which lasted from the middle 1950s to the early 1990s. Lifetime employment is a business practice that basically hires workers until retirement. Even though no legal requirement stipulates that

Japanese companies provide such lifetime employment to every worker, this practice has prevailed due to the postwar labor shortage and case law which limits employer's right to dismiss workers. In other words, Japanese business had already met one of the most critical social demands with which the CSR concept expects corporations to cope. A more serious problem is the polarization of the labor market between regular and nonregular employees. Almost half of Japan's current workforce is classified as nonregular[10]. Improvement of their working conditions is rarely mentioned in Japanese CSR discussions.

4. Underlying CSR policies

One underlying CSR policy is the internalization of externalities in welfare economics[11]. Companies do not always bear the negative costs incurred on the side of stakeholders due to market malfunctions, which causes overproduction. In basic economics, the necessity of taxation and legal regulation is usually cited as a means to optimize production. However, social problems are usually complex and corporate activities are individual and diverse, so it is difficult to find a "one fit for all" solution. The political initiatives related to CSR encourage or even force corporate managers to find a solution suitable for their corporation by raising their awareness of the responsibility for stakeholders' interests through public discussion and other kinds of pressures from stakeholders or the NGOs representing them. Such a policy can be justified by the premise that every success of private corporations owes a debt to the stakeholders and the world.

Policy debates on CSR are not limited to the internalization of externalities. As indicated by the fact that unemployment was one of

---

[10] For the data and the current policy discussion, *see* http://www.mhlw.go.jp/stf/seisakunitsuite/bunya/koyou_roudou/part_haken/index.html.

[11] Iwai Katsuto and Komiyama Hiroshi, *Kaisha ha Shakai wo Kaerareru* (President Inc. 2014): pp. 14-15.

the triggers of the CSR debate in EU, the CSR concept was designed to encourage corporations to cope with various social problems that are not attributed to them or to even substitute for governments and other public institutions whose ability to adjust the interests of various members of the society has been challenged by globalization. This aspect of the CSR discussion goes beyond the internalization of (positive) externalities, as it is not self-evident, however, why private corporations will, or have to meet this expectation using their own resources to solve social problems that they themselves do not incur.

Both of these aspects underlying the CSR policy debate have been overlooked in Japanese business practices, where the CSR theme is often broached in management studies. Interest in such contexts is focused on how to exploit the maximum use of corporate social contributions for marketing and public relations. There only such examples are mentioned that seem successful from a marketing perspective, and less attention is paid to what the CSR concept expects from business, and whether these examples really satisfy it.

Moreover, in management theories the shareholders of corporations are often treated as merely one of the stakeholders who exercise some influence on corporate managers. Such an approach tends to underestimate the power on corporations wielded by the shareholders who can elect members to the board of directors.

II. Corporate governance in Japan and its recent development

1. Shareholder-oriented model

No provision in Japanese corporate law specifically defines a company's social responsibility. The Japanese Company Act has not adopted a codetermination system like Germany, either. All members of the board of directors are appointed at meetings of shareholders[12]. The board of directors appoints and controls management in turn. Board members assume the responsibility of operating the business for the corporation's interests. According to prevailing theory, the board should promote the interests of the shareholders except during financial crises when they should also consider the interests of the creditors[13].

This does not necessarily mean that corporations pursue commercial profit at the expense of other stakeholders, since the long-term success of the business usually depends on the cooperation and the reputation of other stakeholders. If shareholders pressure the management to pursue short-term profits and the capital market fails to evaluate long-term negative effects, then it will be difficult for management to ensure the business's long-term success, considering the interests of other stakeholders.

During the postwar decades, the management of Japanese listed corporations was free from the pressure of shareholders due to cross-shareholding and the limited liquidity of the undeveloped capital market. This structure changed in the late 1990s when banks and corporations began to sell their cross-holding shares due to accounting standards that required that financial products be evaluated based on their market value. When stock prices plummeted in 1990, the shareholding ratio of foreign investors began to consistently rise[14]. This tendency was spurred by the increased stock liquidity due to the sale of the cross-holding shares just mentioned. This structural change, which has made the management of listed corporations more vulnerable to pressure from the capital market

---

[12] Companies Act Art. 329 Sec. 1.

[13] *See, for example*, Egashira Kenjiro, *Kabushikikaishaho* (7th ed. Yuhikaku 2017), pp. 24-25; for the recent discussion, *see* Osugi Kenichi, "Kaisha ha Darenomonoka," in *Shojiho No Atarashii Soseki* (Shojihomu, 2014), p. 1.

[14] For the statistics, *see* the share ownership survey of the Tokyo Stock Exchange, https://www.jpx.co.jp/english/markets/statistics-equities/examination/01.html.

because the management can no longer fully control the outcomes of shareholders' meetings, is now being exposed to the threat of hostile takeovers and other types of shareholder activism.

2. Hedge fund activism

Especially in the United States and the United Kingdom, a new type of shareholder activism is emerging. One of its characteristics is that, although acquirers buy shares in the offeree company, they do not achieve control of the target company but only exercise pressure on management to some structural or strategic changes to help their company become more profitable and resell the stock relatively quickly[15]. It is difficult to grasp the current situation of such activism in Japan as long as contact with management is informal. Despite the often-expressed notion that activism remains unestablished in Japan, a recent empirical study positioned Japan as the country with the second most activism behind the United States[16].

Hedge funds that do not acquire control of the target corporation need the support of other shareholders to enforce their proposals. As a result of a proposal of hedge funds, if a strong rise in share prices is expected, it might be supported by other shareholders. This could happen even if the proposal is at the expense of the company's sustainable growth and the long-term negative effects on its stakeholders. It remains to be seen whether such behavior by hedge funds will be neutralized by the voting behavior of other institutional investors.

3. Stewardship code

In 2014, a working group established at the Financial Services

---

[15] *See, for example,* Lucian Bebchuk et al., "The Long-term Effects of Hedge Fund Activism," *Columbia Law Review* 115 (2015): p. 1085.

[16] Marco Becht et al., "Returns to Hedge Fund Activism: An International Study," *ECGI Finance Working Paper* 402/2014 (2017).

Agency announced a stewardship code, which should function as a code of conduct for institutional investors[17]. It recommends that institutional investors comply with these standards of action. However, institutional investors are not required to comply. The institutional investors who adopt the code is expected to publish a report on a comply-or-explain basis, which means that if they do not comply with any part of the code, they must explain why. 227 institutional shareholders have already adopted this code as of April 5, 2018[18].

Following the British model, the stewardship code requires that institutional investors actively engage with the companies in which they invest to enhance the enterprise value and the sustainable growth of companies on middle and long-term bases. The code is designed to encourage institutional investors to seek dialogues. In its current version, which was revised in March 2017[19], the stewardship code also encourages collective engagement, in which several institutional investors act together[20]. Regarding the exercise of voting rights, the amended code requires that the status of exercising voting rights be announced at annual general meetings for each target company and its agenda[21].

A code is expected through which institutional investors aim for long-term growth of the corporations in which they invest, not short-term benefits. This promotes the first aspect of the CSR policy: the internalization of externalities.

---

[17] The Council of Experts on the Stewardship Code, Principles for Responsible Institutional Investors (Japan's Stewardship Code): To promote sustainable growth of companies through investment and dialogue (April 7, 2014).

[18] For the data, *see* https://www.fsa.go.jp/en/refer/councils/stewardship/20160315.html.

[19] The Council of Experts on the Stewardship Code, Principles for Responsible Institutional Investors (Japan's Stewardship Code): To promote sustainable growth of companies through investment and dialogue (May 29, 2017) (hereafter cited as Code).

[20] Code, Guidance 4-4.

[21] Code, Guidance 5-3.

4. Growing ESG investment

In Japan, ESG investment has only recently increased, which considers the social, environmental, governance factors as well as financial ones. The turning point came in 2015 when the Japanese public pension fund, GPIF, signed the Principles for Responsible Investment (PRI)[22]. GPIF is a public pension fund, reportedly the largest of its kind in the world[23]. Due to the volume of its assets, its signature on the PRI greatly impacted both investors and the listed corporations. Growing ESG investment will promote the second aspect of the CSR concept (the substitution for government functions), because the listed companies will proactively meet social needs to gain higher reputations.

It would be too optimistic to stop here and argue that in this way, corporations will partly substitute for government functions to solve social problems. Japan's public pension scheme, which collects funds from every citizen starting at the age of 20 and guarantees an old age pension to each one, might suffer from a lack of financial resources in the near future because of Japan's aging population. Under the current government, in 2014 GPIF changed the allocation of its assets and shifted some of its funds from bond markets to stock markets to seek higher yields[24]. In this way, Japanese pension schemes are becoming more dependent on the stock market. Political pressure is being exerted on the government to raise stock prices and the payout ratio of the listed companies in the mid- and long-term. Meeting social needs and creating profit is very difficult in the world where there are many stakeholders

---

[22] *See* http://www.gpif.go.jp/operation/esg.html; for the growing importance of ESG investment in Japan, *see* Mizuguchi Takeshi, ESG toshi (Nihonkeizaishinbun Shu'pansha, 2017).

[23] For the recent statistics, *see* Willi Towers Watson, *Pensions & Investments* (September 2017), p.36.

[24] For its midterm investment strategies, *see* http://www.gpif.go.jp/operation/foundation/portfolio.html.

and NGOs that seek different values, some of which are probably contradictory.

5. *Prepared reform of company act*

Due to the increased presence of activist shareholders, institutional shareholders and ESG investments, the management of listed corporations must meet the complicated expectations of the capital market. Shareholder meetings will be more important opportunities for the stakeholders who hold shares in listed companies, directly or indirectly, through their representatives to express their wishes and for management to explain its business strategies and persuade shareholders to support them.

A company law subcommittee of the Legislative Council of the Ministry of Justice is now discussing corporate law reform[25]. One topic is to make it mandatory for listed corporations to electronically send invitations to shareholder meetings to reduce the time required to print and send such notices and enable early dispatches to ensure that foreign institutional investors have enough time to review the agenda[26]. Another topic is how to prevent the abusive use of the shareholder's right to propose agendas. But developments relating to CSR have not been discussed or how company law responds to these developments, since the CSR concept has not been treated with urgency in the field of corporate law yet. This may change in the near future.

---

[25] For the discussion at the Company Law subcommittee of the Legislative Council, *see* http://www.moj.go.jp/shingi1/housei02_00297.html.

[26] Tentative Proposal of the Company Law Subcommittee (February 14, 2018) Section 1, available at http://www.moj.go.jp/shingi1/shingi04900348.html.

CSR and Data Protection: Recent Development in Taiwan

Lung-Sheng Chen

Associate Professor, Department of Law, National Chung Hsin University

J.D., School of Law, Washington University in St. Louis, Missouri, U.S.

Dr. Hsiang-Yang Hsieh

Partner, Formosa Transnational, Taipei, Taiwan

J.S.D., School of Law, Washington University in St. Louis, Missouri, U.S.

I. Introduction: How Data Protection Matters

In this digital age, one can hardly dispute the value of information privacy and data protection. But for corporates and their lawyers, the question that needs to be explored is how data protection matters in the real business world. In other words, companies and private organizations doing businesses are always thinking how data protection matters to their business practices. Most companies consider data protection as a burden and even obstacle. Some researchers even claim that data protection law imposes undue burdens on their freedom in discovering new ideas and scientific findings. Thinking privacy and data protection in this way, most lawyers working with companies and research institutions thus take data protection seriously only for compliance purposes. For them, their legal advises on data protection law will be focusing on the minimum requirements that their clients should meet in order to keep their clients away from any liabilities or legal troubles.

In this paper, we argue for a different and much more positive approach to data protection law. We argue that data protection matters to corporates not merely because of compliance purposes, but also because a corporate's data protection practice is essential to maintain its consumer's trust in its products and services. Let's consider Facebook's recent data leak scandal. Facebook recently is under attack due to the data leak scandal.[1] This high profile event well indicates the importance of data protection to corporates. Mark Zuckerberg, CEO of Facebook, testified in the hearing of the US Congress,

> *Overall, I would say that we're going through a broader philosophical shift in how we approach our responsibility as a company. For the first 10 or 12 years of the company, I viewed our responsibility as primarily building tools that, if we could put those tools in people's hands, then that would empower people to do good things. What I think we've learned now across a number of issues—not just data privacy, but also fake news and foreign interference in elections—is that we need to take a more proactive role and a broader view of our responsibility. It's not enough to just build tools. We need to make sure that they're used for good. And that means that we need to now take a more active view in policing the ecosystem and in watching and kind of looking out and making sure that all of the members in our community are using these tools in a way that's going to be good and healthy. So, at the end of the day, this is going to be something where people will measure us by our results on this. It's not that I expect anything that I say here today—to necessarily change people's view. But I'm committed to getting this right. And I believe that, over the coming years, once we fully work all these solutions through, people will see real differences.[2]*

---

[1]   *See e.g.*, Emily Commander, *Cambridge Analytica Suspends CEO in Data Row* (March 21, 2018), http://www.euronews.com/2018/03/21/cambridge-analytica-suspends-ceo-in-data-row, accessed April 10, 2018; Sallyann Nicholls, *The Facebook data leak: What happened and what's next*, http://www.euronews.com/2018/04/09/the-facebook-data-leak-what-happened-and-what-s-next , accessed April 10, 2018.

[2]   Transcript of Mark Zuckerberg's Senate hearing dated April 10, 2018, https://www.washingtonpost.com/news/the-switch/wp/2018/04/10/transcript-of-mark-

As Zuckerberg pointed out in his testimony, companies' responsibilities are not limited to offering services and products to customers, but extended to ensuring their services and products are used in a good, right way.

The lesson learned from this scandal, however, is more than this. Many users, and regulators, have been taking anxious reactions to this scandal. Many corporates thus were reminded again of how data protection matters to their consumers' trust in their business practices. This is probably why some IT companies have long declared consumer data protection as a vital part of their corporate social responsibility.[3]

In this regard, privacy law professors Richards and Hartzog has argued that trust is at the core of information privacy and data protection.[4] As they argue, trust is essential to our digital lives. They explain their argument by stating,

> *So much of modern networked life is mediated by information relationships, in which professionals, private institutions, or the government hold information about us as part of providing a service......*
> *We see them when we share sensitive personal information with Internet service providers (ISPs), doctors, banks, search engines, credit card companies, and countless other information recipients and intermediaries. We also see them as we get information via large and small computers to access apps, social media, and the Internet at large.[5]*

They thus propose a different approach to understanding privacy

---

zuckerbergs-senate-hearing/?noredirect=on&utm_term=.7abccda6c495, accessed May 3, 2018.

[3] Irene Pollach, "Online Privacy as a Corporate Social Responsibility: An Empirical Study," *Business Ethics: A European Review* 20, no. 1 (January 2011).

[4] Neil Richards & Woodrow Hartzog, "Taking Trust Seriously in Privacy Law," *Stan. Tech. L. Rev.* 19 (2016): pp. 431, 433.

[5] Ibid.

law from the perspective of trust, claiming that privacy protection is essential to building trust that is core of virtually most relationships.[6]

Professors Richards and Hartzog's privacy and trust claim suggests that privacy or data protection should not be considered a mere non-disclosure rule that forbids unauthorized disclosure/use of someone's personal data. Instead, privacy and data protection law should lay down a foundation for an individual to share information with anyone that this individual finds necessary, especially with anyone that this individual would like to build a relationship. This relationship is diverse, including one's relationship with intimate partners, and with professionals such as lawyers and doctors. Trust, then, comes back to our discussion. Without privacy protection, or trust, that prevents others from using or disclosing the shared information, no one will be able to freely build up a relationship with others, including friends, partners, professionals, and customers.

We thus argue that data protection matters to corporates in terms of customer trust. Thinking data protection in this way suggests the point we would like to make in this paper—companies should consider data protection as part of their corporate social responsibilities. By doing so, we argue that data protection should go beyond the law and rest on a social culture that is supportive of data protection values. We thus consider how the law and the social norms shape private companies' data protection practices. First, we explore the experiences in the European Union and the United States. In particular, we look into the EU's General Data Protection Regulation and the US FTC's privacy jurisprudence. We offer comparative observations and identify evolving social norms in data protection law.

After that, we go back to the case of Taiwan. We first give an overview of Taiwan data protection law and turn to court cases where

---

[6] Ibid., at 435.

companies were held jointly liable for their employees' unauthorized use/collection of consumer data. By doing so, we are trying to explore empirical evidence supporting our argument that data protection should be recognized a social norm that is shared by the society and private organizations and companies.

Finally, we propose a set of ethical rules that should be followed by the companies whose business practices involve collection/use/analyze of personal data. Though not part of the laws and regulations, these ethical rules should be honored by companies on a voluntary basis and considered as their social responsibilities.

II. Data Protection in Practice: The EU and the United States

1. *The EU General Data Protection Regulation*

The EU General Data Protection Regulation (GDPR)[7] will become effective on May 25, 2018, replacing the European Directive on Data Protection[8]. After the effective date, the GDPR will be one of the most important legal documents binding information practices in the EU and many other countries around the world, including Taiwan.

Article 5.1 of the GDPR sets forth a set of principles governing data collection/use/disclosure. These principles includes: "lawfulness, fairness and transparency," "purpose limitation," "data minimization," "accuracy," "storage limitation," "integrity and confidentiality," and

---

[7] Regulation of the European Parliament and of the Council on the protection of individuals with regard to processing of personal data and on the free movement of such data.

[8] Directive 95/46/EC of the European Parliament and of the Council of 24 October 1995 on the protection of individuals with regard to the processing of personal data and on the free movement of such data.

"accountability."[9] Generally speaking, the GDPR requires personal data to be "processed lawfully, fairly, and in a transparent manner."[10] Also, the GDPR mandates that personal data be "collected for specified, explicit and legitimate purposes and not further processed in a manner that is incompatible with those purposes."[11] It is noteworthy that the GDPR sets forth some restrictions on data subjects' consent, making companies not to exclusively rely on their data practice on data subject consent.[12]

2. US: FTC Privacy Jurisprudence

In the United States, the Federal Trade Commission (FTC) has been playing a very important and active role in regulating consumer data protection matters. The FTC is a U.S. federal independent agency with statutory authority in protecting consumers and enhancing competition.[13] In particular, the FTC has developed a set of detailed rules that govern the data practices of private companies.

According to the FTC, the FTC found its legal basis for stepping in and regulating consumer privacy matters in "Section 5 of the Federal Trade Commission Act, which prohibits unfair or deceptive practices in the marketplace."[14] "This broad authority allows the Commission to

---

[9] GDPR, at art. 5.

[10] Ibid.

[11] Ibid.

[12] Paul M. Schwartz & Karl-Nikolaus Peifer, "Transatlantic Data Privacy Law," *Georgetown Law Journal* 115 (2017): p.144.

[13] Federal Trade Commission, 2014 Privacy and Data Security Update (2015), http://www.ftc.gov/reports/privacy-data-security-update-2014, accessed March 1, 2015.

[14] Federal Trade Commission, Privacy & Data Security Update (2017): An Overview of the Commission's Enforcement, Policy Initiatives, and Consumer Outreach and Business Guidance in the Areas of Privacy and Data Security: January 2017 – December 2017 (January 2018), https://www.ftc.gov/system/files/documents/reports/privacy-data-security-update-2017-overview-commissions-enforcement-policy-initiatives-consumer/privacy_and_data_security_update_2017.pdf, accessed April 11, 2018.

address a wide array of practices affecting consumers, including those that emerge with the development of new technologies and business models."

The FTC has been assuming a very important role in regulating data protection matters. According to privacy law professors Solove and Hartzog, the FTC has been developing a common law-like privacy jurisprudence.[15] As they have noted, the FTC has in many specific cases found a "deception" offense in the practices of many private entities because of their breaking of privacy policies (promises). In the cases of this kind, through its exercising statutory authority to regulate a business' deception practice, the FTC aims to keep a business to honor its own promises, such as "promises to maintain confidentiality or to refrain from disclosing information to third parties;" "promises to only collect data consistent with the company's privacy policy;" "promises to provide adequate security for personal data;" "promises to maintain anonymity;" and "promises not to disclose personal data to third parties by selling in bankruptcy proceedings."[16] According to the FTC, the FTC has filed more than 60 actions against companies that were allegedly involved in unfair or deceptive practices.[17]

The FTC privacy jurisprudence in the deception cases is helpful to ensure an individual's privacy in sharing because it allows an individual (an Internet or social network user) to have more privacy expectation in the online social network context. As the FTC points out, the goals for its privacy policies and enforcement actions are "to protect consumer's personal information and ensure that consumers have the confidence to take advantage of the many benefits of products offered in the

---

[15] Daniel J. Solove & Woodraw Hartzog, "The FTC and the New Common Law of Privacy," *Columbia Law Review* 114 (2014): pp. 583, 586.

[16] Solove & Hartzog, Ibid., at 629.

[17] Federal Trade Commission, *supra* note 14, 4.

marketplace."[18] Keeping the social network companies to honor their privacy policies (promises) allows an individual to have a space, forum, or platform upon which this person is able to ensure (and expect) what will happen to the information he/she shares online and what is the consequence if the information goes beyond the context in which he/she wants to share the same information.

3. Evolving Privacy Norms

Considering the EU GDPR and the US FTC privacy jurisprudence together helps us identify an involving privacy norm. The experiences in the EU and US of enforcing data protection law reminds us that privacy law and data protection law could not function just as a set of non-disclosure rules. In particular, the EU GDPR requires data collectors and users to be bound by a set of data principles; the US FTC mandates companies to keep their promises that they made in return of data subject's willingness to disclose their personal data. By doing so, both the GDPR and FTC privacy jurisprudence are offering an individual a foundation, under which this individual will be able to share/disclose his/her personal information with an understanding that the shared information will be used/processed as expected.

In this digital age, people (younger generations, particularly) like to share with friends or the public their views or private lives in the social media context. At the same time, however, people appreciate a virtue of being forgotten when they no longer want the shared information to be accessed by others.

The solution to the concern of this sort cannot be just a nondisclosure rule. Instead, a set of confidentiality rules that allows us to choose our own audience is essential for us to share with people we trust certain private matters that reflect our intellectual activities, but at the

---

[18] Ibid., at 1.

same time leave us with a space to keep these matters from the audience we do not expect.[19] A new privacy norm, thus, has been evolving—in addition to withholding the information or disclosing it, we must have some alternatives to these two extreme choices in order to have a meaningful freedom of thought, discussion, speech, and other intellectual activities.[20]

III. The Case of Taiwan

1. Taiwan's Personal Data Protection Act

We now go back to the case of Taiwan. Taiwan has a one-piece legislation, the Personal Data Protection Act (PDPA), setting forth a comprehensive data protection scheme that governing government agencies and private entities. Generally speaking, any use, collection, or processing of personal data is permissible only if the use, collection, or processing has been authorized by laws or regulations, or has been approved by data subjects.

2. An Empirical Look of Taiwan Case Law

Many court cases have been reported where individuals successfully sought monetary damages for unauthorized use or disclosure of their personal data. We found some of these court cases, where companies were held jointly liable for their employees' unauthorized use/collection

---

[19] Neil M. Richards & Jonathan King, "Big Data Ethics," *Wake Forest Law Review* 49 (2014): pp. 394, 413 (arguing, "Much of the information in intermediate states that we share is private data that we share in trust, expecting them to be confidential. Confidentiality is a kind of privacy that is based on trust and reliance on promises in the context of relationship").

[20] Neil M. richards, Intellectual Privacy: Rethinking Civil Liberties in the Digital Age 5 (2015).

of consumer data, to be illustrative of our arguments here.

For instance, in its judgment Year 2017 Su Tzi No. 2204, dated December 8, 2017, the Taipei District Court held the Post Office shall be jointly liable for its employee's unauthorized use of consumer data. The plaintiffs in this case were consumers of the Post Office's banking service. They alleged that one of the Post Office's employees conducted an unauthorized check of their financial data. They claimed that the Post Office shall be liable for the unauthorized use, basing on Article 188.1 of Taiwan's Civil Code, under which an employer shall be jointly liable for any infringing activities of its employees if the infringing activities fall within in the scope of the employees' job duty. The Post Office, in response, defended itself by arguing that the Post Office has done everything to prevent its employees from doing anything that were against data protection law. In particular, the Post Office established that the Post Office has offering many data protection training sections to the employee who misused the plaintiff's personal data. The court in this judgment found what the Post Office has done was not enough to help the Post Office get rid of its joint liabilities. According to the court, there were many other measures that the Post Office might have taken to prevent its employees from misusing consumer data, such as a set of internal control mechanisms that control and supervise its employees' compliance of data protection law obligations. The Post Office's failure of taking such actions, the court continued, made the Post Office liable for its employee's wrong-doings.

In another judgment Year 2016 Su Tzi No. 5255, dated April 28, 2017, the Taipei District Court held a stock trade company jointly liable for its employees' authorized use of its consumer's financial data, including the consumer's name, telephone number, and address. Relying on a similar theory, the court found that this stock trade company did not take any possible measures to prevent its employees from misusing its consumer's personal data. The court thus concluded that the company shall be jointly liable for its employees' authorized use of consumer data.

3. Lessons Learned

These court cases remind us of at least two points. First, companies shall be well aware of their obligations set forth by data protection law. Second, more importantly, the obligations imposed by data protection law are sometimes imprecise. Imprecision of data protection makes companies to face risks of being held liable for their employee's violations of data protection requirements.

The lessons learned from the Taiwan court cases indicate that companies shall take data protection as their corporate social responsibilities. This leads to the core of our argument in this paper— data protection shall go beyond the law and, moreover, for companies, they shall do more than their obligations required by the law.

IV. Conclusion: Ethical Information Principles

According to a study by business ethics professor Irene Pollach, "only a small proportion of the largest IT companies comprehensively address privacy as a social responsibility. In the sample, we find both companies that have taken a number of relevant actions to address user privacy and companies that have only taken one or two concrete measures, but nevertheless present privacy as part of their CSR program."[21] Based on her findings, she concludes that information privacy is "rather new on the CSR agenda, currently playing only a minor role."[22]

Based on our arguments in this paper, we would like to propose a set of ethical information principles that we argue companies, especially companies doing businesses online, shall embrace as their CSR.

---

[21] Pollach, *supra* note 3, 98.

[22] Ibid., 88.

According to Aguilera and other authors, companies accept CSRs for reasons including: (1) moral reasons, (2) stakeholder relationship, and (3) self-interests.[23] Here, we argue that companies shall accept ethical information principles as their CSRs for morality and self-interests. As the recent case of Facebook has shown, companies' voluntary adherence to privacy ethical rules will not only help the companies to get away from legal troubles, but also help them gain customer trust.

Our proposed ethical information principles include at least:[24]

1. a consumer has never waived his/her data protection right altogether by just giving consent to disclose his/her personal data.

2. in the context where products or services offered by companies involve professional areas, such as health care, a set of confidentiality rules applies to information and data shared/disclosed with a consumer's expectation that the shared information/data will be kept in confidential.

3. a company should make its data protection practice transparent and accountable.

---

[23] Aguilera, R.V., Rupp, D., Williams, C.A. and Ganapathi, J., "Putting the S back in CSR: A Ultilevel Theory of Social Change in Organizations," *Academy of Management Review* 32, no. 3 (2007): pp. 836-863.

[24] Richards & King, *supra* note 19, 408-422.

CSR vs "Business and Human Rights" Approach with Some Experiences in Korea

Prof. Dr. Sang-Soo Lee

Sogang University School of Law

I. Preface

The concepts of "Corporate Social Responsibility" (CSR) and "Business and Human Rights" (BHR) are often discussed, yet lack a clear distinction. The former refers to a corporation's responsibility towards society, and the latter towards human rights. Both are recent developments and impose unprecedented obligations on corporations. Are they two different expressions for the same phenomenon, or are they distinct with different aims and methodologies? Or do they both have the same goal, but with different approaches? What is, and should be, their relationship? Are they complementary or mutually exclusive? This article attempts to answer these questions.

Before discussing the relationship between them, we should first show what is meant by CSR and BHR as neither is clearly defined. The difference in definition will lead to drastically different conclusions. Accordingly, this article focuses extensively on developing a proper definition for each term, and then demonstrates the actual and normative relationship between them. Following the definitions proposed here, the paper briefly examines the current CSR and BHR developments in Korea.

II. Emergence of CSR and BHR

1. ISO 26000 in the History of CSR

The literal meaning of CSR is that corporations owe a duty to act responsibly vis-à-vis the general public, and not just to their shareholders. Broadly defined, one can trace back the CSR discourse more than a century. Intensive discussion on CSR, however, can be found beginning in the 1950s. Howard Bowen, who was referred to as Father of CSR by Archie Carrol, published his monograph Social Responsibilities of the Businessman in 1953.[1] He argued that the day when profit maximization was a sole criterion of business success was rapidly fading (p.52), and that businessmen should take social responsibilities in educating the American public, human [or worker] relations, local community relations, government relations, productivity, efficiency and expansion, economic stability, competition, and conservation of national resources (pp. 54-67). While he did not use the exact term "corporate" social responsibility, he deserves to be called father of CSR because he conducted comprehensive theorization of CSR, which included CSR phenomena, background, contents, criticism and counter-criticism, and policy proposals.

One of the influential documents in CSR controversy is Milton Friedman's essay of 1971.[2] After a long discussion on the meanings of social responsibility of businesses[3], he conclusively argued that "there is one and only one social responsibility of business—to use its resources

---

[1] Howard R. Bowen, *Social Responsibility of the Businessman* (University of Iowa Press, 2013).

[2] Milton Friedman, "The Social Responsibility of Business is to Increase its Profits," *New York Magazine* 13 (Sep 1970).

[3] Friedman did not use the exact term "corporate" social responsibility, and instead he used social responsibility of "business" by which he actually meant social responsibility of "corporate executives". From this fact we know that CSR was not widely used before 1970.

and engage in activities designed to increase its profits so long as it stays within the rules of the game, which is to say, engage in open and free competition without deception or fraud."

His essay has relevance for this article at least at two points. Firstly, he drew a very clear distinction between what is and what is not CSR. For Friedman, CSR includes activities which benefits workers, consumers or society in general at the cost of corporate owners. Businesses which ostensibly pursue social benefits but actually are motivated only by economic corporate profits, he argues, should not be called CSR, for they are nothing but "hypocritical window dressing". Secondly, Friedman openly denied the value of CSR by arguing that corporate executives do not have any social responsibility beyond profit maximization.

Friedman's writing was one of the clearest definitions of CSR and at the same time one of the most powerful attacks against CSR, for his argument did not remain constrained to academia but rather powerfully influenced the business world to ignore CSR. He was actually the leader of neo-liberalist economic theory which dominated the latter half of 20th century with the policy of deregulation and economic globalization. The ideology of the day was that businesses should be managed only in accordance with the principle of shareholder profit maximization as described by Friedman.

While the discussion of CSR was not totally stopped since 1970s,[4] we had to wait until the 1990s to see the noticeable emergence of CSR activities among corporations. Neo-liberalism, essentially anti-CSR, ironically triggered CSR movements in the society in two ways. At first, neo-liberalistic businesses, which ignored social consequences of their activities, caused many social problems and conflicts. Secondly, the public governance gap broadened by deregulation and economic globalization

---

[4] Archie B. Caroll, "Corporate Social Responsibility: Evolution of a Definitional Construct," *Business and Society* (Sep 1999): pp. 273 ff.

needed to be filled by someone, and big corporations emerged as quasi-public entities filling the gap.

Since the 1990s, a large number of corporations, especially global transnational corporations (TNCs), joined the CSR movement. Typically they made CSR policy commitments and communicated their CSR performances in sustainability reports periodically. The number of CSR initiatives skyrocketed. CSR itself became a business market. Various academic works, including stakeholder theory[5], emerged and prospered. Business schools began to deliver CSR lectures on a regular basis. Today, no major corporations dare to openly deny that they have some form of social responsibility. It seems that CSR has been successfully mainstreamed although it still has a long way to go.

Despite these developments, the prosperity of CSR was accompanied by its disorderly growth and lack of cohesive conceptualization. The International Organization for Standardization (ISO), as the most experienced international organization for standardization, played a leading role to make a standard modality of CSR out of diverse CSR notions, the final product being Guidance for Social Responsibility, known as ISO 26000.[6] ISO 26000 clearly focuses on social responsibility of "corporations", even though its coverage is not limited to corporations but includes all types of organizations. The motives for ISO 26000 was in the first place to standardize various CSRs at the international level. In fact, social responsibility for all types of organizations included in ISO 26000 was an expanded version of CSR applied to other types of organizations. In addition, the ISO 26000 is the most authoritative document on CSR currently available for many reasons. First, it took the ISO, the most qualified organization in standardization, nearly 10

---

[5] Edward Freeman, *Strategic Management: A Stakeholder Approach* (Cambridge, 1984).

[6] ISO (International Organization for Standardization), *Guidance for Social Responsibility*, First Edition, ISO 26000, 2010.

years (2001-2010), to prepare, draft and finalize the text. In addition, ISO 26000 was actually the outcome of a succession of discussions and agreements among a huge number of CSR stakeholders, which included 99 ISO members, 40 international organizations and 450 experts on CSR. Furthermore, there is no other comprehensive documents on CSR. Considering these factors, ISO 26000 is surely one of the best starting points to gain a conceptual understanding of CSR.

2. UN Guiding Principles on Business and Human Rights in the History of BHR

The notion of BHR is no less murky than that of CSR. The broadest understanding of BHR implies responsibility of corporations toward human rights. It is difficult to pinpoint when such understanding emerged, but it cannot be traced back before the middle of the 20th century because the term human rights itself was only widely emerging from that point.

The first expression which suggested the emergence of the notion of BHR can be found in the preamble of the Universal Declaration of Human Rights. It declares "every individual and every organ of society ... shall strive ... to promote respect for these rights and freedoms." While the term "every organ of society" in this sentence may be interpreted to include corporations, no evidences was found that the expression was intended to include corporations at the time of drafting or adopting the Declaration. The notion of BHR appeared much later.

Documents which focused on BHR came into existence in the 1990s. International non-governmental organizations (NGOs) began to publish reports which exposed human rights violations allegedly committed or aided by TNCs. In 1998, Amnesty International announced "Human Rights Principles for Companies", which recognized companies' responsibility to contribute to the promotion and protection of human rights, then pointed out important business-related human rights issues. This is one of the earliest forms of BHR discourse in the world.

The United Nations (UN) started its public discussion from the end of 1990s. UN Global Compact (UNGC), inaugurated in 2000, recognized corporate responsibility to support and respect human rights and not to be complicit in human rights abuses. But UNGC can better be categorized as a form of CSR because the coverage of UNGC is not limited to human rights issue.[7]

In 2003, a full-fledged BHR document appeared in the UN, i.e. "[Draft] Norms on the Responsibilities of Transnational Corporations and Other Business Enterprises with Regard to Human Rights"[8] (the Norms). The Norms tried to impose legally binding human rights obligations on TNCs. Although it was finally dismissed by the Human Rights Committee after heated disputes among the member states, its importance as a leading approach to BHR should not be underestimated for it showed a strong intention to hold corporations accountable for human rights abuses or complicity in them. As will be seen later in this article, the pursuing for corporate accountability is the critical feature that differentiates BHR from CSR.

The discussion on and frustration of the Norms only revealed the huge gap among the participants of BHR disputes. Their differences were so wide and deep that any further discussion among them seemed impossible. As the confusion caused by the proliferation of various forms of CSR led to the enactment of the ISO 26000, BHR disputants also

---

[7] Ramasastry admits UNGC is typically categorized as a CSR initiative, but she prefers to posit it in the context of BHR pointing out that it adopted international human rights norms. Anita Ramasastry, "Corporate Social Responsibility Versus Business and Human Rights: Bridging the Gap Between Responsibility and Accountability," *Journal of Human Rights* 14(2015): pp. 237-259.

[8] UN, Norms on the Responsibilities of Transnational Corporations and Other Business Enterprises with Regard to Human Rights, U.N. Doc. E/CN.4/Sub.2/2003/12/Rev.2, 2003.

badly suffered from the absence of a common understanding of BHR. Considering the wide gaps and intensity already found in the disputes, establishment of common ground on which to move forward would be extremely difficult, if not impossible.

This task was commissioned to the esteemed John Ruggie. After 6 years of hard work, Ruggie, as Special Representative for UN Secretary General, successfully produced a comprehensive document on BHR entitled the "Guiding Principles on Business and Human Rights: Implementing the United Nations "Protect, Respect and Remedy" Framework" (UNGP).[9] Without making any reference to CSR, UNGP focused only on "Business and Human Rights" issues. Ruggie's real contribution to BHR movement lies not in the fact that he made such a comprehensive text itself, but in the fact that he made the text embraced by almost all the stakeholders in the BHR field. UNGP was not only endorsed by the UN Human Rights Council unanimously, but also welcomed and adopted as a common platform on BHR by other international and domestic entities, including EU, OECD, World Bank, human rights NGOs etc. Through these broad support and uptakes, UNGP actually became such an overwhelming standard for BHR in the world. That is why UNGP can be the most appropriate starting point in conceptual understanding of BHR.

III. Corporate Responsibility in CSR and BHR

1. Contents of ISO 26000

According to ISO 26000, the objective of social responsibility is to contribute to sustainable development, or to achieve sustainability

---

[9] UN, "Guiding Principles on Business and Human Rights: Implementing the United Nations 'Protect, Respect and Remedy' Framework", HR/PUB/11/04, 2011.

for society as a whole and the planet (p. vi). To achieve the objective, corporations are expected to address 7 core subjects: organizational governance; human rights; labor practices; the environment; fair operating practices; consumer issues; and community involvement and development.

In the human rights chapter, it writes that a corporation has the responsibility to respect human rights within its sphere of influence. To respect human rights, corporations should exercise due diligence to identify, prevent and address actual or potential human rights impacts resulting from their activities or the activities of their business relationships (p. 25). The list of human rights to be respected by corporations includes civil political rights and economic, social and cultural rights as well.

The latter part of ISO 26000 provides guidance on putting social responsibility into practice within corporations, including due diligence to identify its social responsibility, integration of social responsibility in management processes, communication on social responsibility etc.

2. *Contents of UNGP*

UNGP is composed of 3 pillars: state duty to protect human rights; corporate responsibility to respect human rights; and access to remedies. With Reference to the international human rights law regime, it underlines a state's legal obligation to protect individuals or groups against human rights abuses by third parties, including business enterprises.

UNGP dictates that business enterprises should respect all of the internationally recognized human rights, regardless of its size, sector, operational context, ownership or structure. "To respect" means that corporations should avoid infringing on the human rights of others and address adverse human rights impacts with which they are involved (Guiding Principle 11). Corporations are expected to know and show that they respect human rights, by making a policy commitment to human rights; exercising human rights due diligence to identify, prevent, mitigate and account for how they address their impact on human rights; and providing victims with a remedy mechanism (comment of Guiding Principle 15).

3. Comparison at a glance between CSR and BHR

The most conspicuous difference between ISO 26000 and UNGP lies in their objectives. The objective of the former is to encourage corporations to make contributions in achieving sustainability for society as a whole and the planet, whereas the latter simply aims to prevent corporations from adversely impacting human rights. The difference leads to the different coverage of ISO 26000 and UNGP, meaning that human rights issue is only one of 7 core subjects in the ISO 26000.

But the similarity between the two texts cannot be left unnoticed. In fact, the human rights chapter of ISO 26000 is almost the same as UNGP itself, not only in terms of its substantive content but also in key terminology. Both talk of corporate responsibility in regards to respect, due diligence, and remedies. This impressive similarity came from the fact that ISO 26000 was drafted in coordination with John Ruggie's UNGP team.[10] With this feature in mind, BHR might be regarded as a part of CSR.

The similarity between ISO 26000 and UNGP is not limited to the human rights chapter of ISO 26000, because not only the human rights chapter but also all the other core subjects of ISO 26000 such as governance, labor, environment, consumer, and community relations are in fact human rights issues addressed in UNGP, either directly or indirectly. In addition, both ISO 26000 and UNGP offer due diligence as an implementation mechanism. Despite their difference in their

---

[10] John Ruggie, *Just Business* (W.W. Norton & Company, 2013), p. 163.

committed objectives, both documents' requirements for corporations are very much overlapping. The gap between CSR and BHR might not be as wide as one might think, as far as we make use of ISO 26000 as a representing text of CSR and UNGP as that of BHR.

IV. Convergence of CSR and BHR?

If CSR and BHR demand similar behaviors from corporations, what is the use of having two different expressions? Can they converge toward each other, or even can they be integrated into one expression?

Florian Wettstein, taking notice of the disconnection between CSR and BHR, tried to find way to integrate them for their synergies and complementary aspects.[11] According to his arguments, CSR scholars regularly deal with human rights problems, but only marginally, and understand human rights as a matter of virtue and beneficence or even philanthropy and charity. They usually underline the tendency of voluntariness in CSR. Wettstein criticized UNGP's approach to human rights as minimalistic, in a sense that it focuses on the responsibility to respect human rights only, i.e. the responsibility to "do no harm", shying away from the fundamental moral nature of human rights obligations. For him, human rights in a more fundamental sense must be understood as moral concepts and thus as moral rights, implying that corporations have not only negative human rights responsibilities but also positive ones. Human rights, by nature, require responsibilities to protect and realize as well. In this context, he continues, the normative ground for human rights obligations is the existence of human rights itself, and such obligation, under certain circumstances, can and should be distributed to corporations which have the capacity to discharge the obligation. He

---

[11] Florian Wettstein, "CSR and the Debate on Business and Human Rights: Bridging the Great Gap", *Business and Ethics Quarterly* 22, no.4 (October 2012).

called his idea "capacity-based human rights obligation" (P. 755), which contrast with harm-based human rights obligation adopted by UNGP. If corporate human rights obligations in BHR were so defined as he did and CSR took human rights more seriously and as a matter of justice, the difference between CSR and BHR would be blurred, leading to their convergence or even integration.

I admit that Wettstein persuasively showed the possibility of integrating CSR and BHR "at the theoretical level". But other questions remain: is it desirable to converge or integrate CSR and BHR "in the real world"? To answer this question requires deeper understanding on the differences between CSR and BHR beyond simply comparing ISO 26000 and UNGP in text.

V. Differences between CSR and BHR

1. Advocates and Logic of CSR

The distinguishing features of CSR can be traced from looking at by whom and under what logic CSR has been advocated. CSR, from its inception, was developed mostly by business management scholars. They are the persons who began to argue that businesses should make positive contributions to the society in general or take into consideration the interests of various stakeholders beyond legal requirements, instead of benefitting shareholders only. The main audience they have in mind are corporations or business executives.

Then how do the CSR scholars persuade businessmen to adopt CSR policy? CSR discourses provide several common answers on the question. The first points to a social license to operate. Some business activities require community acceptance and support as a prerequisite to operate in certain locations or sectors. In obtaining such acceptance and support CSR activities are one of the most useful and available means.

The second refers to CSR as a risk management. If a company is found to have committed social or environmental crimes or disasters during its business activities, the company's reputation can be seriously damaged, immediately leading to its financial loss. Thirdly, CSR can be a business case. In other words, active response to meet the society's demands may bring to companies various chances for its continuous growth or new business opportunities.

If CSR activities are motivated only by such impetus, they are not CSR at all in the Friedman's sense, for, as seen above, ostensibly socially responsible activities motivated only by economic interests is nothing but "hypocritical window dressing". Social license, risk management and business case can be regarded as means to maximization of shareholder profits. It is about the lowest level of social responsibility in Carrol's CSR pyramid, i.e. "economic responsibility".[12] Here is no place for morality or ethics. As far as CSR is defined as something other than economic consideration, ostensibly social activities motivated only by social license, risk management, and business case cannot be subsumed under the CSR umbrella. Actually Friedman's demonstration of CSR includes only such management which was conducted at the expense of corporate profits. The examples are such as price deduction for fear of inflation or hiring of the "hardcore" unemployed. For him only such behaviors deserve to be called CSR.

Here another question can be raised. Is it proper to adopt Friedman's CSR definition? In other words, is it proper to say that business activities motivated only by economic causes such as social license, risk management and business case must not be called CSR? My answer is no. Firstly, people commonly consider such behaviors as CSR. So excluding such behaviors from CSR would not correspond to daily

---

[12] Archie B. Carroll, "The Pyramid of Corporate Social Responsibility: Toward the Moral Management of Organizational Stakeholders," *Business Horizons* (July-August 1991).

practices of CSR language. Secondly, corporate activities motivated by social license, risk management and business cases have different in nature from the activities motivated by blatant pursuit of economic profit. CSR is historically unique activities of corporations pushed by various social expectations beyond those required by law and which are moral in nature.[13] Now corporations are expected or pressured to properly respond to these social and moral requirements, even if they remain profit-oriented entities. While the fundamental motivation of corporations to exercise CSR might be economical, the expectation of society is moral in nature. We can further argue that corporations might become moral entities if they internalize the moral norms which were imposed through outer social pressure. Therefore, Friedman's definition which excluded business activities motivated solely by economic concern from CSR is not a proper reflection of current CSR practices and consequently does not help us in understanding CSR phenomena in society.

In sum, CSR is, in essence, corporate response to society's expectation or pressure for business corporations to make positive contributions to various stakeholders or society in general beyond the law. As such, CSR by definition cannot be specifically enforced by the law, even though the law may promote CSR by providing CSR-friendly business environments or other incentives.

2. *Advocates and Logic of BHR*

If CSR is a discourse of business management scholars, BHR discourse was begun in the 1990s by human rights activists and human rights law scholars.[14] BHR focuses on human rights violations which arise

---

[13] Prominent CSR scholars started their CSR discussion by point out that heightened corporate attention to CSR has not been entirely voluntary. Michael E. Porter and Mark R. Kramer, "Strategy and Society: the Link between Competitive Advantage and Corporate Social Responsibility," *Harvard Business Review* 12(2006 Dec): p. 80.

[14] When Clapham discussed human rights in private sphere, corporate human rights

in relation with business activities. It contrasts abusive corporations with human rights victims. It highlights the fact that corporations as human rights abusers have rarely been punished or sanctioned, and that human rights victims have been left without remedy. It is not a matter or virtue but that of justice. BHR is not something just to be recommended, but rather to be seriously enforced. As such it has strong tendency to mobilize legal methods.

BHR takes advantage of the fact that human rights are well recognized in the international community. International human rights regime provides not only general principles on human rights but also highly systemized and detailed human rights instruments. The existence of firm human rights instruments is one of the strong points of BHR, which is not the case with CSR.

Based on the international human rights law, the state duty to protect human rights emerges. Actually most BHR advocates emphasize the inevitability of state intervention to enforce corporate human rights responsibility especially through legislative and judicial measures. In this sense BHR has a strong legalist tendency by its nature.

All the characteristics of BHR above is well reflected in UNGP, which expressly recognizes corporate responsibility to respect all the internationally recognized human rights regardless of a corporation's scale, ownership etc. It is minimalistic in a sense that it addresses only corporate responsibility to "respect" human rights, setting aside the responsibility to protect and fulfill. Although UNGP itself is a soft law (or recommendations), UNGP manifestly stresses the importance of a state's engagement to protect human rights and the importance of judicial remedies.

---

issues was not of major concern. Andrew Clapham, *Human Rights in the Private Sphere* (Clarendon Press, 1993). More intensive discussion on business and human rights appears with Ratner. Steven R. Ratner, "Corporation and Human Rights: A Theory of Legal Responsibility," *Yale L.J.* 111(November 28, 2001): p.443.

In sum, BHR aims to hold corporations accountable for their human rights abuses. It takes a minimalistic and legalistic approach in the sense that it focuses on the negative human rights responsibility and legal intervention in corporate human rights abuses. Recent discussions on human rights treaties in UN reflect these core conceptions of BHR.

3. *BHR and the Minimalistic Approach*

As seen above, the UNGP's minimalistic approach was criticized by Wettstein (p. 741). He argued that the UNGP should have adopted the notion of a positive human rights duty instead of a minimalist obligation because human rights by nature require a positive duty from any entities, including corporations, with the "capacity" to discharge human rights obligations. As far as we admit that human rights as a social value has a "moral" nature, his argument is very impressive, at least in theory. Still it seems that his argument takes too little consideration of BHR in the contemporary context. The current BHR is not about corporate failure to fulfill positive human rights obligations, but about adverse human rights impacts by corporations. At the time when the latter is at issue, the expansion of corporate human rights obligations to include the former would blur the most urgent tasks for BHR advocates. In addition maximalist approach would make it extremely difficult to impose legal responsibility for human rights on the corporations. Adoption of minimalism by UNGP does not seem the result of either coincidence or ignorance. That is not to say that BHR, necessarily or preferably, leads to a minimalist approach, but rather that there exists a group of BHR advocates who opted for a minimalist approach for strategic reason and that they are at the center of BHR discourses. In sum, I argue that the minimalist approach is one of core features of current BHR. As a matter of proper definition of BHR for further discussion, I don't adopt Wettstein's thinking, even if I admit that his proposal may prevail in the future.

4. Definitions of CSR and BHR

The above discussion attempts to demonstrate that there exist fundamental differences between CSR and BHR despite facial similarities. In particular, CSR and BHR are advocated by different groups of persons with different objectives and different means in achieving those objectives. The following summarizes typical CSR and BHR approaches, taking into consideration the differences depicted above.

CSR has various characteristics in that it is: led by business management scholars; engages corporations; is duty-oriented; involves corporate-driven activities; is open-ended duty bound; utilizes a maximalist approach; asks corporations to do something; aims for a positive contribution to stakeholders and society in general; allegedly pursues virtue and well-being; opposes state regulations; and is conservative, if social development through construction is a core characteristic of conservatism.

Typical characteristics of BHR are that they are: led by human rights law scholars; engage human rights victims; are rights-oriented; include victim-driven activities; are pre-determined duty bound; utilize a minimalist approach; ask corporations not to do something; provide accountability for human rights abuses; pursue justice; are legally binding and enforceable; require state intervention to punish corporations civilly or criminally; and are left-leaning, if social development through criticism is a core characteristic of the left.

As seen above, CSR and BHR are two distinct types of approaches to corporate responsibility. These definitions are "ideal type" (Idealtypus) in the Weberian sense because these concepts are extracted from empirical data with the purpose of description and explanation of social phenomena. Using such definitions, we can describe various forms of CSR and BHR which are confusing but yet coexist in the world. For example, an initiative may speak of CSR but actually be practicing BHR, or vice versa. Some may make a comment that the UNGP is not fully BHR-oriented. Now that we have definitions of CSR and BHR, we are ready to discuss the relationship between them.

VI. The Relationship between CSR and BHR

If CSR and BHR are so defined, what is the relationship between them and what should it be. Does the one has anything to do with the other? Are they mutually supporting or mutually exclusive? Can they converge towards each other and could they even be integrated into one notion?

As the definitions have already shown, the two have critically different objectives and approaches with different philosophies. So far they seem to coexist without meaningful interactions. Then what should be their relationship? Should they be integrated as argued by Wettstein?

Above all, it is improper for one party to give up its own position to join the other party. For example, we cannot persuade CSR advocates to give up CSR and to join BHR movement. It would be as absurd as persuading business school professors to stop being business scholars to become legal scholars. Similarly, BHR advocates cannot desert BHR to join CSR. Such demands amount to the denial of one party's identity and existence.

Another compelling reason not to take only one of the two comes from the fact that CSR and BHR have different social roles independent of each other. For example the termination of CSR would leave serious consequences to society. It would mean that we have to stop believing in the good will of businessmen and stop making better corporations through social pressures. CSR's destination may be so gracious and so high that the contemporary law cannot cover it completely. It can only be pursued step by step. It is true that many corporations fail social expectation and often get involved in egregious human rights violations, but we still have many reasons to believe that corporations are moving forwards to a better society and that such progresses are the result of continuous efforts to push them in that direction. This is the most fundamental reason why we should not really discard the idea and ideal of CSR.

In the same manner, we should not weaken or stop BHR. Even if we acknowledge that corporations are making tremendous social contributions, we cannot left unpunished human rights abusers. Human rights victims should be properly remedied, civilly or criminally. BHR is a matter of justice and is a minimum requirement for us to maintain our moral balance. BHR requires strict laws with effective enforcement mechanisms because we cannot expect this mission can be reached simply through corporate voluntarism.

If neither CSR nor BHR should be weakened or discarded, then is it possible to make a selective integration of the merits of CSR and BHR? It would extremely difficult, if not impossible, because many of their characteristics are mutually exclusive. Often times they actually conflict with and harm each other. For example CSR advocates sometimes attempts to frustrate legal approaches taken by BHR groups[15], and the latter often depreciate or are cynical about the motives and performance of the former. Regardless of the possibility of their integration, it seems more proper to admit the differences and good-will of each and to let them do their best independently in the pursuit of social development. This proposal resembles a political field where the right and left coexist and compete with each other. They might have many shared political objectives in broad sense, but they keep differentiating themselves from each other in terms of ways to reach them. Their unique contribution to the society comes from their difference in ideas and approaches for the better society. Similarly

---

[15] Shamir argues that CSR is one of the strategies to shy away from legal accountability. Ronen Shamir, "Between Self-Regulation and the Alien Tort Claims Act: On the Contested Concept of Corporate Social Responsibility," *Law and Society Review* 38(December 2004): pp. 635, 649.

CSR and BHR are two different ways to corporate responsibility. As such the difference between them should be preserved and even encouraged. The communication between them surely benefit both, but the integration of them seems not possible, nor desirable.

VII. CSR and BHR in Korea

1. CSR in Korea

CSR seems to enjoy wide acceptance in Korea. Although CSR in Korea is very often equated with corporate philanthropy or voluntary activities of employees, not only global TNCs but also most large corporations, including public enterprises, claim to stand for CSR. Many are regularly reporting their CSR performances in sustainability reports. The Korean government translated OECD Guidelines on Multinational Enterprises as early as 2011. The Korean Standard Association translated ISO 26000 and provides CSR training programs. Disclosure on non-financial information[16] and Stewardship Code of National Pension Fund[17] are under discussion. These days the idea of "creating shared value" (CSV), proposed by Michael Porter, is expanding in place of CSR discourse.[18]

However the actual impact of CSR is very difficult to verify. The number of sustainability reports and the amount of corporate philanthropy have drastically increased in the last decade, as shown in the Figures below. Best practices in CSR and related awards are often

---

[16] A bill requiring public corporations to report non-financial information in annual report was proposed at the National Congress, but not adopted.

[17] Last year the Korea National Pension Service announced to adopt stewardship code for shareholder activism as a way to practice socially responsible investment (SRI).

[18] Michael Porter, "The Role of Business in Society: Creating Shared Value," *Badson Entrepreneurship Forum* (2011): p. 7.

reported in mass media and CSR conferences.[19] But the overall impact of CSR on the corporate culture and various stakeholders remains obscure, which leads some to turn to an alternative approach, i.e. BHR.

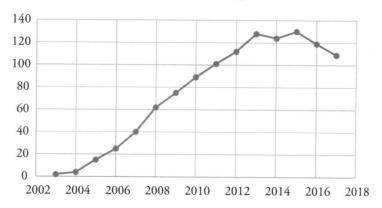

Figure 1 : Number of sustainability reports in Korea
Source: Korean Sustainability Conference, http://www.ksi.or.kr/ksi/5011/subview.do.

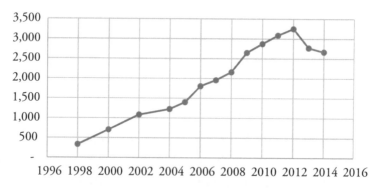

Figure 2 : Amount of corporate philanthropy (billion Korean Won)
Source: The Federation of Korean Industries, 2015 Report of Corporate Social Contribution, p. 2

---

[19] CSR award was organized by, for example, Ministry of Trade, Industry and Energy, Korea Trade-Investment Promotion Agency, Korea Employers' Federation, UN Global Compact Network Korea, and some commercial media such as Hankyung Business.

2. BHR in Korea

BHR in Korea is mostly led by human rights specialists in NGOs or academia. They are addressing human rights abuses by corporations with reference to international BHR norms which arose in the last decade. Their activities include advocacy works and a series of researches on human rights abuses committed by Korean companies abroad. Scholars made comments on the international BHR trends and interpreted various corporate incidents from the BHR perspective. One article, analyzing high-voltage transmission tower disputes which lasted more than 10 years with two deaths in protest, mobilized the notions of BHR.[20] Another article which dealt with workplace deaths and injuries of subcontractors attempted to prove the responsibility of prime contractors, Hyundai Heavy Industry, citing the UNGP.[21] An NGO, which dealt with workplace casualties at Samsung Electronics, appealed to the international community by framing the incidents from the BHR point of view.[22] In this way international BHR discourse and norms began emerging in Korea.

However, many victims and NGOs in Korea have few grievance mechanisms through which to pursue human rights remediation. They conduct street campaigns to attract media attention, or appeal to the National Contact Point (NCP) process under OECD Guidelines for

---

[20] Sang S. Lee, "The Structure of Large-Scale Human Rights Violations Committed by Business Enterprises: A Qualitative Case Study on Disputes over the Power Cable Construction at Milyang," *Law and Society* (Korean Journal) 48(2015).

[21] Sang S. Lee, "Corporate Responsibility for the Human Rights Abuses Committed in Supply Chains : A Proposal to Reduce the Workplace Injuries of Subcontract Workers in the Hyundai Heavy Industry Shipyard," *Law and Society* (Korean Journal) 52(2016).

[22] An NGO, *Banolim* (Half-step Forward), which was organized in 2007 to support a victim of industrial disease, received 50 death reports and more than 100 injuries in Samsung Semiconductor factory in Korea. Its struggle for remedy is still going on, expanding its front globally.

Multinational Enterprises, without any success. Many people and workers whose lives were seriously harmed in relation with business activities are still suffering without proper care. They includes villagers damaged by ocean pollution by Samsung Heavy Industry,[23] victims of the Yongsan Disaster,[24] and victims of forceful suppression of labor strike in Ssangyong Motors[25] etc. Formal legal process over these incidents are finished, but victims' struggles and sufferings remain. The Korean law falls short of protecting human rights of those workers and ordinary people. This is the gap to be filled by BHR initiatives in Korea.

BHR initiative by the Korean government merits special attention. Especially The Korea Human Rights Commission showed a great interest in the UN's BHR activities. In addition to the translation of the UN Framework on BHR (2008) and UNGP into Korean immediately after their publications, the Commission has funded many research projects on BHR.[26] It published tools for corporations to respect human rights.[27] It regularly participated in the UN Forum on Business and Human Rights, with its chairperson making speeches. Recently, it played an important role in inserting BHR chapter into the 3rd Korean National Human Rights Action Plan (2019-2023), with reference to the UN Guidance to National Action Plan for Business and Human Rights.[28] Furthermore,

---

[23] In 2007, Samsung Heavy Industry caused the 19000-ton crude oil leakage in the offshore of Tae-An. Villagers are still suffering from the incident.

[24] In 2009, 6 person (1 policeman included) died during the suppression of the residents who resisted Yongsan District redevelopment project.

[25] In 2009, the conflict over the sale and restructuring of Ssangyong Motors resulted in 28 deaths (14 suicides included).

[26] For example, the Commission funded: Field research on the human rights violations committed by Korean corporations abroad; Research on the human rights condition in SMEs; Research on the best practices and institutions of foreign countries in terms of business and human rights etc.

[27] Korea Human Rights Commission, *Guideline and Checklist for Human Rights Friendly Management*, 2014.

[28] UN Working Group on Business and Human Right, *Guidance on National Action*

the Commission is pushing hard public enterprises to declare human rights policy commitments and to exercise human rights due diligence as suggested in the UNGP and the Commission's Guideline.[29]

However, some precaution is necessary in evaluating the governmental BHR initiative. Although they made clear commitment to BHR in Korea, I suspect that what they mean by BHR is not the same as the BHR defined in this article. For their emphasis lies not so much in corporate accountability for victims as in persuasion for corporation to respect human rights during their business. In fact, the government prefers to use the term "human rights management", instead of "business and human rights." It seems that their BHR is the human rights version of CSR because they persuade corporation to respect human rights with little concern on human rights victims or corporate accountability. In other words, it seems to me that the government is not advocating BHR but CSR. As a result, the discrepancy between BHR of the Commission and BHR of human rights advocates is almost as wide as the gap between CSR and BHR as defined in this article.

In sum, the BHR movement in Korea is only in its nascent stage. While the current Korean government has a strong tendency towards democracy and human rights issues, no visible progress is seen in terms of BHR in a strict sense. Government efforts to reach human rights victims by Korean corporations abroad is almost nonexistent. Human rights language is rarely used in the conflicts between corporations and suffering victims. Korean BHR movement is still so weak that it cannot draw the government's attention and is easily ignored by corporations. This kind of

---

Plans on Business and Human Rights, November 2016.

[29] Recently the Korean government decided to insert human rights factor in evaluating the performance of independent public organizations, including public enterprises. They are asked to make human rights policy commitments and exercise human rights due diligence. So far 24 independent public organizations have made public policy commitments to human rights in their management.

stories are not limited to Korean society. Corporate impunity is at issue at the every corner of the world, whether it be in developing countries or in developed countries.[30] For all of us there remains a long way to go before we see BHR play its role as a remedial mechanisms for the corporate human rights abuses.

VIII. Conclusion

This article attempts to show the actual and normative relationship between CSR and BHR. As their relationship depends on how CSR and BHR are defined, a considerable portion of this article was dedicated to discerning similarities and differences between CSR and BHR. Based on this, the paper proposed a set of their definitions respectively and analyzed their relationships, with the following findings:

Firstly, ISO 26000 and UNGP can be starting points for identifying the basic features of CSR and BHR.

Secondly, ISO 26000 and UNGP have common interest in corporate human rights responsibility and due diligence process as a method to reach their objectives. This similarity alludes the probability of integration of CSR and BHR, which was actually offered by Wettstein.

Thirdly, CSR and BHR take distinctive, even mutually contradictory, approaches in adding new corporate responsibilities. I argue that they are inherently different ideas from each other. CSR is corporate response to social pressure which demands corporations to make positive contributions to stakeholders or the society in general, whereas BHR tries to stop corporate human rights abuses by holding corporations accountable for their human rights abuses. This definition is

---

[30] Regian E. Rauxloh, "A Call for the End of Impunity for Multinational Corporations," *Tex. Wesleyan L Rev.* 14(2008): p. 297; Michael J. Kelly, "Ending Corporate Impunity for Genocide: The Case against China's State-Owned Petroleum Company in Sudan," *Or. L. Rev.* 90(2011): p. 413.

an "ideal type" in a Weberian sense, for it reflects reality and is intended to be used for the description and analysis of social phenomena.

Fourthly, we should not adopt Friedman's definition of CSR. His insistence to conceptually exclude profit-oriented social management from CSR hinders us from having a realistic view to CSR

Fifthly, Wettstein's proposal to integrate CSR and BHR should be objected to. While his argument is theoretically persuasive, he takes too little notice of historical context where CSR and BHR has emerged and worked.

Sixthly, the Korean government are seemingly very active in BHR initiatives but actually adopts CSR approach, which leaves human rights victims unattended. It is a BHR failure which comes from the confusion between BHR and CSR.

Lastly, the normative relationship between CSR and BHR should be their independent development without further effort to converge or integrate them. CSR and BHR have different social roles, which can best be played when they work separately. What is to be pursued is not the integration or selection between CSR and BHR but the independence and cooperation between them.

Corporate Social Responsibility and Social Enterprises: A Comparative Study between Taiwan and the United Kingdom

Prof. Dr. Ta-Wei Kuo

School of Law, Fu Jen Catholic University

I. Introduction

In recent years, Corporate Social Responsibility (CSR) and social enterprises have attracted global attention. CSR is a business approach that companies take responsibility for their impact on society.[1] A traditional view of the company suggests that the primary responsibility of a company is to its owners or shareholders. That is, companies are responsible for merely maximizing financial returns for their shareholders. However, CSR requires companies to adopt a broader view of its responsibilities that includes not only shareholders, but many other stakeholders including consumers, employees, communities, and others. It aims to ensure that companies conduct their business in a way taking account of their social, economic and environmental impact.

Basically, CSR are precursors of the newly emergent social enterprise movement. In general, social enterprises are businesses that apply commercial strategies to achieve specific social objectives, rather than to realize profit for shareholders. Although CSR and social enterprises share some common features, there are important distinctions between them. The aim of CSR is that companies should voluntarily engage in socially

---

[1] *See* Eric C. Chaffee, "The Origins of Corporate Social Responsibility," *U. Cin. L. Rev.* 85(2017): p. 353.

beneficial activity, so it is up to each company to decide the extent of their social responsibility. In contrast, social enterprises have an obligation to take account of social considerations and have a social purpose as their primary purpose[2]. Social enterprises have been developing rapidly in both Taiwan and the United Kingdom in the past decade.

In contrast to CSR and social enterprises in Taiwan, CSR and social enterprises in the United Kingdom are well-developed. Accordingly, this article will first consider the British perspective and recent developments concerning corporate social responsibility. Then, it will discuss the legal framework for social enterprises in the United Kingdom. Finally, it will examine the current regulatory framework regarding CSR and social enterprises in Taiwan. This article aims at drawing lesson from the United Kingdom experience that might be adopted to the Taiwanese context.

II. The development of CSR in the United Kingdom

In the United Kingdom, the modern concept of CSR emerged in the 1970s[3]. Three major reasons can be attributed to the emergence of CSR in the United Kingdom. The first reason is the development of CSR in the United States. The second reason is the United Kingdom joined the European Union (then known as the European Economic Community) in 1973. The implementation of EU Treaties had significant influence on the conception of the company within the EU framework. The third reason is the promotion of CSR by the British government and

---

[2] *See* Thomas Kelley, "Law and Choice of Entity on the Social Enterprise Frontier," *Tul. L. Rev.* 84 (2009): pp. 337, 348-352.

[3] *See* Kevin.Campbell and Douglas Vick, "Disclosure Law and Market for Corporate Social Responsibility," in *The new Corporate Accountability: Corporate Social Responsibility and the Law*, ed. Doreen McBarnet, Aurora Voiculescu and Tom Campbell (2007), p. 241.

private organizations. Many companies are aware of the importance of CSR[4].

Although the spirit of CSR is encouraged, the major challenge to CSR is that there is still not a standard definition and it lacks an officially endorsed assessment standard. Further, the primary duty of directors under the British company law is only to the body of shareholders as a whole. The general common law position is that directors must act in the interests of the company and the interests of the company are viewed as those of the shareholders collectively. Accordingly, directors in running the company must do so in such a way as to maximize the interests of shareholders as a whole. However, it results in the question whether directors are permitted to use corporate assets to serve stakeholders beyond their shareholders.

Prior to the enactment of the Companies Act 2006, Section 309 of the Companies Act 1985 (the predecessor of Section 172(1)(b) of the Companies Act 2006) contained a general provision instructing the directors of a company to consider the interests of the employees in the performance of their functions[5]. Generally speaking, good treatment of employees is thought to generate greater productivity and loyalty. Section 309 of the Companies Act 1985 might provide express authority for companies and directors to consider the interests of their employees. Nevertheless, it was unclear whether Section 309 of the Companies Act 1985 recognized the interests of the employees separating from the interests of the shareholders or whether it required the directors to consider the interests of their employees in the course of promoting the interests of the shareholders[6]. Further, whether companies and their

---

[4] *See* Saleem Sheikh, *Corporate Social Responsibility Law and Practice* (1996), 13.

[5] Companies Act 1985. s.309.

[6] *See* Paul L. Davies & Sarah Worthington, *Gower and Davies' Principles of Modern Company Law* (10th ed. 2016), 512; Saleem Sheikh, A Guide to the Companies Act 2006(2008), 404-408.

directors should have a wider responsibility, above the legal minimum standard, to other stakeholders such as customers, the environment and local communities, and whether managers and directors ought to be entrusted with the discretion to determine the nature and extent of this responsibility were also ambiguous[7].

Due to the awareness that the Companies Act 1985 was complex and became outdated, the British government set up the Company Law Review Steering Group ("CLRSG") in 1998[8]. The main objective of the CLRSG was to modernize the British company law and to provide a simple, efficient and cost-effective framework for business activities in the United Kingdom. With regard to CSR, the CLRSG proposed to adopt the "enlightened shareholder value" approach in its company law review. The enlightened shareholder value approach is based on the principle that the objective of a company is to create value for its shareholders, but in order to achieve this objective it is necessary to form long-term cooperative relationships with the various stakeholders[9]. Under the enlightened shareholder value approach, directors of a company shall not only perform in the best interests of shareholders, but also take account to other stakeholders' interests[10].

After the enactment of the Companies Act 2006, the concept of enlightened shareholder value is incorporated into Section 172 of the Companies Act 2006. Section 172 of the Companies Act 2006 provides:

1. *A director of a company must act in the way he considers, in good faith, would be most likely to promote the success of the company for the*

---

[7] *See* Ibid.

[8] *See* Saleem Sheikh, *A Guide to the Companies Act* 2006(2008), 25-26.

[9] *See* Paul L. Davies & Saraw Worthington, *Gower and Davies' Principles of Modern Company Law*, 501-513.

[10] Ibid.

benefit of its members as a whole, and in doing so have regard (amongst other matters) to-

i.   *the likely consequences of any decision in the long term,*

ii.   *the interests of the company's employees,*

iii.   *the need to foster the company's business relationships with suppliers, customers and others,*

iv.   *the impact of the company's operations on the community and the environment,*

v.   *the desirability of the company maintaining a reputation for high standards of business conduct, and*

vi.   *the need to act fairly as between members of the company.*

2.   *Where or to the extent that the purposes of the company consist of or include purposes other than the benefit of its members, subsection (1) has effect as if the reference to promoting the success of the company for the benefit of its members were to achieving those purposes.*

3.   *The duty imposed by this section has effect subject to any enactment or rule of law requiring directors, in certain circumstances, to consider or act in the interests of creditors of the company[11].*

Section 172 of the Company Act 2006 requires a director to act in the way which he/she considers, in good faith, would be most likely to promote the success of the company for the benefit of its shareholders as a whole and sets out a non-exhaustive list of six factors which a director must consider. In other words, Section 172 of the Companies Act 2006 attempts to introduce the concept of CSR into the company law framework[12].

According to Section 172(1) of the Companies Act 2006, directors

---

[11] Companies Act 2006, s.172.

[12] *See* Paul L. Davies & Sarah Worthington, *Gower and Davies' Principles of Modern Company Law*, 501-513.

have to act in determining the likely consequence of any decision on a long-term basis, rather than a short-term basis[13]. Further, because not all companies formed under the Companies Act 2006 are aimed at maximizing the benefit of their shareholders, Section 172(2) of the Companies Act 2006 deals with the question of altruistic, or partly altruistic, companies such as community interest companies. For those companies whose objectives consist of or include purposes other than the benefit of their shareholders, the directors must act in the way they consider, in good faith, would be most likely to achieve those purposes. It indicates that the primary objective of a company may not simply maximize the value of the company or the benefit of its shareholders, and the directors could engage in other socially responsible objectives[14]. Moreover, Section 172(3) of the Companies Act 2006 recognizes that in certain circumstances the duty to promote the success of the company may be displaced and the directors may have to consider or act in the interests of the creditors of the company[15]. For example, Section 214 of the Insolvency Act 1986 provides that if a company in insolvency proceedings is found to have traded when there is no reasonable prospect of avoiding insolvent winding up, its directors may be liable for wrongful trading. The court may order such directors to make a contribution to the company's assets[16]. In this case, the duty to promote the success of the company may be modified by an obligation to consider or act in the interests of the creditors of the company when the company is insolvent or nearly so.

In order to inform shareholders of the company and help them to evaluate the director's performance, the CLRSG recommended that all

---

[13] Companies Act 2006, s.172(1).

[14] Ibid., s.172(2).

[15] Ibid., s.172(3).

[16] Insolvency Act 1986, s.214.

companies of significant economic size (the majority of public companies and large private companies) publish an Operating and Financial Review ("OFR") as part of their annual reports. The OFR is a form of narrative report, in which companies need to describe future strategies, resources, risks and uncertainties, including policies in relation to employees and the environment[17]. However, the OFR was replaced with a requirement to prepare a Business Review by the British government in 2006. This decision was taken on the basis that it would help relieve the regulatory reporting burdens for companies. Section 417 of Companies Act 2006 stated that all directors of quoted companies must produce a business review in their annual reports The primary objective of the Business Review is to inform shareholders of the company on how directors have performed to "promote the success of the company" as provided under Section 172 of the Companies Act 2006[18].

In August 2013, the British government enacted the Companies Act 2006 (Strategic Report and Directors' Report) Regulations 2013 for the strategic report and directors' report. It inserts new Sections 414A to 414D into the Companies Act 2006. At the same time Section 417 of the Companies Act 2006, which required the directors to produce a business review of the company's activity, has been repealed[19].

According to Section 414A of the Companies Act 2006, unless the company is entitled to the small company[20] exemption, the directors of a company must prepare a strategic report for each financial year of the company. For a financial year in which the company is a parent company

---

[17] *See* Paul L. Davies & Sarah Worthington, *Gower and Davies' Principles of Modern Company Law*, 716.

[18] *See* Saleem Sheikh, *A guide to the Companies Act* 2006(2008), 881.

[19] *See* Paul L. Davies & Sarah Worthington, *Gower and Davies' Principles of Modern Company Law*, 717-719.

[20] According to Section 382 of the Companies Act 2006, a company is small if it meets two of the following criteria: (a) Turnover: Not more than £10.2 million; (b) Balance sheet total: Not more than 5.1 million; (c) Number of employees: Not more than 50.

and the directors of the company prepare group accounts, the strategic report must be a group strategic report relating to the entities included in the consolidation[21]. The group strategic report may give greater emphasis to the matters that are significant to the undertakings included in the consolidation, taken as a whole[22].

Section 414C(1) of the Companies Act 2006 states that "the purpose of the strategic report is to inform members of the company and help them assess how the directors have performed their duty under section 172 (duty to promote the success of the company)[23]." The strategic report should reflect the collective view of the company's directors. It must contain a fair review of the company's business. That is a balanced and comprehensive analysis of the development and performance of the company's business in the period and of its position at the end of it and must contain a description of the principal risks and uncertainties facing the company. In addition, the strategic report should also contain a description of the principal risks and uncertainties the company faces[24]. The review must, to the extent necessary for an understanding of the development, performance or position of the company's business, include analysis using financial key performance indicators and, where appropriate, analysis using other key performance indicators, including information relating to environmental and employee matters[25]. 'Key performance indicators' are factors by reference to which the development, performance or position of the company's business can be measured effectively[26]. A company qualifying as medium-sized for a

---

[21] Companies Act 2006, s.414A.

[22] Ibid., s.414A(4).

[23] Ibid., s.414C(1).

[24] Ibid., s.414C.

[25] Ibid.

[26] Ibid., s.414C(5)

financial year does not need to include non-financial information[27].

For quoted companies, the strategic report must disclose further information. It must contain the main trends and factors likely to affect the future development, performance and position of the company's business and information about environmental matters including the impact of the company's business on the environment. The strategic report should also address the company's employees, social, community and human rights issues, including information about any policies of the company in relation to those matters and the effectiveness of those policies. If the strategic report does not contain the information on environmental matters, employees and social, community and human rights issues, it must state which of those kinds of information it does not contain[28].

Besides, in the case of a quoted company the strategic report must contain a description of the company's strategy and of the company's business model, and a breakdown showing at the end of the financial year the number of persons of each sex who were directors of the company, the number of persons of each sex who were senior managers of the company (other than those who were directors) and the number of each person of each sex who were employees of the company[29]. However, a company is not required to disclose information in the strategic report about impending developments or matters in the course of negotiation if the disclosure would, in the opinion of the directors, be seriously prejudicial to the interests of the company[30].

In order to implement Article 1(1) and (3) of the EU Non-

---

[27] Ibid., s.414C(6).

[28] Ibid., s.414C(7).

[29] Ibid., s.414C(8).

[30] Ibid., s.414C(14).

Financial Reporting (NFR) Directive[31], the British government enacted the Companies, Partnerships and Groups (Accounts and Non-Financial Reporting) Regulations 2016[32] inserting two new sections, Section 414CA and Section 414CB, into the Companies Act 2006. Although the quoted companies have already disclosed specific information on the company's strategy, business model, human rights and gender diversity in their strategic report, Section 414CA of the the Companies Act 2006 imposes a reporting obligation on large public-interest entities, such as listed companies and qualifying partnerships, banks, insurance undertakings and other companies, to disclose relevant non-financial environmental and social information in their strategic reports[33]. Section 414CB sets out the content of the non-financial information statement, which includes environmental matters, the company's employees, social matters, respect for human rights, and anti-corruption and anti-bribery matters[34].

In short, Section 172 of the the Companies Act 2006 requires directors to have regard to a range of interests in discharging their duty to promote the success of their company. Under the current framework, the primary goal of directors is to promote the success of the company in the collective best interests of the shareholders. Nevertheless, directors must take into account non-shareholder interests when considering, in good faith, what will best promote the success of the company. Therefore Section 172 of the Companies Act 2006 can be viewed as a guidance for those companies engaging in CSR. Further, Section 172 also links to the

---

[31] Directive 2014/95/EU of the European Parliament and of the Council of 22 October 2014 amending Directive 2013/34/EU as regards disclosure of non-financial and diversity information by certain large undertakings and groups Text with EEA relevance.

[32] SI 2016/1245.

[33] Companies Act 2006, s. 414CA.

[34] Ibid., s.414CB.

reporting requirements set out in the Companies Act 2006. As stated earlier, the strategic report has three main objectives: (1) to provide an analysis of the company's past performance; (2) to describe the principal risks the company faces and how they might affect its future prospects; and (3) to provide insight into the company's business model and its main strategy and objectives.

III. Regulation of Social Enterprises in the United Kingdom

Social enterprises have been entering the British economy for many decades. In general, social enterprises collapse the traditional barrier between profit and nonprofit organizations, and straddle the border between the public and the private sector. The founders of social enterprise could face difficulties when operating within traditionally legal frameworks. On the one hand, the regulations were not sufficiently flexible to provide a regime which was also attractive to those who wanted to make a profit as well as pursued social purposes. On the other hand, it could not ensure whether companies that were designated "social enterprises" did indeed pursue social goals. Accordingly, this might call for a special legal framework to provide a distinct and easily recognized legal identity for social enterprises, and to impose restrictions on what companies may do as long as they are classified as social enterprises. Based on the above reasons, the British government enacted the Companies (Audit, Investigations and Community Enterprise) Act 2004 to establish a special legal framework for social enterprises[35]. Before the enactment of this Act, social enterprises could take various legal forms and they did not have a distinct legal identity. The society did not have a clear

---

[35] *See* Paul L. Davies & Sarah Worthington, *Gower and Davies' Principles of Modern Company Law*, 10; Janet Rosser, *Tolley's Company Law Handbook* (23rd ed. 2015), 229.

understanding of what social enterprises were. The Companies (Audit, Investigations and Community Enterprise) Act 2004 creates a new type of company for social enterprises, the Community Interest Company (CIC), to provide a distinct and easily recognized legal identity for social enterprises[36]. The legal structure of CICs is designed to encourage people to establish social enterprises that benefit local communities, rather than being focused on generating a profit for the company's shareholders.

CICs are regulated in a similar way to ordinary companies but are intended as a not for profit distribution company. Companies that are formed as CICs or become CICs are formed under the Companies Act 2006 and are subject to the general framework of the company law[37]. A CIC can be either a companies limited by shares or a company limited by guarantee[38]. However, CICs differ from ordinary companies in that they must have clear social objectives. A company wishing to register as a CIC should be approved by the Regulator of CICs and is not an excluded company. Excluded companies are companies which are (or when formed would be) political parties, political campaigning organizations, or subsidiaries of a political party or of a political campaigning organization[39]. A CIC is required to have a name ending with an approved designation. For public limited companies, the designation is "Community Interest PLC", while for other companies, it is "Community Interest Company", or "CIC", or the Welsh equivalent[40]. These designations must not be used by companies which are not CICs. Further, it must submit a "community interest statement" to the Regulator of CICs, containing a declaration that the company's activities

---

[36] *See* Ibid.

[37] *See* Ibid.

[38] Companies (Audit, Investigations and Community Enterprise) Act 2004, s.26.

[39] Ibid., s.35. *See also* Janet Rosser, *Toliey's Company Law Handbook*, 230-31.

[40] Ibid., s.33.

will be carried on for the benefit of the community and an indication of how it is proposed that such activities will have that effect[41]. In order to become a CIC, a company must also satisfy the community interest test. A company meets the community interest test if a reasonable person may consider that its activities are being carried on for the benefit of the community[42].

One of the main features of a CIC is the asset lock. For the purpose of ensuring that CICs use their assets and profits only for the benefit of the communities they serve, there are restrictions on how they can dispose of their assets. These restrictions are known as the "asset lock[43]."

If any assets are to be transferred out of the CIC, that transfer must meet one of the following requirements: (1) it must be made at market value; (2) it must be transferred to another asset-locked body[44] which is specified in the CIC's Articles of Association; (3) it must be transferred to another CIC with the CIC Regulator's approval; (4) it must be otherwise made for the benefit of the community[45].

Although the legislation permits a CIC to pay dividends to its shareholders if the CIC is limited by shares rather than by guarantee, the payment of dividends is subject to a statutory cap set by the Regulator of CICs[46]. The dividend cap may strike a balance between encouraging people to invest in CICs and the principle that the assets and profits of a CIC should be devoted to the benefit of the community. Nevertheless, the dividend cap does not apply if the shares are held by an asset-locked

---

[41] See Janet Rosser, *Toliey's Company Law Handbook*, 232-234.

[42] Companies (Audit, Investigations and Community Enterprise) Act 2004, s.35(2).

[43] See Janet Rosser, *Toliey's Company Law Handbook*, 237.

[44] An asset-locked body means a community interest company, a charity, a permitted registered society or a body established outside the United Kingdom that is the equivalent to those persons.

[45] See Janet Rosser, *Toliey's Company Law Handbook*, 237.

[46] See Ibid., at 238.

body specified in the Articles of Association, or held by an asset-locked body not specified in the Articles of Association, but the Regulator of CICs has consented to the payment of the dividend[47].

Before October, 2014, the dividend cap previously had three elements: (1) the dividend per share cap linked dividend payments to the paid up value of the share; (2) the maximum aggregate dividend cap limited the total dividend declared in terms of the profits available for distribution; (3) the capacity to carry forward unused dividend payments for up to 5 years[48]. The dividend per share cap and the capacity to carry forward unused dividend payment to future years was removed in October 2014. Now the dividend cap has a single element called the maximum aggregate dividend cap. The maximum aggregate dividend cap is retained at 35%[49].

Moreover, there is also a restriction on the level of interest that a CIC may pay on a loan where payment is dependent on the company's profits (i.e. any rate which is linked to the company's profits or turnover or to any item in the balance sheet of the company)[50]. The current interest cap is 20% of the average amount of a CIC's debt, or sum outstanding under a debenture issued by it, during the 12-month period immediately preceding the date on which the interest on that debt or debenture becomes due[51].

In the event of liquidation, the CIC legislation does not interfere with the standard liquidation proceedings, but there is one major exception. The exception is where some of the company's property remains after satisfaction of the company's liabilities. Normally, these

---

[47] *See* Ibid.

[48] *See* Ibid., at 239-40.

[49] *See* Ibid., at 240.

[50] *See* Ibid.

[51] *See* Ibid., at 241.

residual assets would be distributed to the shareholders, but in the case of a CIC the legislation limits distribution to shareholders, who cannot receive more than the paid up value of their shares[52]. If any residual assets remain after such distribution to shareholders, they must be distributed as follows. (1) if the Articles of Association specify an asset-locked body to which any remaining residual assets of the company should be distributed, the remaining residual assets will be distributed to that asset-locked body in such proportions or amounts, as the Regulator of CICs directs; (2) if the Articles of Association do not specify an asset-locked body, the remaining residual assets will be distributed to such asset-locked body (or bodies), in such proportions or amounts, as the Regulator of CICs directs; (3) if the Regulator of CICs is aware that asset-locked body specified in the Articles of Association is being wound up, or receives representations from a member, or director, of the CIC stating that it is not an appropriate recipient of the remaining residual assets and the Regulator of CICs agrees with those representations, then the remaining residual assets will be distributed to such asset-locked body, in such proportions or amounts, as the Regulator of CICs directs[53]. In other words, any remaining residual assets must be used by the CIC for public or community benefit.

A CIC is subject to the usual accounting and reporting requirements of the Companies Act 2006 and is also required to submit an annual CIC report to the regulator. The CIC report must contain a fair and accurate description of the manner in which the company's activities during the

---

[52] That is, what was paid to the company in respect of their shares, including both the nominal value of the share and any premium paid to the company.

[53] *See* Janet Rosser, *Toliey's Company Law Handbook*, 254. When considering issuing such a direction the Regulator must: (a) consult the directors and members of the CIC to the extent the Regulator considers practical and appropriate to do so; (b) have regard to the desirability of distributing assets in accordance with any relevant provisions of the company's articles; and (c) give notice of any direction to the CIC and liquidator.

financial year have benefited the community. It also includes details concerning directors' remuneration, dividends declared, and interest paid on any capped loans[54].

Basically, the Regulator of CICs should monitor whether CICs comply with the law. Stakeholders or shareholders can complain to the Regulator of CICs and the Regulator of CICs can take further steps. The Regulator of CICs may investigate the affair of a CIC or appoint any person (other than a member of the Regulator's staff) to investigate the affairs of a community interest company on behalf of the Regulator[55]. The Regulator of CICs may also authorize members of his own staff to carry out an investigation[56]. The investigator may require the company or any other person to produce such documents (in whatever form) or provide such information as they may specify. Failure to comply with a requirement may be treated as contempt of the court[57].

Further, the Regulator of CICs may by order require a CIC to allow the annual accounts of the company to be audited by a qualified auditor appointed by the Regulator (at the Regulator's expense). On completion of the audit the auditor must make a report to the Regulator of CICs on such matters and in such form as the Regulator specifies[58].

The Regulator of CICs will take account of all information and complaints received in respect of CICs and where necessary seek further information. The Regulator of CICs will attempt where possible to resolve any problems informally with the CIC concerned but if this is not possible the Regulator of CICs will resort to the appropriate enforcement action.

---

[54] Companies (Audit, Investigations and Community Enterprise) Act 2004, s.34.

[55] Ibid., s.42.

[56] Ibid., Sch.3 para.5.

[57] *See* Janet Rosser, *Toliey's Company Law Handbook*, 257.

[58] Companies (Audit, Investigations and Community Enterprise) Act 2004, s.43.

The Regulator of CICs may bring civil proceedings in the name and on behalf of a CIC where its shareholders or directors have failed to do so. However, before instituting civil proceedings, the Regulator of CICs must give written notice to the company stating the cause of action, the remedy sought, and a summary of the facts on which the proceedings are to be based[59].

In addition, the Regulator of CICs can by order remove or appoint a director of a CIC where: (a) there is misconduct or mismanagement in the administration of the company; (b) it is necessary to protect the company's property; (c) the company is not satisfying the community interest test; or (d) the company does not carry on any activities in pursuit of its social purpose[60]. It is intended to ensure that the board of the company has the expertise to remedy the default. The Regulator of CICs may also by order appoint a manager to take control of specified aspects of the company's affairs that are giving cause for concern. The person appointed may be anyone whom the Regulator of CICs thinks appropriate, other than a member of the Regulator's staff[61].

The Regulator of CICs also has the power to vest in trust the property of the CIC. This is intended to provide a means of protecting the assets of a CIC if they are seen to be at risk. The Regulator of CICs has to appoint one of the Regulator's staff as Official Property Holder who, under the direction of the Regulator, will deal with the property on behalf of the company[62].

---

[59] Ibid., s.44.

[60] Ibid., ss.45-46.

[61] Ibid., s.47.

[62] Ibid., s.48.

IV. CSR and Social Enterprises in Taiwan

In Taiwan, CSR has significantly evolved in the past several decades. With an increasing trend of attention devoted to CSR in businesses all over the world, Taiwan's government and self-regulatory organizations follow international practices in promoting CSR.

In 2010, the Taiwan Stock Exchange (TWSE) and Taipei Exchange (TPEx) announced "Corporate Social Responsibility Best Practice Principles for TWSE/TPEx-Listed Companies (CSR Best Practice Principles)" and "Ethical Corporate Management Best Practice Principles for TWSE/TPEx-Listed Companies" as the soft law for driving Taiwan's listed companies to practice CSR. According to the CSR Best Practice Principles, TWSE/TPEx listed companies are advised to follow the principles below to implement CSR: (1) Exercise corporate governance; (2) Foster a sustainable environment; (3) Preserve public welfare; and (4) Enhance disclosure of CSR information[63].

Besides, the CSR Best Practice Principles suggests that "The directors of a TWSE/TPEx listed company shall exercise the due care of good administrators to urge the company to perform its corporate social responsibility initiatives, examine the results of the implementation thereof from time to time and continually make adjustments so as to ensure the thorough implementation of its corporate social responsibility policies. The board of directors of a TWSE/TPEx listed company is advised to give full consideration to the interests of stakeholders, including the following matters, in the company's performance of its corporate social responsibility initiatives: (1) Identifying the company's corporate social responsibility mission or vision, and declaring its corporate social responsibility policy, systems or relevant management

---

[63] Article 4 of Corporate Social Responsibility Best Practice Principles for TWSE/TPEx-Listed Companies.

guidelines; (2) Making corporate social responsibility the guiding principle of the company's operations and development, and ratifying concrete promotional plans for corporate social responsibility initiatives; and (3) Enhancing the timeliness and accuracy of the disclosure of corporate social responsibility information. The board of directors shall appoint executive-level positions with responsibility for economic, environmental, and social issues resulting from the business operations of a TWSE/TPEx listed company, and to report the status of the handling to the board of directors. The handling procedures and the responsible person for each relevant issue shall be concrete and clear.[64]"

For the purpose of performing CSR, listed companies are advised to establish an exclusively (or concurrently) dedicated unit in charge of proposing and enforcing the CSR policies, systems, or relevant management guidelines, and concrete promotional plans and to report on the same to the board of directors on a periodic basis. In addition, listed companies are advised to adopt reasonable remuneration policies, to ensure that remuneration arrangements support the strategic aims of the organization, and align with the interests of stakeholders. It is also advised that the employee performance evaluation system be combined with CSR policies, and that a clear and effective incentive and discipline system be established[65].

Since the CSR reports have become a channel as equally important as financial reports for disclosing information about business performance, the CSR Best Practice Principles also suggests that listed companies shall fully disclose relevant and reliable information relating to their CSR initiatives to improve information transparency. Relevant information relating to CSR which listed companies shall disclose includes: (1) The policy, systems or relevant management guidelines,

---

[64] Ibid., Article 7.

[65] Ibid., Article 9.

and concrete promotion plans for corporate social responsibility initiatives, as resolved by the board of directors; (2) The risks and the impact on the corporate operations and financial condition arising from exercising corporate governance, fostering a sustainable environment and preserving social public welfare; (3) Goals and measures for realizing the corporate social responsibility initiatives established by the companies, and performance in implementation; (4) Major stakeholders and their concerns; (5) Disclosure of information on major suppliers' management and performance with respect to major environmental and social issues; (6) Other information relating to corporate social responsibility initiatives[66]. Further, listed companies shall adopt internationally widely recognized standards or guidelines when producing CSR reports, to disclose the status of their implementation of the corporate social responsibility policy. It is advisable to obtain a third-party assurance or verification for reports to enhance the reliability of the information in the reports. The reports are advised to include: (1) The policy, system, or relevant management guidelines and concrete promotion plans for implementing corporate social responsibility initiatives; (2) Major stakeholders and their concerns; (3) Results and a review of the exercising of corporate governance, fostering of a sustainable environment, preservation of public welfare and promotion of economic development; (4) Future improvements and goals[67].

In 2013, the Financial Supervisory Commission (FSC) announced a five-year Corporate Governance Roadmap as a guideline for promoting corporate governance and CSR policies in Taiwan. In November 2014, the TWSE and TPEx, under the FSC's instruction, required listed companies from the food processing, financial and chemical sectors with paid-in capital more than NT$10 billion, as well as companies which

---

[66] Ibid., Article 28.

[67] Ibid., Article 29.

have over 50% of their total revenues coming from food and beverage businesses, to prepare CSR reports annually starting in 2015. The obligation to publish a CSR report now is expanded to smaller listed enterprises with paid-in capital of more than NT$5 billion[68].

Although CSR in Taiwan has received increased attention and recognition in the business community, Article 1 of Taiwan's Company Act provides that "The term "company" as used in this Act denotes a corporate juristic person organized and incorporated in accordance with this Act for the purpose of profit making[69]." It may be an obstacle impeding companies from better implementing CSR. As stated earlier, in the United Kingdom, the Companies Act of 2006 adopts the so-called "enlightened shareholder value" approach, which requires directors to "have regard to" a range of stakeholder interests as they promote the success of the company for shareholders. In view of this, the "Steering Committee of Company Act Reform"(公司法全盤修正修法委員會)[70] recommends to add a provision which allows the directors of a company to consider the interests of stakeholders under the Taiwan's Companies Act[71]. Recently, Taiwan's government proposes an amendment draft to the Company Act, wherein a supplement to the for-profit clause in Article 1 provides that "the company may behave in a manner that promotes public interests, so as to properly fulfill its social responsibilities." Through a supplement to the for-profit clause in Article 1 of the Company Act,

---

[68] Article 2 of the Taiwan Stock Exchange Corporation Rules Governing the Preparation and Filing of Corporate Social Responsibility Reports by TWSE Listed Companies; Article 2 of the Taipei Exchange Rules Governing the Preparation and Filing of Corporate Social Responsibility Reports by TPEx Listed Companies.

[69] Article 1 of the Company Act.

[70] Taiwan's company law scholars set up a "Steering Committee of Company Act Reform" in February 2016 with many participants from multiple industries, government and universities to study each relevant topic extensively and propose amendments to the Company Act.

[71] http://www.scocar.org.tw/pdf/section3.pdf.

the directors in running the company may consider the interests of the stakeholders rather than merely the interests of shareholders.

With regard to social enterprises, the Taiwan's Executive Yuan announced the Social Enterprise Action Plan in 2014 to promote and encourage people to engage in social enterprises. According to the Social Enterprise Action Plan, there are four ways to develop social enterprises in Taiwan: (1) Deregulation: To create a friendly legal environment for social enterprises; (2) Networking: To promote and build a social networking platform for different groups of social enterprises at home and abroad; (3) Financing: To provide multiple channels of funding through angels, VCs, credit guarantees, etc.; and (4) Incubation: To build an incubation mechanism for social enterprises and establish a professional support system[72].

As mentioned earlier, founders of social enterprises often face difficulties when operating within existing legal frameworks. This is because traditional company law and the structures it provides for typically inhibit companies' ability to prioritize a social mission over the interests of shareholders. Although Taiwan's government encourages people to establish social enterprises, the lack of appropriate legal framework for social enterprises will challenge the development of social enterprises. In contrast, the British government has established a special legal framework for social enterprises and opted to create new legal forms that can be used for social enterprises. This does not remove the ability to continue to use traditional legal forms, but adds an additional option to founders of social enterprises. This article suggests that Taiwan shall emulate the British model to establish an appropriate legal framework to support and stimulate the development of social enterprises.

---

[72] https://www.ey.gov.tw/Upload/RelFile/26/716149/8d8b6be7-0e21-4a37-9c72-871e28b325d2.pdf.

V. Conclusion

Today, CSR and social enterprises have become hot topics worldwide. In order to promote CSR and social enterprises, on the one hand, the British government has adopted the "enlightened shareholder value" approach into Section 172 of the Companies Act 2006 which requires directors to consider the stakeholders' interests in discharge their duty to promote the success of their company. On the other hand, the British government enacted the Companies (Audit, Investigations and Community Enterprise) Act 2004 to establish a special legal framework for social enterprises. In contrast, Taiwan appears not to consider this problem in a meaningful way. The current Taiwanese laws pertaining to CSR and social enterprises need to be reviewed and amended on a comprehensive basis in order to create a more orderly, transparent, fair and efficient system in Taiwan.

On Policy Guideline and Corporate Social Responsibility through Financial Tsunami : The Case of Taiwan

Dr. Hsin-Chang Lu

Associate Professor, Department of International Business,
National Taiwan University

I. Introduction

Right after the financial tsunami occurred in 2008, the expectation for prospects of banking reform and various proposals for re-regulation in the financial sectors worldwide were highly welcomed at the time. Ten years later, we tend to find that most governments in the developed world are cautious at best and did not live up to the promise to mend the financial structure, in need of great repair[1]. More than that, critical legal cases are ignored profoundly and often dismissed from the court systems at the outset.

How can this ever happen after drastic harm caused by continuous financial crisis at the turn of this century? Well, lack of immediate response from the formal institutions might come with good reasons as economic growth does rely on the intermediating role played by the banking sector and active risk taking. No need to mention that court ruling often based on post assessment and is at its best an inefficient approach to serve justice afterwards. As such, a balanced mix of preventive activities and cares assigned ex ante among financial

---

[1] https://www.bloomberg.com/news/articles/2018-02-09/ten-years-after-the-crisis-banks-win-big-in-trump-s-washington.

beneficiaries cannot be over emphasized.

What matters most is proper split of benefit and cost to all sides involved through the end of any investment projects. However, recent banking scandals such as Wells Fargo or Citi, over charging transaction fees and required interest payment, keep reminding us of the peril in self auditing and strength of consumers' awareness. Gradually policy and law makers have learned to set the "default options" in various financial services so as to enhance the consumers right and to assist the fulfillment of the administrative duty.

Other than starting ex post a lengthy period to recover losses through the legal procedure, it's getting common in the light of Corporate Social Responsibility (CSR) to encourage enterprises on comprising and improving in the well beings of society's endeavors[2]. One may wonder if there be reasons to argue for responsibility delegated to the corporate sector. For instance, won't there be room for sound practice of CSR, especially through the relevant process of decision making about the protocol of services and product design?

Out of positive selection process, say under a proper market competition, we may wish to see that CSR is infiltrating into the formation of corporate culture so as to mold company visions and spark stakeholders' involvement as well. As leading groups are getting ready to enrich the quality of community life, their strategy set and choices made would fit coherently for a longer term economic attempt.

On the contrast, some scholars argue forcefully that firms are built to suit interest of their shareholders only. Milton Friedman (1970) stated vividly that businessmen who believed in sharing load of any social duties are no entrepreneurs in a free enterprise system. He wrote straightly from the beginning of that very article, "In fact they are – or would be if they

---

[2] https://search.proquest.com/docview/1948833864/fulltextPDF/FB7927F33EEA4862 PQ/1?accountid=14229.

or anyone else took them seriously—preaching pure and unadulterated socialism. Businessmen who talk this way are unwitting puppets of the intellectual forces that have been undermining the basis of a free society these past decades."

Besides that, within the confine to exercise rationality and independent decision making, trust in business judgment is the central theme of American corporate law. Thus, corporate officers and people in charge are already left free mostly ex ante. Certainly they made a point and speak up loudly all through the past century. It would assume that corporate directors and managers have completed their duties so long as they adopt normal activities and behave rationally in the interests of share owners and corporation.

Sceptics argued that pursuing profit should trounce and managers should act accordingly. Since the late 80's, managerial compensation were increasingly tuned up to some financial yardsticks, be it a direct link to profits, equity or rates of return on some types of assets. This is taken as a stronger alignment between managers and broad interest of shareholders. Although some scholars worry the properness of governance under a loose contractual arrangement, pure financial incentives still dominate before the occurrence of the financial tsunami in 2009.

This line of reasoning admits the deferential judgement of business liability, i.e., it would be impractical to verify legal responsibilities and faults committed out of the decision process. As such, those in charge and benefited most from the corporates might get away easily from accountability and legal obligation. Some researchers focused instead on factors of business lobbying and the ease of law enforcement unto firm performance, namely effects reflected in stock returns and share price volatility (Hochberg, Sapienza, and Annette Vissing-JØrgensen 2009).

In their joint work, the authors evaluate the impact of the Sarbanes-Oxley Act (SOX) by various lobbying behavior of investors and that of corporate insiders. Investors lobbied for stricter implementation, while corporate insiders and business groups lobbied against the extent. An expectation is that SOX would reduce agency problems. The authors do identify firms affected most by SOX as those with insiders more likely characterized by agency problems. Thus investors expected positively regards to the legal impact and lobbied against strategically but not due to concerns over higher compliance costs

The social anxiety and common beliefs would wish for seeking ways out so as to make up the vacuum, be it through the formal mechanism, legal setup and market disciplines formally. However, great thinkers prefer leaving the choice and rights to do to the business enterprises. They doubt the core meaning of CSR based on own beliefs and negative reactions among the related beneficiaries. No need to say that a cardinal principle for CSR to spread in the modern world is rarely found yet.

Yet through comparative studies to examine business details, it is about the right time to call for attention throughout the globe urgently. Related questions include that: can we assume an active role for the public sector to direct and enhance the functioning of CSR? The remaining issues to be examined in this paper go as follows:

1. Is there positive feedback and potential gains collectively among CSR actions adopted across industries within an economy?
2. Will there be serious role to be played by the authority? Can the effort of coordination lead to a better outcome for consumers in particular and the society in the longer run?
3. Should we expand the spectrum of SCRs through the public involvement? If so, under which circumstance and in which direction?

Next section will trace the conceptual development of corporate social responsibility, both for a theoretical construction and timely arguments—sound economic reasons for its very existence, then as now. In the third section, we will go through the transitory period when the problem of consumer bad loans got most attention and became a tough issue in Taiwan. Further comments and conclusion drawn from comparative readings will follow in the last section.

II. Recent development in the light of moral and behavioral concern

An effective governance would require accountability to those in charge for responsible actions. Yet, Milton Friedman (1970) continued his triumphant position, that the goal of business should be constrained to maximize profits solely. He addressed at many surrounding that any democratic societies should implement laws to let the corporations maximize her shareholder returns freely. Some fourteen years after the publication of that news article, his speech was turned into a recording video and televised on the US Public Broadcast System (PBS).

Sadly, recent development in several occasions of corporate scandals since Enron has inspired more studies in corporate governance and social responsibility. It's well understood by now that there exist inefficiencies potentially from tradeoff and conflict of interest under profit maximization. After all, the complexity in modern time and world business already changed a lot. The demand of better corporate governance as well as shifting focus of economic researches is a reaction to scandals and business crises.

Many findings based on model thinking are meant to rule out possibilities of certain wrong doings. In essence, we need to find accountability, one way or another. Despite the suspicion expressed by some economists, CSR has become gradually an unseparated feature in corporate landscape. One would hope that an effective governance out of resetting institutions, both in the private and in public sectors, should make it harder for individuals to get away easily.

As such, more business schools recognize the need to prepare the would-be managers in meeting challenges and various angels of social responsibility. The Interdisciplinary Ethics Applied Center setup in Reeds University, for instance, may serve a good example. It invites philosophers appointed in other departments to give lessons on ethical dilemmas. We will document and review some of the progress made below, including trial efforts conducted in advanced business schools as well. This alternative teaching deepens the complexity of ethical reasoning and moral readiness among class participants.

1. A contrast of judicial ruling and changes in social attitude toward business ethics after the financial crisis

There remains a sharp contrast to policy making and the field of law economics. Both try hard to influence outcomes with different approaches, final attempts and set of behavioral assumptions. Fortunately, studies in ethics learning find that more knowledge of ethical difficulties do prepare students with determination to well-intentioned commitments. One wishes that they would take preventive actions Instead. In the end, less likely will they claim that no harm has been done or it's just beyond their control and authorized actions.

To tender the society better, the emerging field of "behavioral law and economics" also recognizes the importance of rules integrated with default choices. Contrast to the rosy thought, the decision by the US supreme court after hearing the case, CalPERS v. ANZ Securities[3], Inc., may ring an alarm bell for many. It is related to claims of Lehman Brothers bankruptcy[4] and the ruled outcome is crucial indeed. The

---

[3] https://www.reuters.com/article/us-usa-court-calpers/u-s-top-court-buries-calpers-lawsuit-over-lehman-collapse-idUSKBN19H1N8.

[4] On September 15, 2008, Lehman Brothers filed for Chapter 11 bankruptcy with $619 billion in debt. Lehman was the fourth-largest U.S. investment bank with $639 billion in assets and employed more than 25,000 people worldwide at the time. Lehman's bankruptcy filing was the largest by now, dwarfing similar cases such as WorldCom and Enron.

question in harsh dispute is the timing constraint for investors to sue individually, who might have chosen to join with the 2011 class settlement earlier.

CalPERS, the largest pension fund owned by California public employees, wondered of the gain in separate litigation for institutional trader relative to that of going with the class settlement. In the case of CalPERS, it filed a lawsuit in the Northern District of California against Lehman but it was consolidated with others into New York for pre-trial purpose. Is it legitimate for them to opt out later on and sue individually? Most would believe in its right to file a lawsuit separately as it met the three-year statute of limitations.

CalPERS decided to opt out before the class action was settled. We would also put high expectation normally to seek justice done through the legal procedures. Yet much to a surprise, the district court in the case of CalPERS v. ANZ Securities ruled otherwise. The 2nd U.S. Circuit Court of Appeals in New York upheld the District Court's decision. In the end, the California Public Employees' Retirement System was deemed by the Court as waiting too long to sue.

Back to 1974, the Supreme Court then prevailed that the statute of limitations period to sue should not be tolled for all members related. Against the wisdom learnt in the case of American Pipe decades ago, the opt-out after a class action in this case is required to be in a timely fashion. The US Supreme Court granted certiorari to CalPERS' petition after an oral argument held in mid-April, 2017. Shortly, the panel of the Court justices ruled by a 5-4 margin to uphold the decision reached by the federal appeals court.

According to the court records, the administrators by now have distributed around $147 billion of Lehman's holdings to creditors. The responsible banks, such as Bank of New York Mellon Corp (BNY), Royal Bank of Canada (RY.TO), and France's BNP Paribas SA (BNPP.PA), are home free among others. We should watch carefully for the impact of this ruling in the near future.

A similar development occurred where Barkley[5] Capital Inc. was protected from further legal action: first by the agency, the Financial Industry Regulatory Authority (FIRNA), after paying more than $10 million in restitution, including interest, to affected customers, and was fined $3.75 million. In total, 343 of the transactions resulted into a loss for more than $818,000, which was inconsistent with goals specified or risk tolerance rated by its customers. FINRA, overseeing fund management, found that Barclays processed 1,723 fund transactions wrongly, amounted to 39 percent of suspicious accounts reviewed from March to August 2014.

Besides, the Justice Department[6] of the U.S. started a probe targeted 36 RMBS deals created from Barkley Capital, which involved $31 billion worth and more than half of these derivatives went defaulted. This sort of mortgage bonds might have fueled the 2009 financial crisis. The official claimed that loans quality backed on the subprime mortgage deals were less worthy than Barclays had claimed.

Certainly, Barkley denied this allegation from the outset and the strategy paid in the end. They pay $2 billion finally to settle this probe instead of $5 billion at its first request. Notice that top ten banks and financial companies during the subprime crisis paid an amount of 66.6 billion dollars collectively. Not only there is the taboo for "too big to fail" but that together we stand, even in any wrong doing.

2. Modification of class design for MBA programs

Firms in different industries have brought benefits and casualties to the society variously. Over the past decade after global financial tsunami, it has changed dramatically and increased the chance to do harm more widely.

---

5 https://www.reuters.com/article/us-barclays-mutualfunds-settlement/barclays-in-13-75-million-u-s-settlement-over-mutual-funds-idUSKBN0UC18920151229.

6 https://www.bloomberg.com/news/articles/2018-03-29/barclays-agrees-to-pay-2-billion-to-settle-u-s-rmbs-suit.

Business can no longer hide behind the legal status but have to come forward to make some impacts. Most of them did agree on the externality made to the environment at the right start of the industrial revolution.

Concerns other than profit making and worker right are often lumped into the category of corporate social responsibility. How does one compose oneself and make forceful argument upon the alarming call to act responsibly? Changes in beating down resistance came in many ways. Philosophical thoughts can offer different perspectives on ethical dilemmas, which drive a decent talk for ethical reasoning. Meanwhile, emphasis of personal accountability under legal practice and attempt to stand outside the safety net is the key for qualified job completion.

A recent column on Financial Times[7] starts to recognize the speedy spread of MBA courses related to corporate responsibility and social impacts. In the past, they may come under other terms, such as improving good citizenship of the company, making environment friendly investment, creating social sustainability and better income equality, etc. After all, it sounds nothing new really as companies did pay lip service from time to time.

The issue presented requires students in considering the complexity but also making fine decision among competing priorities. Ethics lessons are also integrated into the curriculum of business schools worldwide, particularly on privileged MBA programs. Top notched MBA students in the US are encouraged to learn of related thinking in CSR and debates in ethical issues. Business courses are redefined to incorporate harsh subjects and push MBAs to challenge their team members.

After recognizing the need for graduates of business schools to get a thorough understanding of CSR, some privileged schools also choose to reform programs on their own way. Hundreds of second tier schools in the US and in other developed countries signed into the Principles

---

[7] https://www.ft.com/content/909d3b50-e4a5-11e7-a685-5634466a6915.

for Responsible Management Education by the United Nations as well. Besides encouraging the joint efforts to incorporate business ethics in higher learning, it also comes with a coherent position for a sustainable development under the guideline by the United Nations.

Other than the concurrent topics, privileged MBA programs[8], especially those located in the US, encourage students to undertake social initiatives by forming a joint research project. They use pilot studies to explore possible innovation and solutions related to ethical issues. Universities in return grant some seed money for applicants to work it out and sharpen their cases for further funding. Of course, they do make some differentiation and reserves from their regular MBA programs

What seems striking to some is that on the campus of University of Chicago[9], they also start with social impacts and other innovative programs. These trends to encourage the young generation for doing good are also seen in Stanford and NYT, etc. The message is quite clear that they expect students to look for participation other than in the traditional businesses. After all, an understanding of the ethical judgment in advance will lead to a higher chance for a longer term achievement.

They may go as far to understand charitable giving and examine corporate initiatives under CSR. It helps improving the social skill other than attempt to run social enterprises or work for charities in the future. As acting unethically is likely to be detected and punished through the

---

[8] The following schools all come with some form of social initiative programs, they are: Columbia U., Duke U. Fuqua, Emory Goizueta, Harvard Business School, Northwestern U. Kellogg, NYU Stern, Oxford Saïd, Stanford GSB, UCLA Anderson, U Penn Wharton, UT Austin McCombs, Yale SOM, Michigan's Ross School of Business and Chicago Booth.

[9] The Rustandy Center for Social Sector Innovation follows the feature of interdisciplinary study and integrates students body of Chicago Booth's to experience-based learning besides business education. Through experimental programs and social events, the center intends to improve odds and will of solving complex social and environmental problems. https://groups.chicagobooth.edu/social/home/.

loss of social recognition and market failure. For one's future career and the concern of company's opportunity, managers should strike a balance and so take social responsibility into proper consideration.

3. The behavioral economics and alternatives for public policy

After Enron, mechanisms reform such as increasing auditor responsibility, requiring income statements cosigned by the CEO's or setup of other rating agencies are tried yet only come out with mediocre results. The limited liability and separate legal status of managerial teams from share owners have benefited mostly over time though it also creates its own problems.

Due to the misaligned incentives and lack of individual accountability in critical details, it cannot exacerbate these problems as whoever manage operation will respond in somewhat predictable ways to the scheme of incentives. Even with closer regulation, joint position and law enforcement across countries, some sort of oversight remains and blow up sometimes. After all, conflicts of interests are common in any formal institutions, distortions and inefficiency built into corporate governance are also determinants for unwanted outcomes.

The approach of behavioral economics has got more attention these days. Based on the line of literature, it argues that people might be affected predictably as to the way information is presented to them. Even two recent Nobel winners don't think otherwise (Akerlof and Shiller, 2016). However, it's already a common practice[10], be it in marketing

---

[10] Examples illustrated by Akerlof and Shiller (2016), the practice of credit card companies using the tendency for customers to spend more is to increase their presence and leave the cost for monthly payment out of sight. Salesmen on the other hand would induce buyers to focus on immediate saving rather than the overall cost. In general, the financial industry learns well and are ready to exploit dislike for risky investments. Thereby the offer of seemly risk free investment vehicle with complicated payoffs make the day by year of 2008.

content, leadership, nursery, magician or show business.

Yet more and more research findings also show the influence of social norm or peer pressure. All it takes is how information presented to the targeted persons. Once presented tactically, it can induce people to act more likely to some specified directions. It can be powerful just like winning one's consent, in which people would behave themselves up to social expectation. Be it for extra contribution to individual savings account (Kast et al. 2012) or events of charitable giving (Frey and Meier 2004), it works closely as prescribed.

Under the status quo, with a legal structure allowing the function of corporate governance, it may alleviate very little of the potential harm. Productive changes are in great need but not a simple task. It also requires full understanding of underlying causes. To ensure sound competition and encourage accountability, for instance, an effective system cannot ignore the important of individual consent, either through higher self-esteem or positive peer pressure, along with the incentives offered to corporate managers. We are left with fewer options to go afterwards.

Fortunately, economists as a bystander can play an assertive role both by seeing these issues in direction of rationality and to clarify the necessary tradeoffs or to identify admissible instance for real improvement. Peeking into Table 1, one will see the huge difference regarding policy attitudes toward interest cap and short term loans. Other than the uses of law and regulation to address at corporate frauds, increasing transparency always comes first. The following issues seem to beg the question somewhat but it is worthy thinking it over and over again:

i. Is there positive feedback and potential gains collectively among CSR actions adopted across industries within an economy?

ii. Will there be serious role to be played by the authority? Can the

Table 1: A comparison of interest cap and fees in various countries

	Effective Date	**Interest Rate Capped at**	**Fees and other details**
Australia, the National Consumer Credit Protection Act (NCCP)	1 July 2013	48% in most districts	Vague in terms, Amendment for fees, drafted 2018
Britain, the Financial Conduct Authority (FCA)	2 Jan. 2015 Reviewed in 2017 for an 3-year extent and planned to review again in 2020.	0.8% daily rate. A loan of £100 borrowed for 30 days and repaid on time will not pay more than £24 in fees and charges.	15 dollars for a default charge No borrower will ever pay back more than twice what they borrowed.
USA on payday loan 24 states legal 9 states no position 17 states prohibited	Most states legislation passed since July 21, 2010	if legal, 36% in most cases District of Columbia 24% in all	Restriction for how many times to roll over, from 0 to 4 times maximal

Source: Compiled by the author from various sources of public files and related news report.

effort of coordination lead to a better outcome for consumers in particular and the society in the longer run?

iii. Should we expand the spectrum of SCRs through the public involvement?

If so, under which circumstance and in which direction?

III. An overview of consumer financing in Taiwan and through the Crisis

The need for innovative financing services and the role of banking sector in any modern society is well understood. Benhabib & Spiegel (2000) establish empirically a positive contribution to economic growth and increasing private investment in a comparative study of five developing countries. They conclude that the size of overall private debts relative to GDP appears to influence the economy through the enhanced total factor productivity. Furthermore, functioning of the banking sector matters in the formation of human capital as well.

Their finding is crucial indeed as trade-led growth did rely on the support of banking service. Besides, continuing progress in the financial sector demand employees to be highly educated. The liberalization of banking sectors in most Asian countries is demanded as high priority in trade talk with the advanced countries. Yet among economic deregulation worldwide, the interaction over the extent of policy adjustment, sound banking regulation needed as well as any misbehaving attempt by some participants are less investigated.

Due to the lobbying efforts in and out of the country and the drive for economic transformation, Taiwan started to make necessary legislative changes in the late 80's to cope with the formation of private banks and encourage activities in merger and acquisition among various financial companies later on.

1. *Financial deregulation and the possibility of over banking in Taiwan*

However, newly formed banks chose to lure top managers from the established competitor in order to speed up their business. They focused more on competing away a sure profit. The golden era out of the relaxed regulation in banking services did not deliver much as originally anticipated. Under the pressure to make a quick return and success, a must for the listing of stock exchange in Taiwan, bankers ceased to pay necessary attention to novice service.

At the start, they would instead seek for more secured earnings, such as to lower interest rates in risky loans, mainly offered to the secondhand housing market and investment in the real estate sector. Lots of the new development were in rural areas or places full of mountain views or alone the sea shores. They all come with great imagination for bright future and users' values. Then there came the hard hit by the 1997 Asian crisis.

Early this century, the complete halt in the housing market as well as lack of opportunities in large scale investment in Taiwan, the banking sector suddenly became saturated with huge cash hoarding. This pressure and hint from policy makers drove the private banks into the sphere of non-collateral lending – credit cards business at first and the creation of so called "cash cards" later on. In the meanwhile, we did anticipate a down turn on the way after the millennials hype as well as a reshuffle for unexpected political turmoil across the strait.

2. The impact of economic downturn and restructuring effort in Taiwan

It resulted in a period with negative growth rate in Taiwan. The increasing unemployment as well as economic downturn occurred in 2003 created a need for more domestic consumption and so for the increase in consumption loan. Many privately owned banks thus lowered the requirement for credit rating and the much needed due process, one way or the other.

Through the innovative use of TV programs and commercials, easing the process for credit approvals became the norm. Several banks behaved similarly and believed aggressively in the law of large numbers so as to lure potential customers. Even the young generation or whoever lack of earning potentials, fast cash along with the smart credit rating led to borrow over the limit. Some banks just took them in without second thought to stay in speedy growth.

Down the road to serfdom, young people and risky debtors, you name it, all became target customers. At last, banks ran into the real problem of nonperforming loans. More than half a million people at the turn of 2006 could not repay their loans and some of them were into insolvency, literally speaking. Some banks did debt collecting on their own while other banks switched to the help of debt collecting services.

The bank sector was more eager to balance their book keeping and covered up cleverly by pretending to help whoever could not pay back with their card debt. Actually, that begged an unaddressed question from the start, namely the proper deeds in defining credit card service and the need for responsible marketing. It often went beyond business ethics to the least and sometimes crossed over the legal boundary. The outcry and spread use of the so called "debt slaves" is referred to people facing with the unstoppable use of revolving credit line into the future.

As mentioned previously, some banks also relied on debt collecting companies to go after debtors. As the collection practices often delegated to outsiders, it became too aggressive or violent. They do not shy away from using forces, such as humiliation in public and occasionally forfeited relatives' properties instead. In the case of Taiwan, one more hurdle occurred as how to offer cures for some people to go bankruptcy. Taiwan's bankruptcy law, dated in 1929, was not possible to deal with bad personal debt practically.

It went soured very quickly as family members may be influenced directly. In the end, the issue of accumulated debt through credit card service became a social problem. Some debtors could not stand up the pressure so as to commit suicide. It called in the attention and action of governmental involvement, especially here in Taiwan. Starting that time onward, this law is also applied to individuals who had no assets.

They might lose jobs as well, due to the social shaming and fear out of taming the reputation of companies. Their family life came to a complete stop and joint owned wealth, such as lands, cars or houses, were forfeited abruptly. Therefore, the original purpose is to target people who cannot repay their debts from the outset to start over. By the way, it's also prevailed in Japan and South Korea about the same time.

3. Attempts to alleviate the debt crisis in Taiwan

Certainly, one may wonder more about the health of financial system because of the nonperforming loans. The active involvement by the governmental bureau at the time should take the financial health as one of the underlying reasons. In 2005, the Taiwanese Finance Supervisory Commission (TFSC) directed banks to create a joint negotiation system to deal with the debtors as Taiwan's bankruptcy law was unable to deal with credit card debt in reality. This regulation office also offers rules to direct the process of regeneration, liquidation and other supplementary provisions.

Part of the fixing jobs by this financial bureau was to double check the soundness of bank action and related to the outsourced service for debt collection. The cases of suicide, increased steadily from 2,172 death in 1997 to 4,406 in 2006, might be part of the reasons for Taiwan government to get involved. The uptrend for middle aged people to commit suicides ceased to grow and dropped by nearly one sixth thereafter.

What could this trend tell us regarding the reality of loans and debt collection effort? High incidence of suicides may come with several reasons but it cannot rule out if the result came from an economic downturn or through terrible debt collection. After several protests made by some legal assistance groups and associations of consumers' protection in Northeast Asian countries, the Taiwanese Legislative Yuan finally passed the Debtors Repayment Regulation in 2006.

As the matter of nonperforming loan became much worse, the newly formed TFSC stepped into the mess and encouraged banks to modify their operation in key areas, including issuing process and notification, grading credit scores, customer record keeping and exchanges as well as responsible marketing with warning messages. There was also a time that banks outsourced sale service for campus visit and lure college students to apply for credit cards. As students ran into the debt increasingly, hiding intent just made it much worse.

After all, parents are always the last person to know about. Thus consumer financial regulation became stricter in protective aspects, from marketing details, personnel training, qualification for credit card application and review of income sources. For instance, card issuers, banks and other institutions, facing with a delinquency rate of 8 percent or higher, are suspended temporarily from issuance of new cards.

Once the consumer loans were overdue for more than half a year, it has to be moved into the non-performing loan within some time length. As a result, banks would be held responsible frequently and screw over unsecured loans closer to the credit rating system. Furthermore, the calculating methods in compounding interest payment and fees applicable, the process to write out none performing loans as well as the outsourced debt collection, were modified with guidelines to help banks avoid some wrong doings or bad intention.

It's well known by now that constant pressure out of financial loss can drive the feeling of stress. Whoever in a bad shape would worried more about the job security and relationship with their family and coworkers. The Regulation passed in 2006 gives some protection for borrowers from losing their homes unexpected during the debt restructuring process. Borrowers can now negotiate on their behalf with their banks and creditors directly. If they cannot reach an agreement, the court can then step in and rule instead.

As revolving balances in Taiwan shrank gradually through 2006, the share of the unsecured loans also declined correspondingly by a margin of 11 percent on a y-to-y basis. No need to say that the collective spending by form of using credit cards also fell. It's amounted to a drop of one seventh as consumers got the lesson well. More people were alert to protect their credit records and shy away from over draft. Thus, the number of outstanding cards cut drastically in half, from 40 plus down to 20 million.

4. *Interesting findings out of past experience in consumers' protection*

In the year of 2000, the Legislate Yuan in Taiwan passed the Financial Institution Merger Act. With the proper changes internally and necessary write-offs, the financial strength by the 14 financial holding companies improved. Their business performance made a gross profit of $193.5 billion by 2010 collectively. A great turn back over the period, indeed.

Certainly, even with caution and declaration required in details further, banks may still bump into some unanticipated results. Foreign experience shows that asset management corporations (AMC's) are in better position to deal with debt problems than banks in general. AMC's were introduced into Taiwan at the time of real estate bubbles occurred in the late nineties. Yet personal debts resulted from credit card are more complicated from other loans. Debtors are often connected to several issuing banks.

As there is more than one creditor normally, it is harder to reach an agreement about debt restructuring plan without some compromising activities over the years. Thus, TFSC advised the bankers association of Taiwan into a Public AMCs to deal with complex issues, named as Taiwan United Asset Management Corporation. At first, it served as a coordinator to avoid conflict of interests at hand. As the card loans were organized into a combined package, creditors integrated into one, it is easier to reach an agreement according to some specified rules.

With the revised ruling and changing situations, the public AMC also avoid collecting repayment from low income households, mentally disabled people and during the unemployment. If requested by the debtors, the agency may help enroll the unemployed into job training, loans for extra help, and psychological counseling. Through the administrative and team efforts, it assisted banks and customers in coping the crisis of bad loans and social trust toward the banking sector.

It's well known that pressure out of financial loss can drive the feeling of stress. Whoever in a bad shape would worried much more about job security and relationship with their bosses, family and coworkers. Therefore, the alleviation of poverty need not be the key factor to kick into the thinking of financial policy. Guideline for better loaning services should try not to drive people with low awareness into a situation of no return.

Thus, over the years the CFSA would steer balanced on duty to cover both ends. They have to anticipate the worst in order to avoid escalation of bad outcomes. Whatever methods adopted in Taiwan would be recommended to neighboring countries and help build up their solutions to alleviate their debtors quest and needs. For instance, the interest cap in Taiwan is into law for nearly ninety years. Yet, the treatment of fees collected by credit card companies might go above the interest cap at 20% then. How can we address the need for sound management of card service and at the same time to adhere to legal rights for borrower protection?

The cases of personal bankruptcies in Japan peaked in 2003 around 250,000 according to some news report. Japanese legal association[11] treasured the past experience in Taiwan and finally passed its own reform. It limited the interest cap from 29 down to 20 percent annually and also

---

[11] They called for a conference to invite consumers group and legal scholars from Japan, Korea and Taiwan. The first conference was held at Kagoshima, Japan in 2006 and the second meeting was held next year at National Taiwan University in Taipei, Taiwan.

how much money to borrow from loan companies. The subsequent decrease of bankruptcy was due to the revision of the lending law, effected in 2006. Later on, it put into full effect in 2010 with an ever lower bound at 15%.

After that, Taiwan side started to reconsider the merits of further decrease in revolving interest cap using the card service. It got legislative support in February 2015 and became in effect with the cap at 15% since September 1, 2015[12]. In the end, the managerial team can deliver a clear message inside their organizations along with policy position. They will operate under the request and focus instead more on their strategy rather than protest in vain and go along with the industrial opinions.

According to the survey conducted by Bankers Association in Taiwan, nineteen banks have an average rate below ten percent in 2017. Bank wide average rate is at 11% while six banks carry with higher within interest mean rate. It turns out that banks do follow academic advice to target customers with different risk. Among all within average rates, the maximal is at 13.23% and that of the minimum is at 7.25%. Apparently banks position themselves with different segment of the market and so face to various default rate of nonperforming loan.

IV. Conclusion

Competitive markets are the policy base for laissez-faire in modern time. Banking liberation in Taiwan for new entry does lead to request for further de-regulation. Some restriction would be deemed as unproductive such as the interest cap and is easily bypassed with novice fee charges. It went sky rocked high later on, which explained partially for the increasing lending in card debt. In the end, it causes more troubles than solving the case of the needed.

---

[12] http://www.cna.com.tw/news/afe/201801080185-1.aspx

This would only dig its own tomb as empirical evidences often point to the opposite direction, especially in the case of consumers financing. There is no easy way to avoid deception and banking frauds, be it due to information asymmetry or lack of managerial incentives. Furthermore, bankers also learn to mimic or even license financial services from overseas counterparts. There exists some time lag for spotting wrong doings before the banking sector won in lobbying effort.

Besides that, normally people may get little social attention and mobilize with disadvantage to use resources into negotiating debt relief. Yet more and more organizations get interested in debt settlement on behave of the disadvantaged. Some may claim for low fees with charity sponsors or better management using the financial technology. It actually makes the issue of debt relief ever harder to pursue. More than often, these groups will become creditors for the unlucky clienteles at some stage. Thus some countries[13] start to prohibit the assistance party becomes or arranges for small loan.

Then the whole process of deregulation would come to a full circle. Rules under continuous check and balance matter. It's therefore quite shocking to read the news that the director for US consumers finance would propose four directions for the future changes. The underlying argument is quite simple that the Bureau is way too powerful.

In essence, countries can learn from each other of their administrative experience from each other and make progress with strong social support. Certainly, studies with fact documented closely and of perspectives are highly welcome at any time. Furthermore, the emphasis

---

[13] Namely Australia in the National Consumer Credit Protection Act 2009, Section 111, Division 7: "prohibits a licensee from providing credit assistance to a consumer in relation to short-term credit contracts. It also imposes requirements on a licensee who makes representations about providing credit assistance in relation to small amount credit contracts. It also prohibits a licensee from making third party unsolicited small amount credit contract invitations."

and spread of corporate social responsibility (CSR) will smooth the process of policy persuasion as well as the administrative positioning. We conclude the research findings in the following:

1. The spread and belief in SRC has positive influence to encourage firm participation. However, the scope of SCR should come through open dialogues so as to double check impact of assumptions adopted and reach a common ground.

2. The joint action under SCR within an industry, if timed well, does have some synergy. As to the coordinating action, be it in which direction to follow, priority as well as properness of the legal aspects, governmental bureaus are better informed and often have the firsthand information and complete knowledge.

3. However, the interruption and guidance made by the public sector should aim to establish and strengthen the functioning of normal business. One must avoid overlooking the expertise and opinion proposed by the professionals.

References

Admati, Anat R. 2017. "A Skeptical View of Financialized Corporate Governance." *Journal of Economic Perspectives, 31*(3): 131-50.

Akerlof, George A., and Robert J. Shiller (2016). *Phishing for Phools: The Economics of Manipulation and Deception*. Princeton University Press.

Benhabib, Jess and Mark M. Spiegel (2000). "The Role of Financial Development in Growth and Investment." *Journal of Economic Growth, 5*, pp. 341-60.

Campbell, John Y. (2016). "Restoring Rational Choice: The Challenge of Consumer Financial Regulation." *American Economic Review, 106*(5):1–30.

Eisinger, Jesse. (May 4, 2014). Why Only One Top Banker Went to Jail for the Financial Crisis. The New York Times Magazine. Retrieved from https://www.nytimes.com/2014/05/04/magazine/only-one-top-banker-jail-financial-crisis.html

Frey, B. S., Meier, S. (2004). "Pro-social behavior in a natural setting." *Journal of Economic Behavior & Organization, 54*, pp. 65–88.

Friedman, M. 1970. "The Social Responsibility of Business is to Increase Its Profits." *New York Times Magazine.* September 13, 1970; reprint in Donaldson, T., P.H. Werhane (eds.), *Ethical Issues in Business. A Philosophical Approach.* Englewood Cliffs, N.J.: Prentice Hall: 217-223.

Hochberg, Y. V., Sapienza, P., & Vissing-JØrgensen, A. (2009). A lobbying approach to evaluating the Sarbanes-Oxley Act of 2002. *Journal of Accounting Research, 47*(2), 519-583. DOI: 10.1111/j.1475-679X.2009.00321.x

Kast, Felipe, Stephan Meier, and Dina Pomeranz. 2012. Under-Savers Anonymous: Evidence on Self-Help Groups and Peer Pressure as a Savings Commitment Device NBER Working Paper No. 18417

Oonagh Anne McDonald, (2016) "Holding banks to account for the financial crisis?", *Journal of Financial Crime, 23*(1), pp. 45-69, Retrieved from https://doi.org/10.1108/JFC-08-2015-0041

Thaler, R. H., & Sunstein, C. R. (2008). *Nudge: Improving decisions about health, wealth, and happiness.* New Haven, CT: Yale University Press.

Stempel, Jonathan (DECEMBER 29, 2015) Barclays in $13.75 million U.S. settlement over mutual funds. REUTERS. Retrieved from https://www.reuters.com/article/us-barclays-mutualfunds-settlement/barclays-in-13-75-million-u-s-settlement-over-mutual-funds-idUSKBN0UC18920151229

Driving Corporate Social Responsibility through the European Corporate Law: An Overview of Consumer Protection

Yen-Te Wu

Associate Professor, Chinese Culture University College of Law

J.D., Washington University School of Law, U.S.A.

I. Introduction

Twenty-plus year, elected member, Oliver Balch transitioned from East of England law making in the European Union to advocacy for integrated corporate reporting with the grassroots, London-based International Integrated Reporting Council (IIRC) pro-business coalition.[1] Nonetheless, the wheels of European accountability legislation and regulations continue to grind against the corporate injustices of firms headquartered, or which operate in member states. However, the wheels of capitalism also continue to grind at the expense of human rights; particularly in multinational corporations, which operate in significantly undeveloped countries.[2] The acknowledgement and implementation of corporate social responsibility by the firm contributes to the achievement of national goals and objectives for sustainable development as well as

---

[1] O. Balch, The Disruptors: How Richard Howitt turned from socialist MEP to transparency tsar (2018). http://www.ethicalcorp.com.

[2] K. Ejumudo. Z. Edo. L. Avweromre & J. Sagay. "Environmental issues and corporate social responsibility (CSR in Nigeria Niger Delta region: The need for a pragmatic approach)," *Journal of Social Science and Public Policy* 4 (2012); E. Hennchen, "Royal Dutch Shell in Nigeria: Where do responsibilities end?" *Journal of Business Ethics* 129, no. 1 (2015): 1-25.

to increased competitiveness as a social market economy[3]. This article provides an overview of corporate social responsibility in the European Union with a case study of the social and economic impact of the Royal Dutch Shell oil excavation activities and performance in the Niger Delta.

1. *Background*

The European Union is credited as being first to fully embrace the corporate social responsibility movement.[4] Adam Smith (1776) supported that *"the wealth acquired in the English cities frequently was used to purchase uncultivated land; and wealthy merchants aspiring toward country gentility became the best of the community improvers"*.[5] However, modern speculators describe the European corporate social responsibility policy agenda as "broad, but undeveloped".[6] The European Commission defined corporate social responsibility as *"a concept of the firm's voluntary integration of environmental and social concerns into the fabric of the business operations and interactions with stakeholders"*.[7] In 2011, the European Commission redefined corporate social responsibility as *"the enterprise responsibility for impacts on society"* to reflect the objectives of Enterprise 2020 Initiative.[8] In addition to defining corporate social responsibility, a major challenge has been the achievement of balance between corporate social responsibility regulation enforcement and the

---

[3] R. Mullerat. Corporate Social Responsibility: A European Perspective. (2013). Miami-Florida-European Union Center of Excellence. Ocean Portal. Gulf Oil Spill (2017).

[4] Ibid.

[5] A. Smith, A. *An Inquiry into the Nature and Causes of the Wealth of Nations* (London: Methuen, 1776), III.4.3.

[6] R. Zandvliet. "Corporate social responsibility reporting in the European Union: Towards a more univocal framework," 18 *Colum. J. Eur. L. F.* 38 (2011).

[7] European Commission. Corporate Social Responsibility. (2002). http://www.pwc.com.

[8] Ebncsr. New EU Definition on *CSR Mirrors Enterprise 2020 Aspirations*. The European Business Network for Corporate Social Responsibility (2011).

unique circumstances of the multinational corporation.

A major legal issue with cases of corporate misbehavior on a global scale has been the rights of certain courts to hear corporate irresponsibility claims filed against companies which operate abroad.[9] Until recently, the courts of the United Kingdom declined to hear cases against the multinational company subsidiary whose parent company was incorporated in the United Kingdom, disowning responsibility of jurisdiction over the firm's operations based upon the doctrine of *forum non-conveniens*.

Civil jurisdiction was meant to govern corporate offenses abroad amidst conflicting local and global interpretations of law. The limitations to extraterritorial applications of federal and state laws have only constrained the application of universal civil jurisdiction to a certain degree.[10] The evolution of European colonialization of indigenous lands to occupations in the name of global enterprise has been criticized in the context of "institutional arrangements" and human factors which directly affect significant environmental change.[11]

Corporate corruption has been universally regarded as a significant contributor to the violation of human rights and the exploitation of

---

[9] Luna, M. The role of the state, multinational oil companies, international law & the international community: Intersection of human rights & environmental degradation climate change in the 21st century caused by traditional extractive practices, the Amazon Rainforest, Indigenous people, and universal jurisdiction to resolve the accountability issue. Master's Thesis 167, 2015; R. Zandvliet. "Corporate social responsibility reporting in the European Union: Towards a more univocal framework," 18 *Colum. J. Eur. L. F.* 38 (2011); D. Wallach, D. "The irrationality of Universal Civil Jurisdiction," *Georgetown Journal of International Law* 46 (2015): 803-835; Jain, A. "Universal civil jurisdiction in international law," *Indian Journal of Human Rights* 55, no. 2 (2015): 209-237.

[10] D. Wallach, D. "The irrationality of Universal Civil Jurisdiction," *Georgetown Journal of International Law*.

[11] Luna, M. The role of the state, multinational oil companies, international law & the international community.

natural resources; however, the rights to liberty are made available in civil societies in which the government confers to standard laws established in favor of the public good.[12] However, the ratification of treaties on an international scale is complex due to the diversity of state interests.[13] Oftentimes, the annual revenues of multinational corporations is significantly higher than the GDP of the hosting developing country.[14] In the absence of corporate social responsibility, the corporation's revenues reflect a gross exploitation of the developing nation's resources and an abuse of the human rights of the local people. How the multinational corporation obtains and manufactures its product, and under what socioeconomic circumstances pressured national and international law makers and regulators to clearly define and enforce corporate social responsibility standards on a global scale.

2. *Corporate Social Responsibility*

Corporate social responsibility was birthed from both conceptualizations of 'noblesse oblige' and concerns for the long-term sustainability of the physical environment.[15] A common belief emerged that the corporate return to society must be increased to compensate for the corporate impact on society, a belief which has since been endorsed by human rights advocates and environmentalists. The European Commission published a Green Paper, within which corporate social responsibility was described as "an integration of social and environmental issues created by the corporate business operations and the

---

[12] A. Spalding. "Corruption, Corporations, and the New Human Right," *Washington University Law Review* 91, no. 6 (2014): 1365-1428.

[13] Luna, M. The role of the state, multinational oil companies, international law & the international community.

[14] Bantekas. "Corporate Social Responsibility in International Law," *Boston University International Law Journal* 22 (2004): 309-347.

[15] Hirschhorn, N. "Corporate Social responsibility and the tobacco industry: hope or hype?" *Tobacco Control* 13(2004): 447-453.

voluntary interactions with the stakeholders".[16]

The concept of corporate social responsibility was also contrived as a component of organizational management protocols, along with business ethics, stewardship, and corporate governance.[17] The demand for corporate social responsibility regulation was birthed from the social and environment onslaughts of the Industrial Age, as large factories and mills abused both workers and the physical environment in global epidemics of long operating hours, heat, and dust which persisted along with textile production.[18] Modernization increased infrastructure complexity and threatened sustainability requirements with challenges of environmental stress, impact of human use, and interdependencies between industrial components.[19] Engineering projects initiated by large firms in poor countries have been "designed for large-scaled benefits to the foreign investor and the local elite".[20] Thus, the growth of industry compounded corporate governance issues, as the abuses spread from textiles to the transport and oil & gas industries.[21] The growing labor and materials requirements pushed many large firms well beyond the boundaries of respect for the physical environment and basic of human rights.

---

[16] European Commission. Corporate Social Responsibility. (2002). http://www.pwc.com.

[17] Bhaduri & E. Selarka. *Corporate Governance and Corporate Social Responsibility of Indian Companies*. Chapter 2. CSR, Sustainability, Ethics & Governance (2016).

[18] Gliah. History Now. (2017). http://www.gildermanlehrman.com.

[19] D. Owabi et al. "Sustainability strategies in engineering infrastructure maintenance in developing countries: Selected southwestern Nigeria case study," *Civil and Environmental Research* 6, no. 2 (2014).

[20] L. Parsons. "Engineering in Context: Engineering in developing countries," *Journal of Professional Issues in Engineering Education and Practice* 170 (1996).

[21] K. Ejumudo. Z. Edo. L. Avweromre & J. Sagay. "Environmental issues and corporate social responsibility (CSR in Nigeria Niger Delta region: The need for a pragmatic approach)".

3. Corporate Social Responsibility Law in the European Union

The European legislative and regulatory efforts for corporate accountability are broad in scope, encompassing a diversity of concerns for corporate transparency; the overall protection of human rights; the protection of animals and the physical environment; the rights of the consumer; the rights of the workers; and the impact of the firm's operations on the local communities in efforts to generate shareholder wealth.[22] Great Britain and many of the European Union member states have adopted 'comply or explain' code as the corporate governance standard for business operations.[23] Corporations that fail to report and comply with the corporate governance standards are required to explain why the firm has opted out of participation. However, measurements of the effectiveness of corporate social responsibility regulations across Great Britain and the European Union member states remain problematic, as the approach varies between prospective of governing bodies, corporations, and societies.[24] Conflicts in corporate social responsibility assessments begin with the pursuit of a universal definition for CSR and the role of the corporation in modern society.

The 2009 Treaty of Lisbon presents the core values of the European Union in the contexts of human rights, democracy, rule of law, equity,

---

[22] European Coalition for Corporate Justice. (2006). Corporate Social Responsibility. http://corporatejustice.org; C. Utz. Climate Risk Reporting: Pressure Builds For Disclosure by Australian Corporates. (2018); R. Mullerat. Corporate Social Responsibility: A European Perspective. (2013). Miami-Flor Ida-European Union Center Of Excellence. Ocean Portal. Gulf Oil Spill. (2017); Ebncsr. New EU Definition on CSR Mirrors Enterprise 2020 Aspirations. The European Business Network for Corporate Social Responsibility (2011).

[23] IFC. CG Updates: Corporate Governance Group (2015).

[24] M. Jankalova. "Approaches to the evaluation of Corporate Social Responsibility," *Procedia Economics and Finance* 39 (2016): 580-587; IFC. CG Updates: Corporate Governance Group. (2015).

and human dignity.[25] However, corporate social responsibility has been defined based upon ethics, stakeholder, and human rights platforms which generally encompasses the stakeholders of the organizations, constituent groups with ongoing interests in the operations of the firm; and the communities within which the firm operates.[26] CSR-Europe described the primary elements of corporate social responsibility activities as environmental, community and human rights relations, and within the workplace, or human resources relations.[27] This perspective has been used by local community initiatives to confront corporations with high records of environmental pollution and low levels of community philanthropy.

Elements of European corporate social responsibility regulation typically address the accountability of the firm in the contexts of philanthropy as well as the interests of business ethics, the law regarding the business operations and annual reporting, and the impact on the local and national economies.[28] The fundamental tenets of European corporate social responsibility regulation define the elements of philanthropy, ethics, legal duty, and economic duty:[29]

- Philanthropic Responsibility—The assumed responsibility of

---

[25] Ibid.; EBNCSR. New EU Definition on CSR Mirrors Enterprise 2020 Aspirations. The European Business Network for Corporate Social Responsibility, (2011).

[26] S. Bhaduri & E. Selarka. *Corporate Governance and Corporate Social Responsibility of Indian Companies*. Chapter 2; M. Jankalova. "Approaches to the evaluation of Corporate Social Responsibility," *Procedia Economics and Finance* 39 (2016): 580-587.

[27] EBNCSR. New EU Definition on CSR Mirrors Enterprise 2020 Aspirations. The European Business Network for Corporate Social Responsibility (2011).

[28] IFC. CG Updates: Corporate Governance Group. (2015); EBNCSR. New EU Definition on CSR Mirrors Enterprise 2020 Aspirations. The European Business Network for Corporate Social Responsibility, (2011).

[29] K. Bello, A. Jusoh. & K. Nor. "Corporate Social Responsibility and Consumer Rights Awareness: A research agenda," *Indian Journal of Science and Technology* 9, no. 46 (2016).

voluntary demonstrations of high level, good citizenship behaviors, to include the commitment of a percentage of the corporation's earnings toward the betterment and overall good of society.

• Ethical Responsibility—The Corporation is responsible for ongoing demonstrations of commitment to the codes of ethics established by the firm and by the society within which it operates; and an ongoing avoidance of unethical, immoral activities.

• Legal Responsibility—The Corporation is responsible for business operations and conduct in compliance with the rules, regulations, and laws set forth by applicable local, state, national and global institutions.

• Economic Responsibility—The Corporation is responsible for decision-making that results in increased shareholder wealth; job creation with fair wages; production of quality and feasibly priced goods and services that are desirable to the consumer.

4. Evolution of European Corporate Social Responsibility Law

An increase in reports of violations of corporate social responsibility principles by European and Europe-based corporations has created a heightened interest in regulatory initiatives by the European Union from the close of the 21st century.[30] The 2003 Accounts Modernization Drive amended the Fourth and Seventh Directives on Company Law and increased attention to corporate social responsibility in the areas of accounting and reporting.[31] In 2006, several recommendations were made

---

[30] European Coalition for Corporate Justice. (2006). Corporate Social Responsibility. http://corporatejustice.org.

[31] European Commission. Parliament and Council Directive L 178/16, Amending Directives 78/660/EEC, 83/349/EEC, 86/635/EEC, and 91/674/EEC on the annual and consolidated accounts of certain types of companies, banks and other financial institutions and insurance undertakings, O.J. (L 178) 16 EC, (2003).

to the European Commission in the context of regulations for corporate accountability, improved transparency in reporting, credibility of multi-stakeholder initiatives, increased global CSR regulatory platforms, calls for research on the tenets of corporate social responsibility and impact of violations, and the extent to which social, human and environmental rights are included in corporate investment agreements.[32] The European Commission Directive 2006/46/EC mandated all listed firms in the European Union to submit annual corporate governance statements to the shareholders.

The European corporate social responsibility framework was designed for publicly listed firms integrates soft law, or codes of corporate governance, with legislation in "comply or explain".[33] The IIRC 2010 promoted integrations of governance, social and environmental data with the financial information in corporate accounts.[34] Thereafter, the 2012 European Commission Action Plan was designed to promote long-term economic growth through investments that would strengthen the European corporations and improve long-term sustainability.[35] Table 1 shows how European Law has changed in the past three decades in response to demands for heightened accountability from large firms.

From the open of the new millennium, the European laws in regard to corporate governance and corporate social responsibility have undergone several changes, or revision.[36] The regulation has been modified to not only direct multinationals, but also European small or medium enterprises.

---

[32] Ibid.

[33] IFC. CG Updates: Corporate Governance Group, 5 (2015).

[34] O. Balch, The Disruptors: How Richard Howitt Turned From Socialist MEP To Transparency TSAR. (2018). http://www.ethicalcorp.com.

[35] IFC. CG Updates: Corporate Governance Group. (2015).

[36] European Coalition for Corporate Justice. (2006). Corporate Social Responsibility. http://corporatejustice.org.

Table 1: European Union Corporate Social Responsibility Law

1993, European Commission Eco-Management and Audit Scheme EMAS Regulation 1836/93
1995 European Business Manifesto Against Social Exclusion
1998 CSR Europe Advisory Board
1999, European Parliament call for binding code of conduct for European corporate compliance with environmental standards, appropriate labour practices, and human rights on a global scale
2000, Lisbon Summit; Lisbon Agenda
2001 European Commission Promoting a European Framework on Corporate Social Responsibility; European Commission Eco-Management and Audit Scheme Regulation (EC) No 761/2001 EMAS II
2002, European Parliament vote for new legislation for corporate social and environmental performances and corporate governance for operations in developing nations.
2003, Accounts Modernization Directive; Amendment of Fourth and Seventh Directives on Company Law
2006, European Commission publications: Implementing the partnership for growth and jobs: Making Europe a pole of excellence on Corporate Social Responsibility; and Communication on Corporate Social Responsibility (CSR); European Commission Directive 2006/46/EC
2007, Meeting of the European Alliance Business Social Compliance Initiative
2009, European Commission Eco-Management and Audit Scheme Regulation (EC) No 1221/2009 EMAS III
2010, European Platform Against Poverty and Social Exclusion COM(2010)758; European Academy for Business and Society (EABIS)

(Continued)

2011, New European Commission policy on Corporate Social Responsibility; Renewed strategy for 2011-2014 European Union Corporate Social Responsibility; Brussels, Belgium COM(2011)21 A Resourceful Efficient European
2012, New European Commission research in regard to corporate social responsibility State-of-the-Art in Reporting; European Commission Action Plan
2014 adoption of Directive on Disclosure of Non-Financial and Diversity Information by European Parliament;
2015, European Union Multi-Stakeholder Forum on Corporate Social Responsibility; Brussels, Belgium

Public awareness of corporate social responsibility has increased in the European regulatory bodies from 2014, driving other countries to follow suit.[37] European corporations have displayed more aggressive strategies to objectives that favor the stakeholder, and generated new information sharing resources in the context of corporate social responsibility diffused by European firms.[38] The Australian ASX published *Corporate Governance Principles and Recommendations*, requiring an increase in transparency and communication regarding issues of environmental and climate risks and corporate commitments to environmental sustainability.[39] From 2015, the European Union has enforced the mandatory requirements for all corporations with 500 employees or more to produce environmental reporting in the annual

---

[37] Ibid

[38] R. Mullerat. Corporate Social Responsibility: A European Perspective. (2013). Miami-Florida-European Union Center of Excellence. Ocean Portal. Gulf Oil Spill. (2017).

[39] C. Utz. Climate Risk Reporting: Pressure Builds for Disclosure by Aus Tralian Coporates. (2018).

reports.[40] The 2015 Directive addressed more than 8,000 large, publicly traded firms in terms of disclosure of renewable and non-renewable energy consumption, greenhouse gas emissions, natural resource and land use, and pollution. The Directive provided that corporations who submit misleading or fraudulent reports would be subjected to fines and imprisonment based upon the legal and regulatory parameters of the member state.

5. Case Study of Corporate Social Responsibility: Royal Dutch Shell in the Niger Delta

The social costs of corporate negligence are often so massive that the damaging, costly effects to the community and to the natural environment are irreversible. Business practices that are absent of business ethics force society into an ongoing morality debate, and what business practices are morally defensible.[41] Schrempf-Stirling contributed that the actors of civil society increasingly tend to attribute social responsibility to the corporation solely on the basis of the firm's connection to a particular issue.[42] Between 2008 and 2009, multinational oil mogul, Royal Dutch Shell spilled tons of oil in the Niger Delta during business operations which devastated the natural resources of the local Nigerian community.[43] A settlement of approximately £55m was reached as compensation to the Niger Delta Bodo community, to be distributed as cash settlements to the citizens as well as reinvestments to the local critical infrastructure.

---

[40] European Commission. Parliament and Council Directive L 178/16, Amending Directives 78/660/EEC, 83/349/EEC, 86/635/EEC, and 91/674/EEC on the annual and consolidated accounts of certain types of companies, banks and other financial institutions and insurance undertakings, O.J. (L 178) 16 EC, (2003).

[41] M. Goel, & P. "Ramanathan. Business ethics and corporate social responsibility - Is there a dividing line?" *Procedia Economics and Finance* 11(2014): 49-59.

[42] J. Schrempf-Stirling. "The delimitation of corporate social responsibility: Upstream, downstream, and historic CSR," *Management Faculty Publications* 38 (2012).

[43] BBC News. Shell Agrees $84m Deal Over Niger Delta Oil Spill. (2015).

In January 2013, a ruling was issued against Royal Dutch Shell for the ongoing Niger Delta oil pollution, socioeconomic exploitations, and political chaos that has ignited armed conflicts between the company and the local residents. A history of oil leaks and spills, gas flarings and explosions have haunted the people of the Niger Delta, as Royal Dutch Shell occupies many water and land resources for oil excavation. The company has amassed billions in profits from it oil explorations in the Delta at the expense of the marine life, the drinking water, and many other aspects of the local socioeconomic demographic.[44] Each year, hundreds of spills have been reported in the Delta, and evidenced by black, murky waters and a contaminated water supply.[45] The primary cause of the disasters has been oil pipeline failures, followed by sabotages of the equipment by angry citizens. The corporate governance issues in the Niger Delta begin with the absence of enforced corporate social responsibility policy for Royal Dutch Shell, continues on with the need for an intensive environmental clean-up, and ends with ethical management of the settlement funds.

II. Review of Literature

1. Overview

The review of literature for this article addresses corporate social responsibility policies set forth by the European Commission address contemporary themes in business management, to include ethics,

---

[44] K. Ejumudo. Z. Edo. L. Avweromre & J. Sagay. "Environmental issues and corporate socialresponsibility (CSR in Nigeria Niger Delta region: The need for a pragmatic approach)".

[45] BBC News. Shell Agrees $84M Deal Over Niger Delta Oil Spill. (2015). http://www.bbc.com/news.

business ethics and morality[46]; human rights[47]; creative destruction[48]; stakeholder theory[49]; the adoption of corporate social responsibility strategies and action plans[50]; implementations of responsible supply chain management[51]; reporting requirements for social, environmental, and governance performance[52]; universal civil jurisdiction[53]; and contributions

[46] I. Kant. Groundwork For The Metaphysics Of Morals. Reproduction by Jonathan Bennett. (1785). http://www.earlymoderntexts.com/assets/pdfs/kant1785.pdf; A. Smith, A. *An Inquiry Into The Nature and Causes Of The Wealth of Nations* (London: Methuen, 1776), 16; H. Bowen. *Social Responsibilities of the Businessman* (University of Iowa, 2013); H. Allison. *Kant'S Groundwork for the Metaphysics of Morals: A Commentary* (Oxford Scholarship, 2012); J. Timmerman. "Kantian dilemmas? Moral conflict in Kant's ethical theo-ry," *AGPH* 95, no. 1(2013): 36-64.

[47] K. Ejumudo. Z. Edo. L. Avweromre & J. Sagay. "Environmental issues and corporate social responsibility (CSR in Nigeria Niger Delta region: The need for a pragmatic approach)".

[48] J. Schumpter, J. Capitalism, *Socialism, and Democracy* (New York: Harper & Bros, 1942).

[49] M. Goel, & P. Ramanathan. "Business ethics and corporate social responsibility - Is there a dividing line?" *Procedia Economics and Finance* 11 (2014): 49-59; J. Timmerman. "Kantian dilemmas? Moral conflict in Kant's ethical theory," 36-64.

[50] S. Kraisornsuthasinee. "CSR through the heart of the Bodhi tree," *Social Responsibility Journal* 8, no.2 (2012): 186-198; R. Zandvliet. "Corporate social responsibility reporting in the European Union: Towards a more   univocal framework," 18 *Colum. J. EUR. L. F.* 38 (2011); European Commission. Corporate Social Responsibility. (2002). http://www.pwc.com; European Coalition for Corporate Justice. (2006). Corporate So-cial Responsibility. http://corporatejustice.org; European Commission (2003). Parliament and Council Directive L 178/16, Amending Directives 78/660/EEC, 83/349/EEC, 86/635/EEC, and 91/674/EEC on the annual and consolidated accounts of certain types of companies, banks and other financial institutions and insurance undertakings, 2003 O.J. (L 178) 16 EC); K. Bello, A. Jusoh. & K. Nor. "Corporate Social Responsibility and Consumer Rights Awareness: A research agenda," *Indian Journal of Science and Technology* 9, no. 46 (2016).

[51] S. Bhaduri & E. Selarka. *Corporate Governance and Corporate Social Responsibility of Indian Companies.* Chapter 2.

[52] O. Balch, The Disruptors: How Richard Howitt Turned From Socialist MEP To Transparency TSAR (2018); H. Yeung. F. Huang. X. Liu. Global influence of European Corporate Social Responsibility: China as Case Study. University Of Leicester School Of Law, Research Paper, 15-17 (2015).

[53] Jain, A. "Universal civil jurisdiction in international law"; Luna, M. The role of the

to environmental sustainability.[54] The review of literature for the research was developed using sources from European corporate law agencies and peer reviewed articles in regard to corporate social responsibility and related social theory; European legal codes and principles in the context of best business practices, corporate governance, environmental sustainability, and human rights. Key search terms for relevant literature included "CSR Europe", "ethics", "corporate social responsibility", "stakeholder theory", "business ethics", "European Union", "human rights", "law", "code", "regulation", "constituent group", "multi-stakeholder", "Niger Delta", "universal civil jurisdiction", "morality", "Royal Dutch Shell", and "European Commission".

2. *Ethics in Social Responsibility*

Kant argued that "conflicts between obligations are represented in the relationship between the conflicting obligations; both of which would be cancelled out by one annulling the other".[55] Classical social theorists who followed tended to rally around the definitions of duty and obligation based upon mutual exclusivity, which eliminated the possibility of choice and left society to accept the pains of government and industry by default. Phinney described such phenomenons in the context of acculturation, or the "extent that the individuals of a society have maintained the original culture or adapted to the new culture created by a larger society".[56] However, modern debates on ethics, moral obligation,

---

state, multinational oil companies, international law & the international community; D. Wallach, D. "The irrationality of Universal Civil Jurisdiction," *Georgetown Journal of International Law* 46 (2015): 803-835.

[54] R. Mullerat. Corporate Social Responsibility: A European Perspective. (2013). Miami-Florida-European Union Center of Excellence. Ocean Portal. Gulf Oil Spill. (2017).

[55] I. Kant. Groundwork for the Metaphysics of Morals. Reproduction by Jonathan Bennett (1785). http://www.earlymoderntexts.com/assets/pdfs/kant1785.pdf VI 224.9-11

[56] J. Phinney. "When we talk about American ethnic groups, what do we mean?" *American Psychologist* 51, no. 9 (1996): 921.

and conflicting duties have been shaped by a complete transformation of the world through technology and industrialism; some of which have adulterated Kant's perspective of true obligation. Timmermann argued that Kant "presented himself as a champion of moral thought; identified the supreme tenet of morality in singularity; and defended the imperative against accusations of fantasticalism".[57] However, Allison argued that Kant's perspective is the most significant work in modern philosophy of morality due to the contexts of autonomy of the will, heteronomy, and the self-imposition of moral duty.

Goel and Ramanathan defined business ethics as "concerns for moral principles, decision making, codes of conduct, and governance issues within the business environment" and presented that normative stakeholder theory which draws upon ethics theory confirms the moral responsibility of the[58] firm to all stakeholders.[59] Bhaduri and Selarka supported that corporate social responsibility is based upon ethics, as well as other platforms which generally encompasses the stakeholders, constituent groups, and the local community.[60] Smith argued that "the entire experience of fixed capital maintenance must be excluded from the net revenues of society. Neither the materials nor the required labour can make a part of it at any point".[61] Goel and Ramanathan supported that conceptualizations of social responsibility and business ethics have distinguishable identities, despite the fact they share the same concepts

---

[57] J. Timmerman. "Kantian dilemmas? Moral conflict in Kant's ethical theory," 36-64.

[58] H. Allison. *Kant'S Groundwork for the Metaphysics of Morals: A Commentary.*

[59] M. Goel, & P. "Ramanathan. Business ethics and corporate social responsibility - Is there a dividing line?"

[60] S. Bhaduri & E. Selarka. *Corporate Governance and Corporate Social Responsibility of Indian Companies.* Chapter 2.

[61] A. Smith, A. (1776). *An Inquiry into the Nature and Causes of the Wealth of Nations* (London: Methuen, 1776), II.2.6

that are used in reference to the same codes and debates.[62]

Kraisornsuthasinee supported that corporate social responsibility addresses business profits which come at a social price to others" and that "such cause and effect relationships may be grounded in relativistic perspectives of the law of conditionality and dependent origination".[63] Bello, Jusoh and Nor addressed the link between corporate social responsibility and consumerism from a legal perspective, and described negative ethical consumerism as penal methods applied to corporations which the consumers perceive as socially irresponsible.[64]

3. Defining Corporate Social Responsibility

Schumpterian creative destruction defines the pursuit of a goal or objective beyond the conventions of ethics or morality, in which end justifies the means of creation.[65] The infinite production and destruction of goods that began in the Industrial Age rages on as an innovation mechanism that may hardly be hindered by a social consciousness or harnessed by government regulation. Normative stakeholder theory supports that the internal processes of the corporation directly affect the stakeholders; and therefore, must be regulated by institution on the basis of ethical tenets and moral philosophy.

Howard Bowen was of the first to introduce the concept of social responsibility as a focus of academic research in *Social Responsibilities of the Businessman*, in which he defined social responsibility as *"an entrepreneurial commitment to pursue strategies, make particular decision,*

---

[62] M. Goel, & P. "Ramanathan. Business ethics and corporate social responsibility - Is there a dividing line?".

[63] S. Kraisornsuthasinee. "CSR through the heart of the Bodhi tree," *Social Responsibility Journal* 8, no. 2 (2012): 186-198.

[64] K. Bello, A. Jusoh. & K. Nor. "Corporate Social Responsibility and Consumer Rights Awareness: A research agenda"

[65] J. Schumpter, J. Capitalism, *Socialism, and Democracy.*

or execute such activities that are deemed desirable in the context of societal goals and values".[66] In the 1980s, T.M. Jones defined corporate social responsibility from the perspective of the stakeholder, as *"the notion of obligation owed by the corporation to societal constituent groups outside of the stakeholders, beyond the law, and the stipulations of union contracts... an obligation that must be voluntary in adoption".*[67] Goel and Ramanathan presented that the "normative stakeholder theory in corporate social responsibility based upon ethical philosophy holds that the corporation is "morally responsible" for the concerns of a much larger group, to include the employees and the community.[68] However, Timmerman argued that conceptualizations of the authority of a single moral tenet as a precursor to potential moral conflict are representations of cognitive error.[69]

Bantekas defined corporate social responsibility as "a self-cleansing and self-regulation voluntarily undertaken by the corporation, which may also be referred to as corporate citizenship".[70] Bhaduri and Selarki presented that driving forces of social responsibility are the central theme of corporate social responsibility and which are responsible organizational behaviors.[71] Regulators have concluded that corporate social responsibility must be integrated into the firm's governance and business strategy structures rather than merely added to the company policy.[72] Bello,

---

[66] H. Bowen. *Social Responsibilities of the Businessman.*

[67] T.M. Jones. "Corporate social responsibility revisited, redefined." *California Man Agreement Review* 22, no. 2 (1980): 59-67.

[68] M. Goel, & P. "Ramanathan. Business ethics and corporate social responsibility - Is there a dividing line?".

[69] J. Timmerman. "Kantian dilemmas? Moral conflict in Kant's ethical theory," 36-64.

[70] I. Bantekas. "Corporate Social Responsibility in International Law," *Boston University International Law Journal* 22 (2004): 309-347.

[71] S. Bhaduri & E. Selarka. *Corporate Governance and Corporate Social Responsibility of Indian Companies.* Chapter 2.

[72] M. Goel, & P. Ramanathan. Business ethics and corporate social responsibility - Is there a dividing line? *Procedia Economics and Finance,* 11, 49-59 (2014).

Jusoh and Nor debated as to the driver of corporate social responsibility protocols and efforts; particularly those which target the consumer as the primary stakeholder demographic and identified the firm's justification as the requirement for continuous patronage for sustainability.[73]

Philanthropy has commonly been regarded as a valid manifestation of corporate social responsibility.[74] Yeung, Huang and Liu defined corporate social responsibility as corporate ownership of the company's impact on the local community, society, and the environment in addition to maximization of shareholder wealth.[75] Bello, Jusoh and nor defined corporate social responsibility as the corporate efforts make positive contributions toward local community improvement along with the financial outcomes of the business operations.[76] Jones contributed that corporate social governance is a form of self-governance which encompasses elements of moral imperative, normative constraint, and altruistic incentive, "all in a quest for the corporate social nirvana".[77]

4. Corporate Social Responsibility in European Corporations

Mullerat argued that European corporations have deployed broader, more aggressive approaches to stakeholder-focused objectives, which has produced a substantial pool of information about corporate social responsibility that has been shared and diffused by many European

---

[73] K. Bello, A. Jusoh. & K. Nor. Corporate Social Responsibility and Consumer Rights Awareness: A research agenda. *Indian Journal of Science and Technology*, 9(46) (2016).

[74] S. Bhaduri & E. Selarka. *Corporate Governance and Corporate Social Responsibility of Indian Companies*. Chapter 2.

[75] H. Yeung. F. Huang. X. Liu. Global influence of European Corporate Social Responsibility: China as Case Study. University Of Leicester School of Law, Research Paper 15-17 (2015).

[76] K. Bello, A. Jusoh. & K. Nor. "Corporate Social Responsibility and Consumer Rights Awareness: A research agenda".

[77] T.M. Jones. "Corporate social responsibility revisited, redefined".

firms.[78] The IFC pointed out that a diversity of legal organizational forms exist in the European private, public and non-profit sectors, as well as diversity in executive power delegations in corporate management; therefore, the European Union is challenged to produce codes of governance with universal principles for best practice.[79] Zandvliet contributed that although many corporations in the European Union submit corporate social responsibility reports, additional, more comprehensive, supranational legislative efforts are needful in order to reconcile with more recent, progressive laws enacted by the member states; clarify legal requirements in terms of the scope of corporate social responsibility reports; and to eliminate the majority discretion of firms who currently do not submit any type of corporate social responsibility report.[80]

Yeung, Huang and Liu presented that the number of listings for Chinese firms overseas continues to increase; to include listings on the European stock exchange, which requires compliance with the European corporate law, member state directives, and corporate governance regulation.[81] Moreover, many immigrants from developing nations have entered the European Union and started successful businesses in the member states.[82] However, most foreign firms reject the culture and norms of the host society and pursue the interests of firm and its domestic

---

[78] R. Mullerat. Corporate Social Responsibility: A European Perspective. (2013). Miami-Flor Ida-European Union Center of Excellence. Ocean Portal. Gulf Oil Spill. (2017).

[79] IFC. CG Updates: Corporate Governance Group. (2015).

[80] R. Zandvliet. "Corporate social responsibility reporting in the European Union: Towards a more univocal framework".

[81] H. Yeung. F. Huang. X. Liu. Global influence of European Corporate Social Responsibility: China as Case Study. University Of Leicester School Of Law, Research Paper, 15-17 (2015).

[82] J. Phinney. When we talk about American ethnic groups, what do we mean? *American Psychologist*, 51(9) (1996).

society.[83] Therefore, the development and deployment of corporate social responsibility regulation for foreign investments and operations becomes even more complex, and more difficult to assess and enforce.

The role of the large, industrial firm in society has not changed much from the Industrial Age outside of advancements in technology that have changed the way people work.[84] The IFC reported that many European publicly listed companies have resorted to 'boilerplating' or publishing identical governance reports year after year.[85] However, the outcomes of a Grant Thorton report compiled with data from 2010 to 2011 indicated that corporate social responsibility initiatives have increased globally in the new millennium as corporations have come to realize their value beyond commercialism.[86]

Zandvliet concluded that a European framework for corporate social responsibility, and more specifically, reporting will solicit more positive results from elements which are more univocal; which will strengthen sustainable investment markets, confront firms with potential, confront high potential environmental and social risks in the corporate supply chain and business operations, and effectively meet consumer needs.[87] Consumer rights became an issue in multinational corporate violations of corporate social responsibility standards. Bello, Jusoh and Nor proposed increases in consumer rights awareness which will increase the demand for corporate social responsibility; and subsequently, the positive responses to the increased demand will improve the consumer

---

[83] J. Phinney. When we talk about American ethnic groups, what do we mean? *American Psychologist*, 51(9) (1996).

[84] Gliah. History Now. (2017). http://www.gildermanlehrman.com.

[85] IFC. CG Updates: Corporate Governance Group (2015).

[86] M. Goel, & P. "Ramanathan. Business ethics and corporate social responsibility - Is there a dividing line?".

[87] R. Zandvliet. "Corporate social responsibility reporting in the European Union: Towards a more univocal framework".

perceptions of the corporation.[88]

5. Chapter Summary

European legislative and regulatory initiatives for corporate social responsibility encompasses a broad canvas of legal and social concerns to include the protection of human rights, the environment, the rights of the laborer and the consumer and to govern the firm's operations to minimize devastations to the local communities in efforts to generate shareholder wealth. Ethics, morality, and corporate social responsibility were defined as the interrelationships between the concepts were presented from social, business, and legal theories. Kant and Goel and Ramanathan provided popular conceptualizations of ethics and moral duty, and the identification of society stakeholders.[89] The relationship between corporate social responsibility, profit, and the social costs to society were debated by Adam Smith in *Wealth of Nations*, and by Kraisornsuthasinee[90] and Bello, Jusoh and Nor[91] who described capitalism, consumerism, and ethics in the context of social irresponsibility.

Multinational corporation economic interests have challenged the efficiency and enforcement of universal civil jurisdiction clauses of international law. More specifically, the rights of the local communities and the power of the national governments to prohibit corporate actives that exploit natural resources and damage the local economy have

---

[88] K. Bello, A. Jusoh. & K. Nor. "Corporate Social Responsibility and Consumer Rights Awareness: A research agenda".

[89] M. Goel, & P. "Ramanathan. Business ethics and corporate social responsibility - Is there a dividing line?"; I. Kant. Groundwork for the Metaphysics of Morals. Reproduction by Jonathan Bennett. (1785). http://www.earlymoderntexts.com/assets/pdfs/kant1785.pdf.

[90] S. Kraisornsuthasinee. "CSR through the heart of the Bodhi tree," *Social Responsibility Journal* 8, no. 2 (2012): 186-198.

[91] K. Bello, A. Jusoh. & K. Nor. "Corporate Social Responsibility and Consumer Rights Awareness: A research agenda".

repeatedly come into question.[92] Hirschhorn addressed management theory in regard to the definitions of the stakeholders in relationships between multinational corporations, the company stakeholders, and the stakeholders outside the scope of the company.[93]

Theories of the driving forces of corporate social responsibility regulation and social campaigns were explored from the perspectives of Bhaduri and Selarki[94] and Schumpter's (1942) theory of creative destruction.[95] The IFC provided an update of compliance to European corporate social responsibility regulations and the impact of local initiatives to raise awareness of the social risks involved with supply chain business operations. Relationships between corporate social responsibility were investigated in support of the research of corporate governance abroad and how European firms perform abroad under the authority of foreign governments.[96] Mullerat addressed the impact of corporate activities on the physical environment and the increasing concern for the environment as industrial pollution increases.[97]

---

[92] Luna, M. The role of the state, multinational oil companies, international law & the international community; E. Dan. Volkswagen and the failure of corporate social responsibility, Forbes (2015); A. Spalding. "Corruption, Corporations, and the New Human Right".

[93] Hirschhorn, N. "Corporate Social responsibility and the tobacco industry: Hope or hype?" *Tobacco Control* 13 (2004): 447-453.

[94] S. Bhaduri & E. Selarka. *Corporate Governance and Corporate Social Responsibility of Indian Companies*. Chapter 2.

[95] J. Schumpter, J. Capitalism, *Socialism, and Democracy.*

[96] K. Ejumudo. Z. Edo. L. Avweromre & J. Sagay. "Environmental issues and corporate socialresponsibility (CSR in Nigeria Niger Delta region: The need for a pragmatic approach)"; W. Ebhota. "Engineering Research and Development (R&D) Infrastructure for Developing Economy," *International Journal of Scientific and Technology Research* 3, no. 4 (2014); H. Yeung. F. Huang. X. Liu. "Global influence of European Corporate Social Responsibility: China as Case Study. University of Leicester School of Law, Research Paper, 15-17 (2015).

[97] R. Mullerat. Corporate Social Responsibility: A European Perspective. (2013). Miami-Florida-European Union Center of Excellence. Ocean Portal. Gulf Oil Spill. (2017).

III. Methodology

1. Overview

The methodology for this article is a qualitative case study of corporate social responsibility as it applies to the case of Royal Dutch Shell Petroleum Company oil extraction activities in the Niger Delta. Case study approaches to research has evolved into a "flexible, pragmatic approach to research" that produces "an in-depth, comprehensive overview and outlook of a diversity of disciplines and issues".[98] Further, the case study approach also supports the integration of a diversity of philosophical perspectives.

Harrison et al confirmed that the case study is a desirable approach to investigations of complex social issues in real-world settings.[99] Eckstein contributed that beyond the level of national government, case studies may be found in the context of transnational integrations and phenomena; the specific processes and organizations involved in multinational corporate activities; and the systems associated with international politics and crises in international relations.[100] However, Crasnow argued that research of political science discipline, particularly disciplines of international relations and issues of comparative politics, have evolved to domination in formal research by formal and statistical methods that may or may not be classified holistically as quantitative methods.[101]

---

[98] H. Harrison et al. "Case study research: Foundations and methodical outcomes," *Qualitative Social Research* 18, no. 1 (2017).

[99] Ibid.

[100] H. Eckstein. Case study and theory in political practice. (Eds) Case Study Method: Key Issues, Key Texts. (R. Gomm, M. Hammersley, & P. Foster, 2000). London: Sage Publications.

[101] S. Crasnow. "The role of case study research in political science: evidence for causal claims," *Philosophy of Science* 79, no. 5 (2012).

The general consensus dictates that, with or without the integration of statistical analysis, the case study remains highly regarded as an effective approach to inquiry.[102] Qualitative case studies may also be expanded to include comparative studies of similar and dichotomously contrasting cases to increase the depth of the inquiry and the range of the research. Therefore, the case study for this research includes a comparison of similar cases to the Royal Dutch Shell challenges of jurisdiction and court rulings.

2. Case Study: Royal Dutch Shell Petroleum Development Company in the Niger Delta

Once an oasis, a devastated Niger Delta ecosystem; charred bushes and vegetation from the oil and gas fires, air pollution from gas flaring; and dead fish drifting afloat, down black streams of oil and water has been continuously degraded British and Dutch oil excavations since the close of the 1950s.[103] Between 1933 and 1978, no Senate or Presidential elections were held in Nigeria; but rather House elections occured every 5 years. In 1960, Nigeria gained independence through a coalition government led by Prime Minister Abubakar Balewa.[104] Therefore, the prior to 1960, the Nigerian legal and political infrastructures could be described as immature. The political climate in 20th century Nigeria was unstable and frequently escalated to violence. During the reign of General Sani Abacha between 1993 and 1998, Ken Saro-Wiwa orated and published campaigns against oil company occupations in Nigeria

---

[102] H. Harrison et al. "Case study research: Foundations and methodical outcomes"; H. Eckstein. Case study and theory in political practice. (Eds) Case Study Method: Key Issues, Key Texts. (R. Gomm, M. Hammersley, & P. Foster, 2000). London: Sage Publications.

[103] Business and Human rights; Vaughan, A. (2011). Oil in Nigeria: a history of spills, fines and fights for rights. The Guardian.

[104] BBC News. Shell Agrees $84m Deal Over Niger Delta Oil Spill. (2015).

and the damage caused to Ogoni.[105] In 1995, Ken Saro-Wiwa was tried in the Nigerian judicial system and executed. Nonetheless, the opposition against oil companies, to include Royal Dutch Shell, continued after Saro-Wiwa's death.

British explorations of Nigeria began in the open of the 20th century. In 1936, the Shell D'Arcy Company was founded in Nigeria by the Royal Dutch Shell Group; however, it was not until 1938 that Shell D'Arcy obtained an official license for oil exploration in the region.[106] Moreover, it was not until 1956 that the first well was drilled on behalf of Shell D'Arcy at Oloibiri. Soon after, Shell D'Arcy was renamed Shell-British Petroleum Development Company. In 1956, Nigeria was a British protectorate with joint operations between the British and Dutch oil companies.[107] Early on in the Nigeria operations, accusations of exploitation, disregard for the local natural resources, and government corruption were attached to the revenue flows while some residents of the Niger Delta earned as little as $1 per day.

Since the discovery of oil in 1956, the relationship between Shell-British Petroleum Development Company and the locals of the Elikpokwuodu community has deteriorated steadily to the point of armed conflict and oil spills and fires have reduced the potential sustenance and revenue from natural resources to solely the oil wells. In 1970, a massive oil spill in Ogoniland, Southeast Nigeria contaminated both waterways and local farms, the Shell-British Petroleum Development Company was sued, and thirty years later, in 2000, the company was fined £26 M. However, the dispute raged on, Shell objected to the rulings; and in response, the local opposition kidnapped Shell employees

---

[105] Ibid.

[106] Vaughan, A., Oil in Nigeria: a history of spills, fines and fights for rights. The Guardian. (2011)

[107] Ibid.

and destroyed pipeline equipment.[108] Despite a 1984 court decision to ban excess hydrocarbon burning, oil companies have been granted special permissions to do so in Nigeria under special ministerial concessions. The burnings generate approximately 70 million tonnes of CO_2 annually while reducing the annual Nigerian revenues by £1.5B. The World Wildlife Fund, the Friends of the Earth, and Greenpeace published *Gas flaring in Nigeria: A Human Rights, Environmental, and Economic Monstrosity*, a 35 page report on the activities of Shell Petroleum Development Company of Nigeria Limited in Nigeria.

During the course of hundreds of court cases filed annually against the company, in 2010, Shell acknowledged spilling 14,000 tonnes of oil in the waterways of the Niger Delta from 2009, a figure that increased exponentially each year.[109] The lack of goodwill and corporate governance by Shell Petroleum Development Company in the Nigeria operations has been rooted in the management of cash flows as well as the damage to the environment. Proceeds from the Shell operations that were designated for the improvement of the Nigerian communities went instead to former oil minister of Nigeria, Dan Etete. In 2007, Etete was found guilty of money laundering for Malabu Oil and Gas.[110] The law firm specializing in human rights, Prakken d'Oliveira filed a suit on behalf of the campaign group, Global Witness and others against Shell Chief Executive Ben van Beurden, former Chief Financial Officer Simon Henry, and former Chief Executive Officer Peter Voser.[111]

Amidst the ethnic and political tensions and the violence of Boko Haram, a January 2013 ruling was issued against Royal Dutch Shell

---

[108] Ibid.

[109] Vaughan, A. (2011). Oil in Nigeria: a history of spills, fines and fights for rights. The Guardian.

[110] George, L., Law firm seeks criminal case against Shell and its CEO over Nigeria deal. Reuters. (2017)

[111] Ibid.

Petroleum for the ongoing Niger Delta oil pollution. The court filings demanded an award for environmental damage. Environmentalists charged Royal Dutch Shell with prime contributions to global warming through the gas flarings from the Nigerian oil wells.[112] In 2016, an anti-fraud team raided the Shell headquarters in The Hague as a part of the ongoing investigation.[113] Three independent law suits have been filed against Shell Petroleum Development Company of Nigeria for 2005 oil spills in Ikot Ada Udo, Oruma, and Goi. The oil spills contaminated the fishing ponds and farmlands in the areas, and Royal Dutch Shell failed to execute a full, adequate clean up.[114]

3. Shell Petroleum Development Company of Nigeria in the Dutch Courts

The Dutch courts expressed the belief that the Shell Petroleum Development Company of Nigeria Limited was somewhere between partially and solely responsible for the environmental devastation, socioeconomic exploitation, and political chaos in the Niger Delta. However, Shell argued that the Dutch courts had no jurisdiction over the Nigerian oil field subsidiaries and a Statement of Defense to the Motion Contesting Jurisdiction was filed in the Hague District Court.[115] Conflicts ensued as to where the proceedings should be held. The claims of corporate negligence attracted global attention as photographs of the oil contaminated waters and lands circulated across the Internet. In self-defense, Shell attributed the majority of the damage and resulting charges for pollution to "local miscreants" in the Niger Delta who allegedly

---

[112] Macalister, T. Shell Must Face Friends Of The Earth Nigeria Claim In Netherlands. The Guardian (2009).

[113] George, L. Law firm seeks criminal case against Shell and its CEO over Nigeria deal. Reuters (2017).

[114] Business & Human Rights. Shell lawsuit (re oil pollution in Nigeria). B&H (2016).

[115] Ibid.

seized the company vehicles, purposely damaged the pipes, and lit fires to sabotage the operations.[116] Moreover, Shell accused the stealing of oil for illegal refineries by the locals as the cause of many of the spills.

Although the claims for Ada Udo were affirmed, the courts upheld judgements for some of the defense claims of sabotage, and the cases for Goi and Oruma were dismissed. The Friends of the Earth presented the Amsterdam, Netherlands courts with the assertion that the Royal Dutch Shell oil spills "were not accidents, but rather a pattern of systematic pollution" and "a disregard for the rights of the local Ikot Ada Udo community that has been ongoing for decades".[117] The compensation case was brought in the interests of Friday Alfred Akpan and other Oruma farmers in the Bayelsa estate for pollution caused by the Shell Petroleum Development Company of Nigeria. The United Nations estimated that the Niger Delta clean up will require 30 years of effort by Royal Dutch Shell. Nigerian government corruption was placed on trial along with a lack of corporate governance by the Royal Dutch Shell operations in the Niger Delta.

4. Comparison to Other Corporate Social Responsibility Cases

Kiobel v Royal Dutch Shell Petroleum was brought before the United States Supreme Court in 2012 under the Alien Tort Statute, with a claim that Royal Dutch Shell Petroleum "planned, conspired and facilitated numerous extrajudicial executions, tortuous events and crimes against humanity in the Niger Delta from 1992 to 1995".[118] Amicus curaie briefs were submitted to the United States Supreme Court by

---

[116] Concannon, T. Shell Fights Fires over Niger Delta Oil Spill. Pambazuka News (2004).

[117] Macalister, T. Shell Must Face Friends Of The Earth Nigeria Claim In Netherlands. The Guardian (2009).

[118] 133 S. Ct. 1659, 1670 (2013).

the United Kingdom, Germany, and the Netherlands to support the respondents. The Supreme Court presented that "whether or not, and under what circumstances the Alien Tort Statute, 28 U.S.C. §1350 allows the courts to recognize causes of action for national law violations which occur in the territory of sovereign outside of the United States".[119] The 2010 British Petroleum oil spill, which dumped millions of barrels of crude oil into the Gulf of Mexico is an additional case global extractive operations which are poorly managed and subsequently diffuse pollution inn isolated incidents or systematically. Environmental sustainability has become a legal issue as multinational companies engage in extractive practices all over the world according to a diversity of standards and fluctuating compliance with corporate social responsibility.

Republic of Ecuador v. Chevron Corp, the Sarayaku filed similar claims against the California-based Chevron oil extractions, which exemplified environmental degradation similarities from business practices which systematically abuse the people in the local Lago Agrio community.[120] Table 2 presents a comparison of legal suits filed against multinational companies for negligence in oil extraction operations.

The *Ecuador v Chevron* movement began in 1993, when local residents from multiple tribes in the Amazon collectively filed suit against Texaco. Since then, oil explorations expanded to include Yuca, San Carlos, Rio Aguarico, and Francisco de Orellana.[121] In 2016, the United States Supreme Court ruled in favor of Chevron and denied the request for $8.7 billion in damages for pollution in the Ecuadorean rain forest between 1964 and 1992. The court cited the 28 U.S.C. § 1604 Foreign Sovereign Immunities Act, which supports that "foreign states shall be

---

[119] Ibid.

[120] 2016 BL 179029, No. 15-1088; *Chevron Corp v. Donziger* No. 11-00691.

[121] BBC News. Us Judge Annuls Ecuador Oil Ruling Against Chevron. (2014). http://www.bbc.com/news.

Table 2: Comparison of Oil Company Suits for Negligence in Corporate Social Responsibility

Comparison of Suits for Negligence in Corporate Social Responsibility						
	Oil Company	National	Region	Period	Damages	CSR Outcomes
Niger Delta	Royal Dutch Shell	Great Britain	Ogoniland, Bodo, Port, Ada Udo, Harcourt	2015	$84M	Ruling in favor of plaintiffs
Ecuador	Chevron	United States of America	Lago Agrio	2014	$18.2B - $9.5B	Ruling annulled by US Judge
Gulf of Mexico	British Petroleum	Great Britain	Tamaulipas, Quintana, Veracruz	2013	$1.4B	Ruling in favor of plaintiffs

considered immune to jurisdiction" with the exception of arbitration. Further, the court determined that corruption could be traced to the plaintiffs' legal team, rather than for the corporation.

The oil companies won some and lost some in courts all over the world, as villagers, tribesmen, and indigenous peoples pulled together and a found a voice to formally cite their concerns. An Amnesty International on Colombia report found that "allegations of involvement by British Petroleum, and a private, British-owned security firm potentially violate the human rights of the local communities in Colombia".[122] Moreover, perhaps the greatest travesty of justice in regard to the presence of the Shell-British Petroleum Development Company in Nigeria has not been the occasional spills or corrupt management of revenues; but rather, the company's indifferent attitude towards the blackened streams and

---

[122] Luna, M. The role of the state, multinational oil companies, international law & the international community.

charred woods.[123] The lawsuits that piled into the courts were filled with claims of negligence, no effort put forth to prevent or limit the number of spills due to corruption or breaks in the oil pipes; nor were there many legitimate efforts to clean up the spills as the production rolled on. The communities of the Niger Delta witnessed first-hand how the British and Dutch corporate owners really perceived Nigeria, its people, and its future.

IV. Conclusion

Corporate social responsibility is constituted by driving forces of social responsibility are the central theme of corporate social responsibility and direct organizational behaviors.[124] The outcomes for European corporations who do not incorporate the principles of corporate social responsibility in their business structure and activities include lawsuits based upon claims of environmental degradation and socioeconomic exploitation. Moreover, corporate social responsibility has played a significant role in direction and monitoring of corporate business activities and relationship between Royal Dutch Shell and the Niger Delta communities in the past 10 years. The integration of corporate social responsibility into the European corporate business practices and operations has a limited yet positive affect on the financial performance of the firm.

Corporate social responsibility is dampened by the corporate objective to maximize profits and shareholder profit by any means necessary.[125] Some have concluded that corporate social responsibility has

---

[123] Business & Human Rights. Shell lawsuit (re oil pollution in Nigeria). B&H (2016).

[124] S. Bhaduri & E. Selarka. *Corporate Governance and Corporate Social Responsibility of Indian Companies*. Chapter 2.

[125] E. Dan. Volkswagen and the failure of corporate social responsibility, Forbes (2015).

failed and must be reinvented.[126] European corporate social responsibility laws appear to have failed in the case of the Niger Delta. Tons of crude oil, spilled into the oceans and tributaries each year by multinational oil companies interrupt the current well-being of local residents, fauna, flora, and marine life and threaten the future of vital ecosystems. National governments struggle to establish the appropriate routes of judicial power to manage the claims of gross corporate social irresponsibility that are pending all over the world. Despite the environmental damages from production and the detriment to public health, companies such as British American Tobacco and Phillip Morris have gained front page coverage with accolades in global corporate publications, such as the Asian *Ethical Corporation* magazine.

Reports from the IFC assert that many European corporations engage in 'boilerplating' or publishing identical annual corporate governance reports.[127] Conversely, a Grant Thorton report for the period between from 2010 to 2011 indicated that global corporate social responsibility initiatives are increasing; and that since the open of the new millennium, large corporations have explored their value beyond commercialism. Researchers debate as to the best approach to human rights violations by multinational corporations who forsake pledges of corporate social responsibility; whether the application of universal jurisdiction to claims of violations would substantially reduce the number.[128] Historically, the doctrine of forum non-conveniens

---

[126] Luna, M. The role of the state, multinational oil companies, international law & the international community; E. Dan. Volkswagen and the failure of corporate social responsibility. FORBES, (2015); Jain, A. "Universal civil jurisdiction in international law".

[127] IFC. CG Updates: Corporate Governance Group. (2015).

[128] A. Spalding. "Corruption, Corporations, and the New Human Right"; Luna, M. The role of the state, multinational oil companies, international law & the international community; Jain, A. "Universal civil jurisdic-tion in international law"; D. Wallach, D. "The irrationality of Universal Civil Jurisdiction," *Georgetown Journal of International*

has significantly impacted limitations to the venue of actions for multinational corporations, as the court may elect not to hear a case based upon jurisdiction, forcing the plaintiff to sue in other courts.

Some advocates for the enforcement of corporate social responsibility law criticize the progress of the ongoing global initiatives. Luna asserted that:

> *Global, national, and local legal conventions which serve to protect indigenous sovereignty and indigenous territories whose natural and human resources are continuously subject to extraction and abuse by multinational corporations, and most specifically oil corporations, remain in jeopardy due to ambiguous international legal frameworks which could provide protection by holding these companies to accountability.*[129]

Lawsuits continue to flood the courts with claims of negligence by multinational corporations who continue to produce and generate revenue. The International Petroleum Industry Environmental Conservation Association advocated for "good human rights policies and business practices" to improve the relationship between multinational corporations and the hosting local communities.[130] Spalding proposed that "alternative strategies for enforcement which focus upon the promotion of liberal, democratic institutions and values through ethical cross border commerce" would resolve the "paradox of human rights and corporate corruption".[131]

Law 46 (2015): 803-835.

[129] Luna, M. The role of the state, multinational oil companies, international law & the international community.

[130] M. Goel, & P. "Ramanathan. Business ethics and corporate social responsibility - Is there a dividing line?".

[131] A. Spalding. "Corruption, Corporations, and the New Human Right".

V. Recommendations for Future Studies

This article provided a comprehensive overview of European law, corporate social responsibility, and the degree to which either provide protection to the consumer. The case study of Royal Dutch Shell and the Niger Delta provide some insight into the problems which challenge European corporate legislation which result in negative outcomes from plaintiffs in cases of corporate social irresponsibility. However, future research will benefit of a quantitative study of the economic outcomes from the judicial decisions of European legislators. Moreover, investigations of the status of ongoing cases across the world.

Corporate Social Responsibility and International Trade: The EU's Trade Policy and Trade Agreements

Prof. Takao Suami

Law School, Waseda University, Japan

I. Introduction

This chapter focuses on the relationship between Corporate Social Responsibility (hereafter referred as CSR) and international trade agreements, notably free trade agreements and international investment agreements, and explores the EU's CSR policy in the context of EU trade agreements. The EU policy makers highly evaluate CSR as an important instrument to accomplish its policy goals since the beginning of this century[1]. For the current EU, CSR is a means of not only tackling social exclusion and sustainable development, but also improving the competitiveness of European industries. On the other hand the coverage of the EU trade policy is broad. It deals with various subjects that are not directly related to international trade and investment. The EU trade policy must also keep consistency with fundamental values of the EU such as human rights, labor rights and the environment[2]. Therefore, it is quite natural that EU has reached an idea to combine its trade

---

[1] European Commission, Communication from the Commission to the European Parliament, the Council, the European Economic and Social Committee and the Committee of the Regions, A renewed EU strategy 2011-14 for Corporate Social Responsibility, COM(2011) 681 final (25 October 2011).

[2] European Commission, Trade for all, Towards a more responsible trade and investment policy 5 and 20–26 (October 2015).

agreements with CSR. Recent trade agreements concluded by the EU contain provisions which mention cooperation for the promotion of CSR (hereafter referred as CSR provisions). In my presentation, after surveying the recent trade policy of the EU, I will examine CSR provisions in the EU's recent trade agreements including the EU–Japan Economic Partnership Agreement (hereafter referred as EPA) and tries to clarify how such CSR provisions will contribute to further development of CSR.

II. Intercourse between CSR and Trade Policy in the EU

1. CSR and its Target Subjects in the EU

The EU's notion of CSR has evolved over time from the inception of this century. In October 2011, the European Commission presented its new definition of CSR on the basis of internationally recognized principles and guidelines[3]. According to the Commission, CSR is currently defined as "the responsibility of enterprises for their impacts upon society", and "to fully meet their CSR, enterprises should have in place a process to integrate social, environmental, ethical, human rights and consumer concerns into their business operations and core strategies (….), with the aim of: maximizing the creation of shared value for their owners/shareholders and for their other stakeholders and society at large"[4]. It is noteworthy in the EU's understanding of CSR that according to internationally recognized principles and guidelines,

---

[3] Internationally recognized instruments include OECD Guidelines for Multinational Enterprises, the ten principles of the United Nations Global Compact, the ISO 26000 Guidance Standard on Social Responsibility, the ILO Tri-partie Declaration of Principles Concerning Multinational Enterprises and Social Policy, and the United Nations Guiding Principles on Business and Human Rights.

[4] European Commission, supra note 1, at 6.

CSR covers a wide range of policy subjects like "human rights, labour and employment practices (such as training, diversity, gender equality and employee health and well-being), environmental issues (such as biodiversity, climate change, resource efficiency, life-cycle assessment and pollution prevention), and combating bribery and corruption"[5]. Accordingly, most parts of corporate activities can be associated with CSR.

2. Non-Trade Subjects of the EU's Trade Policy

While the EU trade policy is mainly addressed to ordinary trade and foreign investment issues (TFEU Article 207, para.1), it is a part of the whole EU's external action and guided by the same principles with other aspects of its external action. These principles include democracy, the rule of law, human rights and fundamental freedoms, and respect for human dignity (TEU Article 21, para.1). They derive from the values which constitute the foundation of the EU (TEU Article 2). The European Community was founded as an economic community in the 1950s, but the current European Union has gone much beyond the limits of an economic community. Therefore, EU Treaty demand that the EU should uphold and promote its values to the wider world (TEU Article 3, para.5). The objectives of the EU's external action also include consolidating and supporting democracy, the rule of law and human rights (TEU Article 21, para.2 (b)).

In addition to these values, the EU aims at working for the sustainable development of Europe and a high level of protection of the environment (TEU Article 3, para.3). For this purpose, the TFEU provides for the integration of environmental protection into all other EU policies and activities (TFEU Article 11). The provisions in the EU treaties clearly provide that the EU's policy of sustainable development

---

[5] Ibid., at 7.

covers the territory outside the EU[6].

3. *Consistency between CSR and Trade Policy*

In brief, it follows from the above consideration that the EU trade policy is deeply connected with many subjects covered by CSR. The recent expansion of global supply chains by multinational enterprises is obvious. As a result, the EU's CSR policy has to target actions of European multinational enterprises outside the EU. On the other hand, the EU trade and investment policy on the basis of the above-mentioned values has to work for sustainable development and human rights. Therefore, it is easy to find out some connecting points in the EU between CSR policy and trade policy. Due to the expansion of global supply chains, businesses of all size are increasingly involved in sourcing activities in third countries. These phenomena have necessarily given rise to calls on trade policy to be connected with CSR policy in order to advance sustainable development and human rights agendas. Actually, the European Commission has been positive to the use of trade policy for the promotion of the EU's common values[7].

Drafters of the EU Treaties expected overlap among external and internal aspects of various EU policies. In order to respond to discord among different policies, TEU stipulates in advance that the EU shall ensure consistency between the different areas of its external actions and between these and its other policies (TEU Article 21, para.3). The consistency must be ensures by the aforesaid values and principles, and

---

[6] The EU's external action purposes to foster the sustainable, economic, social and environmental development of developing countries (TEU Article 21, para.2, (d)). The EU policy on the environment shall contribute to promoting measures at international level to deal with regional or worldwide environmental problems, in particular climate change (TFEU Article 191, para.1).

[7] According to the European Commission in 2015, the EU trade policy is understood as an instrument to promote around the world the EU's values like human rights and sustainable development (Commission, supra note 2, at 5).

the EU trade and investment policy must be consistent with broader European values[8]. In its current strategy for trade policy, the European Commission undertook to expand measures to support sustainable development, fair and ethical trade and human rights[9]. This is well indicated by the recent practice that EU bilateral trade agreements are linked to the political framework agreement, which include democracy, rule of law and the respect of human rights as essential elements of the relation.

4. Incorporation of CSR into the EU Trade Policy

As a result of keeping consistency among various policies, CSR has constituted a part of the EU's trade policy for more than a decade. In 2011, the European Commission already expressed that it would promote CSR through its external policies[10]. At that time, the Commission declared its standpoint that it would "continue, through a mix of global advocacy and complementary legislation, to aim at disseminating internationally recognized CSR guidelines and principles more widely and enabling EU businesses to ensure that they have a positive impact in foreign economies and societies" and that where appropriate, it would propose to address CSR in established dialogues with partner countries and regions[11].

Anti-globalists often argue that trade liberalization measures serve only the interests of big businesses at the expense of the socially disadvantaged such as employees, local farmers, small and medium-sized enterprises and indigenous people. Incorporating CSR in trade liberalization measures is usually considered as a way to counterbalance

---

[8] Ibid., at 20.

[9] Ibid., at 22-26.

[10] Commission, supra note 1, at 14.

[11] Ibid.

rights and responsibilities for big businesses[12]. For that reason, The Commission has emphasized CSR in relations with other countries and regions in the world. In other words, in order to combine social and environmental concerns of the civil society with the EU trade and investment policy, the Commission suggests the "reinforcement of CSR initiatives and due diligence across the production chain with a focus on the respect of human rights and the social and environmental aspects of value chains" in the context of a value-based trade and investment policy[13].

As regards Asia in particular, the EU is going to start a project on responsible supply chain in Asia, This is a joint project developed by the EU together with the International Labour Organization (ILO) and the Organization for Economic Co-operation and Development (OECD)[14]. The project will promote CSR and responsible business conduct (RBC) with regard to the environment, decent work and the respect of human rights. The project will be implemented in partnership with six Asian countries including China and Japan, and is scheduled to launch in 2018. Although its content is not entirely clear, we have to give attention to its progress.

III. EU's Trade Agreements and CSR

1. How has the idea on CSR affected the EU's trade agreements?

The EU trade agreements, notably recent free trade agreements

---

[12] Rafael Peels, Elizabeth Echeverria M., Jonas Aissi and Anselm Schneider, Corporate social responsibility in international trade and investment agreements: Implications for states, business, and workers, ILO Research Paper No.13, 3 (April 2016).

[13] Commission, supra note 2, at 20.

[14] EU, Responsible Supply Chains in Asia, Action Fact Sheet.

(hereafter referred as FTAs) and EPAs include non-trade objectives such as human rights and sustainable development. In particular, their chapters on "Trade and Sustainable Development" set out binding commitments to respect both core labour standards and international environmental agreements, and establish dedicated institutions to reinforce transparency and dialogue on the implementation of sustainable development provisions. These chapters generally mention CSR and understand CSR as a useful means to attain sustainable development. The following section will examine how effective these provisions are to promote CSR in the contracting states.

2. *EU Trade Agreements with CSR provisions*

The incorporation of CSR provisions into trade and investment agreements is a relatively recent world-wide phenomenon[15]. It is reported that the US-Peru and Canada-Peru comprehensive FTAs both of which came into force in 2009 are the first agreements to include provisions promoting CSR principles[16]. For example, the former agreement makes reference to CSR as a means of improving labour standards and advancing common commitments regarding labour matters. Since CSR is available in many subjects, the linkage between CSR and government policies has permeated into trade and investment policy too[17]. As a result, CSR provisions in trade and investment agreements have been constantly increasing since around 2010 in particular[18]. Recent agreements such as the Trans-Pacific Partnership (TPP), and the Canada-Burkina Faso

---

[15] UNEP, Corporate Social Responsibility and Regional Trade and Investment Agreements, 25 (2011).

[16] Joshua Waleson, "Corporate Social Responsibility in EU Comprehensive Free Trade Agreements: Towards Sustainable Trade and Investment," *Legal Issues of Economic Integration* 42, no.2 (2015): 143, 144.

[17] Peels and others, supra note 12, at 2.

[18] Ibid., at 8.

Foreign Investment Promotion and Protection Agreement (FIPA) make explicit reference to CSR[19].

The EU is not an exception to such a general trend. In case of recently concluded trade agreements of the EU, CSR is usually mentioned in provisions about trade and sustainable development. Namely, several trade agreements such as the Comprehensive Economic and Trade Agreement with Canada (CETA), and the EU-Vietnam FTA make reference to CSR in their chapters on "Trade and Sustainable Development" and/or "Social Policy and Equal Opportunities"[20]. The Commission has also expressed its intention to focus on the implementation of the sustainable development provisions in the FTAs[21].

The recent inclusion of CSR provisions has been motivated partly at least by the pressure of the European Parliament. While after the entry into force of the Lisbon Treaty, the powers of the European Parliament have been considerably increased in the field of trade and it now

---

[19] Article 19.7 (Corporate Social Responsibility) provides in the context of labour regulations that [E]ach Party shall endeavor to encourage enterprises to voluntarily adopt corporate social responsibility initiatives on labour issues that have been endorsed or are supported by that Party. Article 20.10 (Corporate Social Responsibility) also provides in the context of environment that [E]ach Party should encourage enterprises operating within its territory or jurisdiction, to adopt voluntarily, into their policies and practices, principles of corporate social responsibility that are related to the environment, consistent with internationally recognized standards and guidelines that have been endorsed or are supported by that Party.

[20] Peels and others, supra note 12, at 29-33; For example, Article 9 of the chapter on Trade and Sustainable Development in the EU-Vietnam FTA stipulates that The Parties, in accordance with their domestic policies, agree to promote corporate social responsibility (CSR), provided that CSR-related measures are not applied in a manner that would constitute a means of arbitrary or unjustifiable discrimination between the Parties or a disguised restriction on trade. Promotion of CSR includes among others exchange of information and best practices, education and training activities and technical advice.

[21] Commission, supra note 2, at 24.

participates in trade policy making more than before[22], the European Parliament has since 2010 called for the systemic integration of CSR clauses in all future international trade and investment agreements[23].

Even before the Lisbon Treaty, the inclusion of sustainable development chapters in EU FTAs including provisions on labour standards and environmental standards had occurred[24]. Afterwards the inclusion of CSR provisions in the core text of trade agreements has become an ordinary practice of the EU trade policy under the Lisbon Treaty. In one sense, this progress revealed more legalization on CSR at the international scene. In another sense, however, we have to keep in mind the limits of obligations concerning CSR imposed by these agreements.

First of all, the obligations by CSR provisions are aimed only at the contracting states, namely the host and home states[25], and private companies do not assume any obligations by them. Even under these agreements, the private sector is guaranteed purely voluntary CSR engagement[26].

Secondly, contacting states' commitments with regard to CSR are

---

[22] Jean-Claude Piris, "The Lisbon Treaty," *A Legal and Political Analysis* (2010): 279-287.

[23] Peels and others, supra note 12, at 7; European Parliament resolution of 25 November 2010 on corporate social responsibility in international trade agreements, OJ 2012, C 99E/101; European parliament resolution of 5 July 2016 on implementation of the 2010 recommendations of Parliament on social and environmental standards, human rights and corporate responsibility (2015/2038 (INI)); The EP resolution of 2010 proposes that future trade agreements negotiated by the EU should incorporate a chapter on sustainable development which includes a CSR clause based on the OECD Guidelines for Multinational Enterprises (EP resolution of 2010, para.25).

[24] Waleson, supra note 16, at 157; The 2008 EU-Cariforum Economic Partnership Agreement is the first EU international agreement to include a 'sustainable development' chapter, containing horizontal obligations to respect labour and environmental standards (Ibid., at 158).

[25] Waleson, supra note 16, at 163.

[26] Peels and others, supra note 12, at 11.

generally not hard but soft. In other words, they do not create strict legal obligations for the contacting states to achieve certain results in terms of human rights, environment protection and labour conditions[27]. According to analysis of CSR provisions, there are a number of ways countries could choose to reflect CSR concepts and tools in trade and investment agreements[28]. One option is simply to encourage their use in a non-legally binding manner. Under this arrangement, their governments are required to make efforts to establish a favorable environment for the development of CSR[29]. The second option requires governments to promote particular CSR instruments and tools within trade and investment agreements. Namely, governments need to be more involved in various activities than the first option. For example, they have to set up an institutional framework that can facilitate a dialogue about CSR between the relevant stakeholders. The third approach is for governments to be obliged to "require private companies to adhere to particular CSR principles and tools pursuant to a trade and investment agreement". The feature of this option is to impose legal obligation on private investors to meet certain requirements. Generally speaking, in case of the EU trade agreements, CSR provisions are classified into the first and second categories, because they usually stipulate cooperation in promoting CSR and set up special institutions for monitoring their implementation[30]. The softness of these obligations is also indicated by the fact that normal dispute settlements procedures established under the agreements are not

---

[27] Ibid., at 11.

[28] UNEP, supra note 15, at 31-33.

[29] The Canada–Peru FTA was the first FTA to include an explicit reference to CSR (Waleson, supra note 16, at 163). It introduces a horizontal obligation on the contracting parties to promote a comprehensive set of guidelines with regard to CSR (Ibid., at 164).

[30] Peels and others, supra note 12, at 29-33.

applicable to CSR provisions[31]. Instead, less contentious procedures are applied to disputes concerning the chapter on Sustainable Development[32].

These features are applicable to the EU's trade agreements with Asian countries too. In the next section, I will examine these agreements, in particular the EU–Japan EPA. The EU and Japan finally settled their negotiation for the EU-Japan Economic Partnership Agreement (the EU–Japan EPA) in December 2017 and they are expected to officially sign the Agreement before this summer.

3. *The EU Trade Agreements with Asian Countries*

3.1. The EU–Japan EPA and CSR

i.   Promotion of and Cooperation for CSR

While its preamble does not explicitly refer to CSR, the EU–Japan EPA, like other recently concluded trade agreements of the EU, inserts two provisions explicitly referring to CSR in the "Trade and Sustainable Development" chapter[33].

While both the EU and Japan recognize the contribution of the EU–Japan EPA to promoting sustainable development which covers economic and social development, and environmental protection (Article 1, para.1, and Article 5), in order to achieve this objective, the

---

[31] Waleson, supra note 16, at 159; For example, Article 16, para.1 in the chapter on Trade and Sustainable Development of the EU–Vietnam FTA states that "[F]or any matter arising under this chapter where there is disagreement, the Parties shall only have recourse to the procedures established under Article 16 and Article 17". Normal dispute settlements procedures shall not apply to this Chapter.

[32] Article 16 and Article 17 in the Chapter on Trade and Sustainable Development of the EU–Vietnam FTA.

[33] This chapter targets important non-economic or trade subjects, namely the observance of international environmental and labour standards (Article 3 International labour standards and conventions, Article 4 Multilateral environment agreements, Article 6 Biological diversity and Article 7 Sustainable management of forests and trade in timber and timber products).

EU and Japan also agree to promote CSR. In the first place, CSR is regarded as one of the major means to enhance the contribution of trade and investment to the goal of sustainable development. Namely, both parties agree to encourage CSR on the basis of relevant internationally recognized principles and guidelines (Article 5 Trade and investment favouring sustainable development, (e)), In this context, both the OECD Guidelines for Multinational Enterprises and the ILO Tripartie Declaration of Principles concerning Multinational Enterprises and Social Policy are specially mentioned in the provision. In the second place, while recognizing the importance of cooperation on trade and investment related aspects of environmental and labour policies, the EU and Japan also agree to include CSR as one of the subjects of cooperation between the parties. Namely, the parties "may cooperate to promote corporate social responsibility, notably through the exchange of information and best practices, including on adherence, implementation, follow-up, and dissemination of internationally agreed guidelines and principles" (Article 12 Cooperation).

ii.   Enforcement Mechanism

For the chapter on Trade and Sustainable Development, the EU–Japan EPA sets up a special mechanism for the implementation of their commitments, and excludes the application of normal dispute settlement procedures in that Chapter (Article 16, para.1).

This mechanism is composed of two stages. In the first place, the EU–Japan EPA sets up three institutional frameworks (namely a Specialised Committee, domestic advisory groups and a Joint Dialogue with civil society) for both parties to promote sustainable development[34].

---

[34] Namely, first of all, the Parties will establish a Specialised Committee on Trade and Sustainable Development (hereafter referred to as the Specialised Committee) (Article 13, para.2), The Committee is given the task of reviewing and monitoring the implementation and operation of this Chapter, and seek solutions to resolve differences

These frameworks will be useful to reflect the interests and views of different groups (such as employers, workers and environmental groups) in the society in sustainable development policy making of both parties, and will contribute to harmonization of their implementation.

In the second place, in the event of disagreement between the parties on the interpretation or application of this Chapter, specific procedures prescribed in this Chapter will be applied. These procedures are divided into two stages, namely Government Consultations (Article 16) and Examination by a Panel of Experts (Article 17). First, the party will have recourse to consultations with the other party. If the parties do not reach a mutually satisfactory resolution of the matter concerned, each party may request a panel being composed of three experts to examine the matter concerned. After examination, the panel of experts shall issue a final report to the parties setting out the findings of facts, the interpretation or the applicability of the relevant Articles and the basic rationale behind any findings and suggestions (Article 17, para.5). Finally, the parties will discuss actions or measures resolve the matter in question, taking into account the panel's final report and suggestions. As the wording of "suggestions" indicates, the final report is not legally binding upon the parties.

3.2. Comparative Analysis with Other Trade Agreements

i.   Gradual Progress of CSR Obligations

The Sustainable Development chapter in the EU-Japan EPA is largely modeled upon that in the EU–Korea FTA concluded in 2009.

---

in case of disagreement on the interpretation or application of this Chapter (Article 13, para.3). Secondly, each party organize its own domestic advisory group as a consultative body on economic, social and environmental issues (Article 14, para.1). Thirdly, the parties shall convene a Joint Dialogue with civil society organizations in their territories (Article 15).

The structure of the chapter in the EU–Korea FTA is similar to that in the EU-Japan EPA. In common with the EU–Japan EPA, the EU–Korea FTA not only refers to CSR in the provision for Trade favouring sustainable development (Article 13.6, para.2) but also establishes cooperation on CSR as one of areas for cooperation on trade-related aspects of social and environmental policies (Article 13.10 and Annex 13). Since the reference to CSR is limited only in the context of trade in goods, it appears that CSR in the EU–Korea FTA has narrower coverage than that in the EU–Japan EPA. However, it is doubtful whether or not there is actually substantial gap in terms of CSR obligations between the two agreements. This is because there is no limitation on the scope of CSR cooperation in the EU–Korea FTA.

On the other hand, the EU–Japan EPA is more advanced as to the substance of CSR obligations than the EU–Korea FTA. This is because the former explicitly invokes the OECD Guidelines and the ILO Declaration as examples of internationally recognized principles and guidelines, while the latter does not mention about any concrete documents. References to specific internationally accepted instruments have already become ordinary practice of the EU trade policy as the recently concluded agreements such as the EU–Vietnam FTA and the CETA demonstrate[35], and have the effect of making CSR obligations more concrete and substantial.

ii.   Standardized Enforcement Mechanisms

The effectiveness of enforcement mechanisms is crucial for the

---

[35] The EU–Vietnam FTA agreed in 2016 also refers to the OECD Guidelines for Multinational Enterprises, the UN Global Compact, the ILO Tripartite Declaration of Principles concerning Multinational Enterprises and Social Policy. The Comprehensive and Economic Trade Agreement which came into force in 2017 refers to the OECD Guidelines for Multinational Enterprises in the Chapter on Trade and Sustainable Development (Article 22.3, para.2, b) as well as the preamble.

proper implementation of CSR obligations. As aforesaid, an enforcement mechanism in the EU–Japan EPA combines the monitoring through the special committee with both consultations with governments and recommendations by the expert panel. This type of arrangements has almost become a standard in the EU trade agreements since the EU-Korea FTA[36]. For example, the EU–Vietnam FTA adopted the same arrangements which were composed of a specialised committee with domestic advisory group (Article 15), government consultations (Article 16) and panel of experts (Article 17). However, an enforcement mechanism in CETA is different from the EU standard, because the chapter on Trade and Sustainable Development does not include the expert panel procedure[37].

iii.   Overall Evaluation on the Current State of Affairs

To conclude, the incorporation of CSR provisions into trade agreements has become the established trade practice of the EU. Furthermore, the substance of these provisions has been almost standardized in terms of CSR obligations and enforcement mechanisms for such obligations. In other words, when the EU negotiates a EPA with countries in he Asia and Pacific region in a future, it is likely that CSR provisions in the EU–Japan EPA will serve as a draft proposal for both parties.

3.3. Effectiveness of CSR provisions in the EU's Trade Agreements

It is a controversial issue whether or not CSR provisions in the

---

[36] The EU–Korea FTA already established the structure of these mechanisms (Articles 13.12, 13.13, 13.14 and 13.15).

[37] The structure of CETA is different from other agreements, because the subjects of "Trade and Labour" and "Trade and Environment" are dealt with not by the chapter on sustainable development but by independent chapters. Therefore, the expert panels are provided for by these chapters (Chapter 23 and Chapter 24).

trade agreement are able to have the effect of actually promoting CSR in the contracting states. Some scholars are skeptical of their effectiveness and raise several reasons. First of all, as aforesaid, trade agreements are binding only on their contracting states. As obligations to promoting CSR in the trade agreements is aimed at state practice and their impacts upon multinational enterprises remain indirect[38]. Therefore, Waleson suggests that the investment chapter should directly impose positive CSR obligation on private investors[39]. Secondly, as aforesaid too, CSR obligations on contracting states are not enough to actually promote CSR. These obligations still remain in the scope of obligations to make sincere efforts[40]. Thirdly, many trade agreements provide for quasi-judicial style dispute settlement procedures. However, most of them exclude the sustainable development chapter from the application of their general dispute settlement procedures[41]. As a result, dispute settlement for the sustainable development chapter is less effective than for other areas. It is therefore questionable whether a trade agreement with CSR provisions would be effective as an instrument to enforce a voluntary framework on non-contracting parties, notably multinational enterprises[42]. For example, Wagner insists that due to the lack of effective enforcement, CSR provisions in the three major trade agreements, namely the NAFTA, the Canada–Peru FTA and the TPP, have failed to achieve their purposes[43].

It seems that from the purely legal point of view, these arguments generally hit the right points. However, it is too early to conclude that

---

[38] Waleson, supra note 16, at 168.

[39] Ibid., at 162 and 169–172.

[40] Ibid., at 172.

[41] Ibid., at 173.

[42] Ibid., at 173-174.

[43] Ashley Wagner, "The Failure of Corporate Social Responsibility Provisions within International Trade Agreements and Export Credit Agencies as a Solution," *Boston University International Law Journal* 35(2017): 195, 219-220.

the present CSR provisions would be meaningless for the promotion of CSR. Unlike those skeptics, I am more positive to the meaning of CSR provisions.

First of all, it seems not so decisive whether or not CSR provisions impose legal obligations on private companies. As long as CSR requires them to go beyond their legal obligations, it is impossible for legal obligations to control every aspect of CSR. Even assuming that enforcement mechanisms for CSR obligations are effective, it is unlikely that any violation of the CSR provisions would be brought to dispute settlement procedures, because the level of precision of CSR obligations is generally low[44]. In brief, the overall scheme of CSR does not in essence fit legalistic dispute settlement. This is a reason why most agreements do not apply ordinary dispute settlement procedures to CSR obligations.

Secondly, the idea of CSR functions well in case that private companies are motivated to improve their performances on sustainable development and human rights. When do they have strong motivation to be positive to CSR? It is probable that when its positive participation of the CSR scheme contributes to the improvement of its competitive position in any particular product or service market, a private company cannot help being positive to CSR activities[45]. Therefore, while each market is organized by combination of many elements including legal regulations, consumer awareness, social incentives and traditional moral and culture, the market design of a government is important for the effectiveness of CSR. However, legal regulations are not omnipotent for the satisfactory function of CSR, and they have to be properly blended with other elements. In this context, it must be notable that the inclusion of CSR provisions sends a clear message to peoples in the society.

---

[44] Peels and others, supra note 16, at 14.

[45] Takao Suami, "Kigyo no shakaiteki sekinin (CSR) to Kankyohogo" [Corporate Social Responsibility and Environmental Protection], *Nihon Kokusai Keizai Ho Gakkai Nenpo* [*International Economic Law*] 18(2009): 36–58.

Thirdly, for Japan particularly, CSR provisions in the EU–Japan have great potential. They are not so innovative for the EU, but they are quite new and important for Japan. Before the EU–Japan EPA, Japan has concluded a number of EPAs with countries in different regions. Although they express concern lowering environmental measures and labour standards for the purpose of attracting foreign direct investment[46], however, to my knowledge, all of them refer to neither sustainable development nor CSR. Therefore, the insertion of CSR provisions into the EU–Japan EPA was likely to be made at the initiative of the EU. Practice under the EU–Korea FTA having similar CSR provisions evidences that these provisions have in fact encouraged various stakeholders including governments, civil society and multinational enterprises to participate in discussion for the implementation of international CSR instruments[47]. Definitely, CSR provisions are able to give birth to a new impetus to drive CSR forward. This progress may become a turning point for Japan's CSR policy in the context of trade agreements. For example, similar CSR provisions may disseminate in other trade agreements between Japan and Asian countries. Therefore, we have to pay careful attention to implementation of CSR provisions once the EU–Japan EPA comes into force.

4. *Corporate Social Responsibility (CSR) and Sustainable Development Goals (SDGs)*

In recent times, we can be aware of another development which

---

[46] For example, the Japan–Swiss EPA which came into force in 2009 recognizes that it is inappropriate to encourage investment activities by relaxing domestic health, safety or environmental measures or lowering labour standards (Article 101). The Japan–Thailand EPA concluded in 2007 also recognizes that it is inappropriate to encourage investment by relaxing its environmental measures (Article 111). Other EPAs (such as Japan–Malaysia EPA) contain similar provisions.

[47] Peels and others, supra note 16, at 14–15.

is favorable to CSR. That is the adoption of the UN Resolution on Sustainable Development Goals in 2015[48], In this resolution, the UN General Assembly specified the 17 sustainable development goals and 169 targets to be achieved in the next 15 years.

As the title of the resolution indicates, this resolution expressed its strong commitment to sustainable development in its three dimensions –economic, social and environmental (para.2). The resolution does not explicitly mention about CSR at all. Yet it has contributed much to the formation of a favorable environment for CSR. For example, as means of its implementation, the resolution suggests bringing together governments, the private sector, civil society (paras.39 and 60), and emphasizes the role of the diverse private sector (para.41), Furthermore, it "encourage companies, especially large and transnational companies, to adopt sustainable practices and to ......" (Goal 12. Ensure sustainable consumption and production patters, 12.6). It is not difficult to notice something in common between CSR and SDGs. Therefore, it is likely that CSR and SDGs can reinforce each other to achieve sustainable development in the world.

IV. Final Remarks

CSR provisions in trade agreement still have potential for further development of CSR. In case of the EU–Japan EPA, it fully depends upon the attitude of the EU whether or not CSR provisions are effectively implemented in Japan. As EU Consumers care about the respect of human rights, labour rights and the environment in the way the products are produced, it is important for the EU to ensure responsible management of global supply chains which is essential to

---

[48] General Assembly of the United Nations, Transforming our world: the 2030 Agenda for Sustainable Development, A/RES/70/1 (21 October 2015).

align trade policy with European values[49]. In addition to Specialized Committees (the Specialised Committee on Trade and Sustainable Development is one of them), the EU–Japan EPA also establish a Joint Committee comprising representatives of both parties for the purpose of monitoring its implementation. It is expected that the Joint Committee will discuss various subjects covered by this EPA. Since cooperation for CSR is explicitly mentioned in this EPA, each party is able to bring any CSR issue before discussion at the Joint Committee. Therefore, if the EU wants to do so, the EU will be able to put continuous political pressure on Japan in order to make its CSR policy align with internationally accepted principles. If reality under the EU–Japan EPA really follows such expectation, I will be able to declare the positive function of CSR provisions as a catalyst for promoting CSR.

---

[49] Commission, supra note 2, at 24.

Comparative Analysis of Trade-Labour Linkage in FTAs of the US and EU

Prof. Yoo-Duk Kang

Language and Trade Division, Hankuk University of Foreign Studies

Prof. Bomin Ko

Catholic University of Korea

I. Introduction

International discussions on the trade and labour standards linkage date back to the beginning of the International Labour Organization (ILO) in the early 20th century. The ILO Constitution states in its preamble that "the failure of any nation to adopt humane conditions of labour is an obstacle in the way of other nations which desire to improve the conditions in their own countries". This means that labour conditions in countries could be influenced by exchange of trade in goods and services with their trade partners. Since then, increasing trade and investment between developed and developing countries have stirred international debate on the linkage of trade and labour standards. Many people in developed countries feared job loss to developing countries via relocation of low wage/technology industries, while news about labour exploitation in developing world caused a sensation. In this context, the argument that trade and investment issues should include labour right protection became more convincing.

Protecting working conditions is often included in trade negotiation agenda in order to level a playground for fair competition as well as to protect normative value of human rights (Golub, 1997). Labour standards are the product of social consensus that has been formed endogenously, reflecting the level of political and economic development and social experiences of each country. However, in a situation where trade barriers are considerably lowered in the context of trade liberalization, wage and labour management costs related to the labour standards may affect the international competitiveness of firms. If they are located in countries with low labour standards, they may have an advantage over production costs on the basis of low wages plus low cost related to labour standard. On the contrary, firms in countries with higher labour standards could be in disadvantaged position in international trade. As a result, this disparity in labour standard can create a 'race to the bottom' due to the social dumping (OECD, 1990; UNCTAD, 1994).

Linking trade and labour standards had been discussed in the multilateral trading system and became the object of confrontation between developed and developing countries without making concrete progress (Anuradha and Dutta, 2012). From the viewpoint of developing countries, the linkage of trade and labour standards, which developed countries claim, can be used for the purpose of protectionism. It was regarded as an attempt to interfere with domestic policy through trade negotiations. In this confrontation, the ILO adopted the 'ILO Declaration on Fundamental Principles and Rights at Work and its Follow-up' in 1998 (hereinafter referred to as Declaration of 1998) and introduced the four principles related to labour rights. The Declaration stated also that labour standards should neither be used for a purpose of protectionism, nor for a purpose for questioning comparative advantage of a particular country.[1] Linking trade with labour standards was

---

[1] The official name is 'Declaration on Basic Principles and Rights in the Workplace and its Follow-up' (ILO Declaration on Fundamental Principles and Rights at Work). The four core labour rights specified in the Declaration are as follows.(1) effective recognition of freedom of association and collective bargaining; (2) prohibition of all forms of forced and compulsory labour; (3) effective prohibition of child labour; (4) elimination of employment and occupational discrimination.

discussed on various occasions in the WTO system in the 1990s, but the discussions did not result in any binding rules at multilateral level due to the differences in interests among major countries (Kim, 2001).

One of remarkable trend in international trade in 2000s is the proliferation of regional trade agreements (RTAs). According to the WTO, the cumulative number of RTAs reported to the WTO as of February 2016 is 625, of which 419 RTAs are in effect.[2] More than 90% of RTAs are free trade agreements (FTAs), and many of the FTAs are bilateral. Developing countries used to aim to improve their access to markets of developed countries by FTAs, while developed countries are concerned with to impose their own regulations and standards on developing countries.[3] In this sense, the proliferation of FTAs seems to have created a new era in linking trade and labour standards. This is because it is easier for a developed country to acquire concession from a developing country with regard to the labour standards in a bilateral negotiation than in multilateral negotiation.

In this context, it is meaningful to examine how the US and EU, which are two major economic powers in international trade, link trade and labour standards through their FTAs. The US signed the North American Free Trade Agreement (NAFTA) in 1992 and included its side agreement on labour and the environment into the NAFTA in 1993. Since its FTA with Jordan, concluded in October 2000, the US has included a separate labour chapter in its FTAs. The labour provisions in US FTAs are most far-reaching with conditional regulations that stipulate trade sanction, when the labour standards are not properly respected. The EU, on the other hand, has been reluctant to include strong labour standards in FTAs and tried to protect labour rights by promoting

---

[2] WTO, https://www.wto.org/english/tratop_e/region_e/region_e.htm (accessed on 2016. 05. 18)

[3] Such a strategy, termed "regulatory cooperation", is prominent in the EU's trade policy. See the European Commission (2010, p. 7) for the EU's position on this.

cooperation with FTA partners. However, since the mid-2000s, the EU has gradually emphasized the link between trade and labour standards in the process of implementing more comprehensive FTAs.

This paper examines international the trend on trade and labour standards linkage and reviews its characteristics by analyzing labour - related provisions of FTAs signed by the US and EU from comparative perspective. Both the US and EU have rule-making capacity in the global governance and use this 'regulatory power' in order to acquire advantageous position in trade. In this sense, it is necessary to review FTAs of the US and EU and find their common features and differences.

This paper is organized as follows. Section 2 reviews main arguments for linking trade with labour standards and international discussion among related countries. The section includes literature reviews as well. Section 3 and Section 4 examine the characteristics of the labour clause in the US FTAs and in EU's FTAs respectively. Based on this analysis, Section 5 examines the common features and differences of the labour clauses between US and EU's FTAs and examines the root causes of the differences.

II. Theoretical background

1. *Economic discussion*

Discussions on the linkage of trade and labour standards have been developed in a way that different countries, academic schools and social groups were in confrontation and its debates took place in a mixture of normative, practical and economic perspectives. As discussed in the introduction, the debates divided countries into two groups, the developed and the developing countries. From the economic point of view, they focused mainly on the relations between trade and labour standards and how to maximize welfare. They can be divided into 'unfair competition' and 'race to the bottom' debates.

First, the debate about unfair competition suggests that countries can compete fairly in international trade, only if they have a certain level of 'similar' labour standards. Products produced in countries with low labour standards can have unfair price competitiveness, because their production costs do not reflect the social costs related to the descent working conditions. As a consequence, the countries have a favorable position for increasing export and market share abroad in the short term (Busse, 2002). On the other hand, in the long run, they can suffer from side-effects such as long-lasting under-development in social affairs as well as the deterioration of working conditions. In order to level playgrounds for fair competition and to prevent the adverse effects of worsening labour conditions, it was argued that the WTO should establish an institutional body so that each member countries can include international labour standards into its own trade policy (Elliott 1998; Turnell 2002 ; Aleo 2006).

This view has been raised by developed countries not only for economic benefits, but also for a move to improve working conditions in developing world from an ethical point of view. On the other hand, many argued against the view that lower labour standards can promote exports (Martin and Maskus, 2001; Aidt and Tzannatos, 2002). Most economists recognize that developing countries have a comparative advantage in labour abundant and low technolgy industries, because they are at the low stage of economic development and have a rich workforce in unskilled labour. Therefore, they do not think that low labour standards are a key factor in comparative advantage. Rather, it is pointed out that inclusion of international labour standards in trade agreements is nothing more than "hidden protectionism" of developed countries (Krugman 1994; Bhagwati 2001).

In the same vein, some economists are skeptical about whether strong labour provisions included in the trade agreement will contribute to the promotion of labour rights in the countries concerned. According to them, it is hard to improve the working conditions in developing countries by imposing any rule at international level. The efforts for that should be made in improving productivity and income level in developing countries and eliminating trade barriers (Burtless, 2001; Stern and Terrell, 2003).

The second argument is that international trade tend to exert downward pressure to labour standards and it is necessary to prevent from this by establishing international labour standards. In general, developing countries have low wages and low labour standards, and there is still a motive to lower labour standards in order to attract more foreign investment. This coincides with interests of multinational corporations that are willing to lower production costs and decide to relocate their production base to developing countries. Therefore, labour standards are subject to downward pressure by competition between countries (Anderson 1998; Chan and Ross 2003).

On the other hand, there is a view that the increase in international trade can contribute to the strengthening of labour standards in developing countries. This view is in the same context as the view that productivity and income increase in developing countries can lead to improvement of labour standards. The increase in international trade can be positive for improving labour standards when economic and political developments interact each other and form a virtuous circle. If increasing international trade and investment open a way to higher economic growth and income increase, it is likely that social demands will increase and as a result, it will lead to better labour right protection and ultimately to political development (Davies and Vadlamannatid, 2013). Furthermore, the role of labour cost became less important in investment decisions of foreign firms. It is rather institutional factors such as the quality of labour and the level of governance of the host country that are more important. It means that host countries need to improve labour standards to attract foreign investment in promising industries (Tsogas, 1999).

2. International discussion on trade-labour standards linkage

Since the beginning of the WTO, linking trade with labour standards at multilateral trading system is one of contentious issues. The US and European countries, such as France argued that labour issues should be included in the WTO agenda. The trade and labour linkage was, however, a complex issue amid intricate webs of interests between developed and developing countries. The debates were whether this issue was motivated from humanitarian purpose or hidden protectionism. In particular, the inclusion of labour clauses that could trigger trade retaliation in case of non-respect of labour standards encountered strong opposition from developing countries.

At the WTO ministerial meeting in Marrakesh in 1994, some countries including the US and France insisted that the compliance of basic labour rights be a prerequisite for an WTO membership and an special working group be set up within the WTO secretariat to examine the relationship between trade and labour standards. This suggestion encountered strong opposition, particularly from developing countries. This issue was discussed at the World Summit for Social Development held at Copenhagen in 1995 as an UN Special Session, but opinions diverged between developed countries, and developing countries, such as India, China, Malaysia and Indonesia. The Summit served as a momentum for the international recognition of the four core labour standards (prohibition of forced and child labour, prohibition of discrimination, freedom of association and collective bargaining right), but it failed to reduce differences of opinion between developed and developing countries. The same pattern of disagreement appeared at the WTO Ministerial meeting held in Singapore in 1996. The US insisted on establishing a working group within the WTO to review the relation of internationally recognized core labour standards with trade. This was supported by the EU and Canada. However, this proposal was confronted with the opposition of most of developing countries. The Clinton administration had shown a protectionist attitude on a number of issues and this also created an unfavorable situation for the US proposal within the WTO. The majority of WTO Members shared a view that labour issues should be discussed at the ILO and opposed to the idea of including labour standards to WTO agenda. As a result, the Declaration of Singapore Ministerial Conference only confirmed the principles and the role of the ILO in this regard without any specific description of the link between trade and working conditions. In particular, the paragraph 4 of the Declaration states that "reject the use of labour standards for protectionist purposes, and agree that the comparative advantage of countries, particularly low-wage developing countries, should not be questioned". [4]

This confrontation between developed and developing countries continued at the Ministerial Conference in Seattle in 1999. The US repeatedly asserted its position to establish a working group on trade-labour standards linkage within the WTO, and the EU proposed to establish a rather loose forum with permanent status between the ILO and WTO. On the other hand, developing countries in the WTO, termed 'Group 77' strongly opposed linking trade and labour standards within the WTO. The same phenomenon continued in the Doha Development Agenda (DDA), which began in 2001, and eventually the trade-labour standards linkage was not included in the agenda of the WTO.

The above mentioned episodes provide lessons as follows. First, due to the disagreement between countries, it is difficult to discuss the trade-labour standards linkage within the WTO.

---

[4] https://www.wto.org/english/thewto_e/minist_e/min96_e/wtodec_e.htm.

This issue had been divisive than any other issues. Second, the WTO could not deliver visible outcomes on labour-related issues and this demonstrates well why the DDA has been stagnating under the current system. It is difficult to make progress in negotiation, if both sides of the opposition are large and most developing countries oppose collectively.

3. *Recent trade agreements and labour-related provisions*

Labour provisions have been included in trade agreements such as FTAs. Most of trade agreements with labour provisions are bilateral agreements concluded between developed countries such as the US, EU and Canada on one hand, and developing countries on the other hand in so-called North-South format. According to the ILO (2014), there was no single RTA including labour provisions in 1990. However, the number increased to 12 in 2000 and 43 in 2010. In 2014, total 67 RTAs included labour provisions. This increase is due to the fact that the number of RTAs (either with labour provision or not) had increased in an

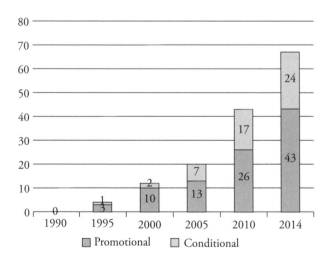

Figure 1: Labour provisions in trade agreements
Source: ILO (2014); Kraatz (2015), p. 4.

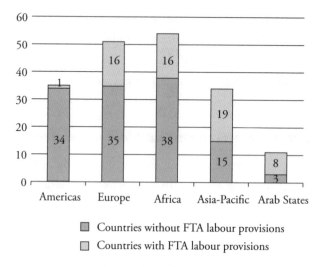

Figure 2: ILO member countries with trade agreements
Source: ILO (2015), p. 20

unprecedented manner since the mid-1990s. But it is clear that labour-related provisions are increasingly included in RTAs.

ILO (2015) reports that one-third of FTAs notified to the WTO from 2005 to 2013 include labour provisions. In this trend, 60% of the 185 ILO Member States have concluded at least one trade agreement that includes labour clauses. It is noteworthy that even FTAs concluded between developing countries (South-South format) include labour provisions and the number of this case has been increasing. As of June 2013, total 16 FTAs concluded between developing countries have labour-related provisions.

As illustrated in Figure 3, the labour provisions included in the FTA can be broadly divided into two groups, one with binding labour provisions and another with promotional (non-binding) labour provisions. Of the FTAs that include labour provisions, 40% have binding labour provisions, while 60% have promotional labour provisions, for example, a declaration of good willingness to protect labour rights and cooperation between authorities concerned. The former uses retreat of reciprocal preferences and eventually a trade sanction as a last resort for imposing labour standards, while the latter mainly relies on dialogue and discussion between authorities, instead of resorting to enforcement action. The main reason why FTAs with labour provisions are divided into two groups is that FTAs that US concluded so far incorporate binding and enforceable labour provisions, while the EU's FTA rely on dialogue with trading partners as a means of enforcing and implementing labour provisions. In addition, FTAs for which both contracting parties are developing countries do not include labour-

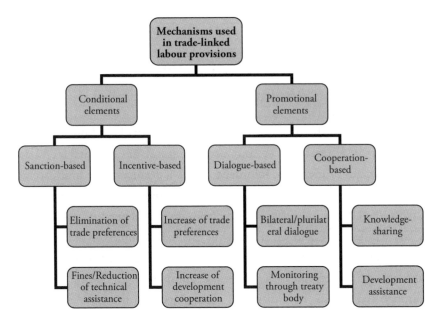

Figure 3: Different implementation mechanisms used in labour provisions
Source: Ebert and Posthuma (2011), p. 4.

related clauses or only have some clauses stating broad and non-binding principles of labour rights.

III. US FTA and labour provisions

1. US FTA Policy

The US entered into an FTA with Canada in 1989 and extended it to Mexico, establishing the North American Free Trade Agreement (NAFTA) in 1994. In the 2000s, the US governments pushed for FTAs mainly with Countries in Central and South America and some East Asian countries seeking preferential market access to US market. As of May 2016, the US has 14 FTAs with countries such as Jordan, Singapore, Korea, and Panama. In October 2015, the US concluded a mega FTA, Trans-Pacific Partnership Agreement (TPP) with other 10 countries in the Asia-Pacific region. Since February 2013, the US has been engaged in negotiating Transatlantic Trade and Investment Partnership (TTIP) with the EU (see Table 1).

Until the early 2000s, the US FTA policy was based on so called 'competitive liberalization' and used bilateral or regional FTAs as breakthroughs or pressures, in order to break a deadlock over multilateral negotiation agenda (Deblock 2005). On the other hand, since the mid-2000s, the US has moved its priority from the multilateral negotiation to FTAs. US-led TPP and TTIP with the EU are examples of this change. Basic motivations of US trade policy in FTAs are to seek market access abroad and to widespread its rules and norms over its trading partners through trade deals. In addition to these objectives, the US FTAs tends to be practical and flexible to reflect particular situations of its trading partners, compared to FTAs of the EU (Horn et al., 2009).

Labour provisions in US FTAs can be well perceived from its New Trade Policy announced on May 10, 2007. This new policy

Table 1: US FTAs with its trade partners

Partners	Category	Date of entry into force
Israel	FTA	August 19, 1985
NAFTA	FTA/EIA	January 1, 1994
Canada	-	January 1, 1989
Jordan	FTA/EIA	December 17, 2001
Singapore	FTA/EIA	January 1, 2004
Chile	FTA/EIA	January 1, 2004
Australia	FTA/EIA	January 1, 2005
Morocco	FTA/EIA	January 1, 2006
Bahrain	FTA/EIA	August 1, 2006
Central America	FTA/EIA	March 1, 2006
El Salvador (March 1, 2006), Honduras, Nicaragua (April 1, 2006), Guatemala (July 1, 2006), Dominican Republic (March 1, 2007), Costa Rica (January 1, 2009)		
Oman	FTA/EIA	January 1, 2009
Peru	FTA/EIA	February 1, 2009
Korea, Republic	FTA/EIA	March 15, 2012
Colombia	FTA/EIA	May 15, 2012
Panama	FTA/EIA	October 31, 2012
FTA signed or under negotiation	TPP: finalized (October 5, 20155) TTIP: under negotiation (de facto suspended) (February 13, 2013 ~)	

Note: (1) Free Trade Agreement (FTA) means agreements for trade in goods based on Article 24 of the GATT, and Economic Integration Agreement (EIA) means a FTA for trade in service for which the legal basis is GATS Article 5. (2) The US-Canada FTA was subsequently absorbed by NAFTA.

Source: WTO, http://rtais.wto.org/UI/PublicAllRTAList.aspx (accessed on May 18, 2016)

includes protective policy orientation of the US Democratic Party that became a majority in US Congress. In addition to conventional trade issues, this policy covers a wide range of issues, such as core labour and environment standards, investment, government procurement and trade adjustment measure such as training and education of workers prior to trade liberalization. With regard to the core labour standards, the policy states that any US FTA partners should recognize and adopt the five core basic labour rights stipulated in the ILO Declaration of 1998 (freedom of association, recognition of collective bargaining rights, prohibition of forced labour and child labour, and prohibition on discrimination in employment and occupation). The policy also makes it clear that US Federal and state governments can ask any tenderers to US public procurement offers to accept five core labour standards and guarantee acceptable wage conditions for employment. Furthermore, the US administration and Congress and are expected to develop a comprehensive program, Strategic Worker Assistance and Training (SWAT) that transcends the existing Trade Adjustment Assistance (TAA) system in the areas of education and training and income support for workers.

The New Trade Policy seeks for aggressive trade liberalization in US trade partners, but it has dual objectives to protect US workers from the US trade liberalization. In other words, by proposing high labour and environmental standards as a prerequisite for free trade talks with the US, it attempts to protect US domestic industries and workers from international competition pressure. This policy reflects the strong position of trade unions, which used to be favorable for the Democratic Party. This means that protecting workers and their economic benefits would be the central part of the US trade policy.

2. US FTA and labour provisions

The US signed the NAFTA in 1992 and then signed a side

agreement on labour and environment in 1993, which was incorporated into the NAFTA as an annex. From the FTA with Jordan in October 2000, all FTAs signed by the US include a separate labour chapter. Since then, the US has inserted more stringent and binding labour provisions into its FTAs than any other developed countries. Its provisions allow to US authority to impose penalties and trade sanctions, when labour conditions deteriorate in trade partners. If the US authority find a foreign firm to violate labour protection, the authority can investigate the case and can prohibit its export to the US.

The main labour provisions in US FTAs are as follows. First, the North American Agreement on Labour Cooperation (NAALC) does not include a provision to prohibit any attempt to lower labour protection in view of promotion of trade and investment. However, the US-Jordan FTA includes an independent labour chapter that stipulates the trade-linked labour standards. Other FTAs of the US since then have similar contents, while there are some differences in their sentences. Second, with regard to 'Dispute Settlement Procedure', the NAALC specifies an arbitral panel, and the maximum penalty set at $ 20 million for the first year and then at 0.007% of the trade volume between the Parties. The US-Jordan FTA introduced for the first time Dispute Settlement Panel and allow to impose trade sanctions according to decisions of the Panel. In subsequent FTAs with Singapore, Australia, Morocco, Bahrain, and Oman, the dispute settlement procedures are divided into three stages as following; Inter-governmental Consultation → Joint Committee → Dispute Settlement Panel. A maximum penalty is fixed up to $15 million per year, and trade preferences are suspended in case of nonpayment of penalty. Thereafter, another FTAs of the US with Chile, Central America, Colombia and Peru have a similar three-stage dispute settlement procedure; Intergovernmental Consultation → Commission →Arbitral Panel.

Table 2: Labour provisions included US FTAs

	NAFTA (1992)	Jordan (2000)	Chile (2003)	Singapore (2003)
Form	Annex	Incorporated into the agreement as a part		
Contents	The Contracting Parties shall: 1. Make efforts to improve 11 labour standards expressed in domestic labour laws and the FTA ⁂ 11 labour standards: ILO core labour standards and internationally recognized labour rights 2. Comply effectively with domestic labour laws 3. Hold discretionary right to allocate labour-related resources 4. Not have rights to enforce labour laws in other contracting parties 5. Guarantee civil rights remedy	The Contracting Parties shall: 1. Make efforts to protect internationally recognized labour rights protected by ILO core labour standards and domestic laws 2. Comply effectively with domestic labour laws 3. Hold discretionary right to allocate labour-related resources 4. Not lower or avoid domestic labour standards in order to promote trade	The Contracting Parties shall: 1. Make efforts to protect internationally recognized labour rights protected by ILO core labour standards and domestic laws 2. Comply effectively with domestic labour laws 3. Hold discretionary right to allocate labour-related resources 4. Not lower or avoid domestic labour standards in order to promote trade 5. Not have rights to enforce labour laws in other contracting parties 6. Guarantee civil rights remedy	
Target	Non-compliance with domestic labour laws in the fields of safety and health, child labour and minimum wage which affect trade	The sanctions may target all non-respect of labour provisions. Possible in case of violation ⁂ General dispute settlement system	Non-compliance with domestic labour laws which affect trade	
Maximum Penalty	First year: $ 20 million Since then: 0.007% of total bilateral trade value ⁂ FTA benefits will be suspended for as long as the penalty is not paid	Affected Parties can impose appropriate sanction	$ 15 million per year; ⁂ FTA benefits will be suspended for as long as the penalty is not paid	

The US-Korea FTA includes an independent labour chapter (Chapter XIX) with 8 sections that covers principle labour right, cooperation and consultation in labour related issues. According to Article 19 (2) of the FTA, the five basic labour rights defined by the ILO Declaration in 1998 should be adopted and maintained in laws and practices. The US-Korea FTA was influenced by the US New Trade Policy above mentioned and US authority can also resort to a trade sanction through the general dispute settlement procedure. On the other hand, Article 19 (8), limits the coverage of the labour provisions to internationally recognized labour rights and minimum wages, working hours, and industrial safety and health-related laws in order to ensure equality of labour laws applicable to the agreement.

3. Characteristics of labour provisions in the US FTA

The FTAs with Israel (1985) and Canada (1988), which the US concluded in the earlier period, did not include labour related provisions. The reason for this may be that both contracting parties are advanced countries, so there would be few contentious labour issues in implementing the FTAs. Besides, the FTA with Israel was motivated by security concerns. On the other hand, with the NAFTA including Mexico, the US turned to a policy of including labour related provisions in its FTAs. NAFTA did not have separate labour clauses in the text of the agreement, but supported by a side agreement, NAALC, to cover labour-related issues. It is since the FTA with Jordan in 2000 that US FTAs have incorporated international labour standards such as the ILO Declarations.

In particular, the New Trade Policy with America agreed in May 2007 between the US Administration and Congress states that the international standards related to various labour and environment should be included in FTAs with trading partners. As a result, the US FTAs since then have the following characteristics in linking trade with labour standards. First, the labour clauses in US FTAs have a coercive nature. Under the US FTAs, ratified before the New Trade Policy, it was hard to impose labour standards on trade partners, because the parties—particularly developing countries—have discretion over resource allocation in the process of enforcing labour laws (Huh, 2007, 3). On the other hand, FTAs concluded under the New Trade Policy have enforceable and binding labour provisions that allow to impose penalties through the general dispute settlement procedures. Second, the ILO Declaration of 1998 was mentioned as symbolic and advisory sense in the past FTAs. But it became mandatory provisions after the New Trade Policy.

IV. EU FTA and labour provisions

1. EU FTA Policy

The EU has implemented 36 FTAs in terms of notification to the WTO. They differ in coverage and effect, but can be categorized into three groups. The first group is association agreements with the Eastern European countries in Balkan. These agreements, which includes trade agreements in goods and services, were conceived as a part of the EU's neighbor policy for potential EU candidates. The second group consists in FTAs with the Mediterranean countries in North Africa and the Middle East. Since 1995, the EU has pushed for the Euro-Mediterranean Partnership with the Mediterranean countries under Barcelona Process and concluded a number of bilateral agreements. These agreements were motivated by diplomatic and development considerations in order to secure stability in EU's neighborhood as well as by expanding trade and investment. EU's trade agreements with African-Caribbean-Pacific (ACP) countries can also be included in this category. The third group is composed of bilateral FTAs concluded with Chile, Mexico, and South Africa in the early 2000s and FTAs negotiated with Korea, Singapore and

Table 3: EU's FTAs

	Country	Category	Date of entry into force
Group 1	Bosnia and Herzegovina	FTA	July 1, 2008
	Moldova	FTA/EIA	September 1, 2014
	Albania	FTA/EIA	December 1, 2006 (G), April 1, 2009 (S)
	Serbia	FTA/EIA	February 1, 2010 (G), September 1, 2013 (S)
	Montenegro	FTA/EIA	January 1, 2008 (G), May 1, 2010 (S)
	Macedonia	FTA/EIA	June 1, 2001 (G), April 1, 2004 (S)
Group 2	Tunisia	FTA	March 1, 1998
	Morocco	FTA	March 1, 2000
	Jordan	FTA	May 1, 2002
	Lebanon	FTA	March 1, 2003
	Egypt	FTA	June 1, 2004
	Algeria	FTA	September 1, 2005
	Israel	FTA	June 1, 2000
	Cariforum	FTA/EIA	November 1, 2008
	Ivory Coast	FTA	January 1, 2009
	Papua New Guinea / Fiji	FTA	December 20, 2009
	East South Africa (ESA)	FTA	May 14, 2012
	Cameroun	FTA	August 4, 2014

(Continued)

	South Africa	FTA	January 1, 2000
Group 3	Chile	FTA/EIA	February 1, 2003 (G), March 1, 2005 (S)
	Mexico	FTA/EIA	July 1, 2000 (G), April 1, 2004 (S)
	Korea	FTA/EIA	July 1, 2011
	Columbia / Peru	FTA/EIA	March 1, 2013
	Central America	FTA/EIA	August 1, 2013
Finalized/ completed	Singapore	FTA/EIA	Negotiation completed (October 17, 2014)
	Canada	FTA/EIA	Negotiation completed (September 26, 2014)
	Vietnam	FTA/EIA	Finalized (August 2015)
Under negotiation (since -)	India (June 2007), Malaysia (October 2010), Thailand (March 2013), Japan (April 2013), USA (July 2013), MERCOSUR (May 2010 resume the negotiation)		

Note: (1) Free Trade Agreement (FTA) means agreements for trade in goods based on Article 24 of the GATT, and Economic Integration Agreement (EIA) means a FTA for trade in service for which the legal basis is GATS Article 5. (2) 'G' means FTA in goods and 'S' for EIA.

Source: WTO, http://rtais.wto.org/UI/PublicAllRTAList.aspx (accessed on May 18, 2016)

Canada later on. These FTAs are different from the ones belonging to the previous two groups. Trade partners are geographically remote countries and the trade deals are motivated solely by commercial considerations, such as a market access. In particular, the EU has been engaged in aggressive FTA policy with non-European countries under its 'Global

Europe Initiative' announced in September 2006. Since then, selection of FTA partners has been driven mainly by economic criteria such as: market potential, level of protectionism and impact and risks as regards present trade partners.

2. Labour provisions in EU's FTAs

The EU began to include labour-related provisions in its FTAs since the mid-1990s. However, until the early 2000s, these provisions were just included as a part in social chapter of the FTAs which mention protection of human right and cooperation between authorities concerned of two parties. On the other hand, EU's FTA with Korea, which took effect in 2011, deals with labour-related provisions in a separate chapter entitled "Trade and Sustainable Development." While the US FTAs includes separate chapters on labour and the environment respectively, the EU FTAs combine labour and environment as one policy area with the notion of 'sustainable development'.

The labour provisions in the EU FTA are different for each FTA. This is mainly due to the fact that the EU's FTAs has been increasingly comprehensive in their coverage and ambition. EU's FTAs concluded in the early 2000s with Mediterranean countries don't include explicit labour provisions. For example, the FTAs with Morocco, Jordan, Lebanon, Egypt and Algeria focus on low-level concessions in trade in goods, and there is no specific reference to the working conditions of the FTA partners or compliance with international conventions. The EU's first FTA with labour-related provisions is the association agreement with Israel which entered into force in 2000. Article 63 of the agreement stipulates that both sides should conduct a dialogue based on mutual benefit' in employment-related social issues. However, it does not refer to any institutionalized committees for the official dialogue, but only mentions ad-hoc expert meetings, seminars and workshops as a form of dialogue. The FTA concluded with South Africa (entered into force in 2000), states in its preamble for the first time that both parties will abide by the ILO principle conventions on various labour issues, and mention in this text that both parties will discuss social issues including labour relations (Article 86). It also specifies freedom of association and collective bargaining, elimination of forced labour, elimination of discrimination in employment and occupation, and prohibition of child labour. The FTA with Chile, signed in 2003, mentions in the body of the agreement the ILO principle conventions for the first time in EU's FTAs. Article 44 of the agreement stipulates compliance with the ILO conventions in employment creation and respect for basic social rights, but there is no mention of specific implementation measures. It is worth noting that for the first time in EU's FTAs, it stipulates the promotion of regular dialogue between the two civil societies (Article 43) and requires that both sides should take part in civil society in dialogue on labour issues. In sum, EU's FTAs have increasingly incorporated labour-related provisions in the 2000s, but most of labour provisions in the FTAs are symbolic without effectiveness.

The EU FTA has gradually included a comprehensive labour clause since the EU-Cariforum FTA with the Caribbean countries in 2008. The preamble to the FTA includes a broad set of principles on human rights as well as a reference to the ILO Core Conventions. It differs from the EU's existing FTAs as follows; first, the agreement places a separate chapter on social issues for the first time in the EU FTA. In addition to complying with the ILO Core Conventions, the Social Aspects also specify compliance with the ILO Declaration on Fundamental Principles and Rights at Work and its follow-up actions. (Article 191). Second, Article 191 of the FTA prohibits measures that weaken domestic societal and labour norms as a means of promoting trade and investment. This provision complements other provision, Article 192 stating that Cariforum countries have the right to regulate in order to establish their own social regulations and labour standards in line with their own social development priorities. Third, the two Parties can seek advice from the ILO for policies to address labour market adjustment and effective implementation of core labour standards. In case of a formal objection, one of both can request that a Committee of Experts, composed of three members, be convened to examine such matter. However, opinions and recommendation of the report presented by the Committee are not binding.

It is from the FTA with Korea, implemented in 2011, that EU's FTAs include an independent and stylized labour chapter. Chapter 13 of the FTA, 'Trade and Sustainable Development', covers a wide range of labour and environment issues related to trade. First, Article 13.4, titled 'Multilateral Labour Standards and Agreements' imposes an obligation to both Parties to comply with international Conventions adopted by international organizations, such as the ILO. Korea has not yet ratified four of the eight core ILO conventions, but Article 13.4(3) notes that "the Parties (Korea) will make continued and sustained efforts towards ratifying the fundamental ILO Conventions". This suggests that all eight ILO Fundamental Conventions will be effectively applied in Korea while some of them are not ratified. In addition, the FTA includes some notable changes compared to EU's previous FTAs as follows. (1) evaluation of the sustainability of the FTA (Article 13.10); (2) establishment of a trade and sustainable development committee composed of senior officials from both countries (Article 13.12); (3) establishment of a civil society dialogue mechanism (Article 13.13), and (4) a Panel of Experts for consultation and settlement of disputes. Accordingly, the EU and Korea have held every year the Committee of Trade and Sustainable Development and Civil Society Dialogue with NGOs and other representatives, since the FTA took effect. One Party can request to a Panel of Expert be convened to examine the matter for which both Parties disagree. However, any decisions made by Panel are only advisory and non-binding as in the case of the EU-Cariforum FTA.

Table 4: Labour-related provisions included in EU trade agreements

FTAs(year of entry into force)	Relation with the ILO Conventions	Coverage of labour provisions	Implementation mechanism
Morocco (2000) Israel (2000) Algeria (2005) Cameroun (2009)	Not found	• Cooperation and dialogue on selective issues related to labour standards	
Chile (2003)	ILO Declaration on Fundamental Rights of Workers (1998)	• Compliance with ILO Core Conventions • Promotion of dialogues and cooperation on labour and social issues • Prioritize respect for basic social rights	
South Africa (2000)	ILO Declaration on Fundamental Rights of Workers (1998)	• Confirm the compliance with ILO Core Labour Standards (CLS) on various labour and social issues	

(Continued)

Cariforum(2008)	• ILO Declaration on Fundamental Rights of Workers (1998) • ILO core labour standards and internationally recognized labour rights	• Comply with ILO Core Labour Standards (CLS) • Confirm that the Parties will not weaken labour-related laws for the purpose of promoting trade and investment	• Consultation and monitoring through participation of stakeholders • Seek for opinions from the ILO for advice if needed • Establish a system for reaching a consensus in case of disagreement • Seek an alternative measure without resorting to retaliation when a dispute cannot be resolved through consultation
Korea (2011)	• High level of labour protection corresponding to international standards • ILO Decent work standard	• Commitment to consult and cooperate with each other on trade-related labour and employment issues for mutual benefit.	• Intergovernmental consultation • Establish a committee for trade and sustainable development • Establish of a panel of experts for policy recommendation • Not use dispute resolution provisions of the FTA in case of disagreement or dispute

Source: Elbert and Posthuma (2011); Anuradha and Dutta (2011), pp. 24-25; author's elabouration based on the FTA texts.

3. Characteristics of labour provisions in EU's FTAs

The chapter 'Trade and Sustainable Development' of the EU-Korea FTA provides a template to EU's other FTAs ahead so that similar labour chapters are included in EU's FTAs signed with Colombia, Peru, Central America, Singapore, Canada and Moldova. It means that labour provisions in the EU's FTAs became more formalized and EU style trade related labour provisions emerged. In linking trade and labour issues, the EU's FTAs tend to impose an obligation to comply with the international conventions (those of the ILO) and emphasize dialogues between both parties at government and civil levels. However, these provisions are neither binding nor enforceable, while those in the US FTAs are mandatory.

These features attribute to the following reasons. First, a number of FTAs concluded by the EU are closely related to the development policy and include a number of bilateral cooperation with weak binding power. In particular, in the case of Partnership Agreements concluded with Mediterranean and Eastern European countries, labour provisions mainly describe EU's possible support and cooperation, listing up mostly basic principles or normative guidelines. Second, above mentioned features reflect EU's traditional preferences or tendency in international relations; the EU used to emphasize dialogue in international relations and seeks to establish a multilateral norm in rather 'ideal' directions. The EU's position in imposing trade-related labour standards abroad focuses on promoting the labour right in its trading partners through 'dialogues'. From comparative perspective, Horn et al. (2009) concludes that the EU is more interested in strengthening the WTO system through its FTAs, while the US tends to seek concrete benefits through bilateral contacts with its trading partners. Third, the weak binding power of labour provisions of the EU's FTAs is inherent in EU's institutional framework. The EU is not a single unified country, but a kind of Sui

Generis confederation of Member States having different interests in many policy areas. All decisions taken at the EU level reflect political compromises between Member States and this may lead to weaker binding power in decisions. Furthermore, it may be difficult to express a strong position on labour-related issues in FTA negotiations, as labour policy belongs to competences of individual Member States. Fourth, EU's FTAs define Civil Society Forums where representatives of civil societies can discuss labour and environment issues. It seems that this is related to the objective to overcome criticisms of current EU system, particularly trade area. In trade policy, the European Commission represents all EU Member States and DG Trade of the Commission takes charges of technical aspects of trade negotiations. Due to this reason, EU's trade policy, termed Common Commercial Policy is beyond any direct control of national parliaments of Member States, which was criticized as 'democratic deficit'. In order to respond to this criticism, the European institutions have made considerable effort to make EU's decision making system more democratic and to invite the participation of civil societies, particular in trade policy. The inclusion of the Civil Forum in the implementation process of FTAs can be understood in this context.

V. Comparison of US and EU approaches

1. Differences in labour provisions and causes

The labour provisions in US and EU FTAs have something in common; both the US ad EU inserted 1998 ILO Declaration on the Fundamental Rights of Workers in their FTA texts. There are also similarities in the implementation process in that FTAs include interactive contacts through bilateral and multilateral channels, civil society and independent panel of experts. On the other hand, as noted above, the most salient difference is that the labour clauses in US FTAs have legally binding and enforcement power, through penalties and withdrawal of tariff preferences in case of non-respect, while those in EU's FTAs are lack of binding forces. They focus mainly on the promotion of labour rights through dialogue or cooperation both at government and civil levels. What causes such differences in trade related labour clauses between the US and EU? Given the FTAs concluded so far and the trade policy in general, we point three backgrounds as answer.

First, EU's FTAs used to be driven by more mixed objectives ranging from market access to development and neighborhood policy, while US FTAs are motivated by concrete benefits such as market access and business opportunities. In the GATT/WTO system, the US used to be the most ardent supporter of strong labour standards. The US insisted to include labour-related issues in multilateral trade negotiations, while developing countries formed allied frontline opposing strongly the US proposal. Therefore, the inclusion of strong trade-related labour clauses in bilateral FTAs negotiations is a reasonable measure from a practical point of view. On the other hand, until the mid-2000s, the EU's FTA policy direction, aware of the WTO system, had been supportive to establishing 'ideal' multilateral norms and in most cases, linked to its development policy. The number of EU's FTAs is three times larger than that of the US and they differ in coverage and ambition in liberalization. In this context, the EU aimed to improve labour standards in general through policy dialogue and cooperation, which are less binding, than imposing sanctions on violations of labour standards in developing countries.

Second, the EU ratified all eight ILO Fundamental Conventions, while the US ratified only two of them, Conventions on child labour and forced labour.[5] As a result, the EU tends to organize labour provisions of

---

[5] The ILO's eight fundamental conventions are as follows: Forced Labour Convention, 1930 (No. 29), Freedom of Association and the Right to Organize Convention, 1948 (No. 87), Right to Organize and Collective Bargaining Convention, 1949 (No. 98), Equal Remuneration Convention, 1951 (No. 100), Abolition of Forced

its FTAs, reflecting more closely ILO's core Conventions. For example, the FTA with Korea and Canada incorporate ILO's Decent Work Agenda into their texts. On the other hand, the US ratified only a part of ILO Conventions on the grounds that they may conflict with US domestic laws. As a result, incorporating the ILO Conventions into US FTAs limits to the declaration of fundamental rights and the rest of the labour standards are covered by US trade laws.

Third, unlike the US, unified federation, the EU has an intermediate form between a federation and confederation of independent States. The external trade policy belongs to competences of the EU, while judicial and home affairs including labour regulation are under competences of Member States. Therefore, an attempt to introduce compulsory labour clauses into trade agreements can face a complex situation in which the EU and Member States have to reassess allocation of powers. In addition, the legal binding power may be weakened in the process of coordinating different interests among the Member States. Once any enforceable labour clauses with sanction is included in a trade agreement, the latter should be authorized by all EU Member States in negotiation process, which make trade negotiations hard to go forward.

2. Spillover effect

Given these differences, it is interesting to examine how much labour provisions of the FTAs have changed labour standards and practices in labour managements in FTA partners. It is difficult to give clear-cut answers, because the implementation period of the FTAs are still short and multiple factors might have contributed to changes in labour standards and practices in partner countries. Based on the FTA

Labour Convention, 1957 (No. 105), Discrimination (Employment and Occupation) Convention, 1958 (No. 111), Minimum Age Convention, 1973 (No. 138), Worst Forms of Child Labour Convention, 1999 (No. 182)

implementation so far, our tentative conclusion is as follows.

The US Government conducted some cooperation projects with different trade partners to support the governance related to labour standards. Starting from an assistance project for Chile in 2004 in the context of the US-Chile FTA, the US launched a number of projects for cooperation and financial assistances (as part of ODA) in labour related areas with the developing countries that concluded FTAs with the US. The assistance projects for Central America and Dominican Republic are examples in this regard. Another successful case is the US-Cambodia Textile Agreement, which has provided quota incentives for textiles in response to the efforts to improve labour standards in Cambodia (Lim Seok-jun, 2013). On the other hand, US FTAs with developed countries such as Singapore, Australia and Korea do not define clearly what kind of cooperation can be done between two Parties and focus more on information changes and open dialogues with civil society. It is expected that binding labour provisions in US FTA could be used as a last resort, after all possible 'soft' measures (ie. information exchange) are used. On the other hand, as the US FTA network is expanding to Southeast Asia through TPP, labour management in East Asian production bases (Southeast Asia) will gradually be affected by US FTA policies regardless of whether host countries have FTA with the US or not.

The labour provisions included in EU's FTAs have shown somewhat 'standardized' pattern in all FTAs since the EU developed the concept of 'sustainable development'. Given the EU's way of emphasizing cooperation and dialogue with the governments (and institutions) of the FTA partner countries as well as civil society, the EU's trade-related standards linkage will work as a constant pressure, while they are not binding. Given that trade policy is now a part of the EU's external policy under Lisbon Treaty, it is not strange to expect EU's trade pressure to its trade partners in a manner of urging to improve labour standards through various forms of meetings and dialogues.

VI. Conclusion

This study reviewed international discussions on the linkage of trade and labour standards and examined the labour standards included in bilateral trade agreements since the 2000s. In particular, we analyzed the labour provisions in FTAs concluded by US and EU, two trade powers most active in setting labour standards through trade negotiations.

The US and the EU have incorporated labour standards in their FTAs in accordance with their principles and objectives of trade policy. The US has included binding and enforceable labour provisions in its FTAs since the NAFTA and this trend became clearer after it announced the New Trade Policy in 2007. Of the RTAs notified to the WTO as of 2014, there are 24 RTAs that include binding labour provisions. Half of these FTAs are concluded between the US and its trade partners. On the other hand, the EU began to include labour provisions later than the US and even so, it developed its own cooperation based approach with non-binding provisions. These differences result from the interacting internal circumstances, such as driving factors of FTAs and institutional set up of the EU.

All recent US FTAs include binding labour clauses, as previous its FTAs and this will create a larger ripple effect than ever. The TPP, concluded in October 2015, stipulates that each Party should adopt the basic labour rights specified in the 1998 ILO Declaration as domestic law. It prohibited to weaken labour regulations in order to promote trade and investment. In case of violation of these requirements, it is possible to initiate a trade sanction through a complaint as existing US bilateral FTAs. Given that the number of TPP members is twelve, the entry into force of the TPP is expected to bring about a major change in trade-labour standards linkages within the Asia-Pacific region. While the US administration withdrew from the TPP, recent protectionist measures announced suggests that the US will stick more to stronger labour standards, if it re-enter into the TPP. In particular, the TPP is likely to act as an external pressure to strengthen labour standards in developing countries with relatively low labour standards in Asia, such as Vietnam and Malaysia. Southeast Asian countries have built their manufacturing bases financed by foreign investment. Due to this reason labour management practices can change dramatically, as the supply chains are intertwined over regions.

The EU have relatively weak labour provisions in its FTAs, but it developed its own model of trade-related labour standards based on cooperation and dialogues with its trade partners. Starting from the FTA with Korea, the EU negotiated FTAs including similar labour provisions. This trend will continue in a number of association and partnership agreements under negotiation. This means that an EU-style labour standard template is established for FTAs. However, the EU has been pushing for FTAs with both developed (Japan and US) and developed countries (Malaysia and India). In this situation, labour provisions in EU's FTAs are likely to be somewhat differentiated according to development level of their counterparts, while main features remain same.

The trade related labour standards in US and the EU FTAs are important for the trade policies and foreign investment strategies in East Asia, particularly for the countries that already implemented FTAs with the US and EU. The FTAs of Korea (US-Korea FTA and EU-Korea FTA) provide an example in this regard.

First, coordinating labour standards with trade partners can lead to a long-term convergence of related domestic rules and practice and it involves not only economic but also social changes. Therefore, labour cooperation with the US and the EU in the labour-related field is an important area for a successful implementation of the FTAs in the long run. Labour provisions in US-Korea FTA are not expected to impose a serious burden for both sides, as Korea incorporated most of the international labour standards into domestic laws. On the other hand, problems may arise if Korea's labour-management relations laws and practices do not match US laws. In case of the EU-Korea FTA, it requires two sides to conduct dialogues between public authorities and between civil societies including NGOs during the implementation process. The content discussed in the dialogue (ie. Civil Society Forum) is not binding, but it can work as an external pressure. For example, the EU's Directive 2014/95/EU stipulates disclosure of non-financial information such as corporate social responsibility (CSR) for companies whose size exceeds a certain level. This issue is constantly mentioned during the Civil Society Forum. This is the example that even non-binding provisions in US and EU's FTAs can affect domestic law and practice of their trade partners.

Second, the US and EU are expanding their FTAs to Southeast Asia and Central and South America, where Korean companies have established production networks. Local production of Korean companies aims to re-export to the US and EU as well as the local markets. Therefore, if the concerned country concludes an FTA with the US and EU, the labour standards of the FTA will be an important consideration in the management. The above-mentioned TPP is an important example in this regard. For example, many Korean companies are now using Vietnam as their production base and recently Korean companies became the most important foreign investors in Vietnam. Korean investments in Vietnam are mainly driven by low labour costs and relatively easy labour management. On the other hand, it is expected that Vietnam will revise domestic laws to strengthen the labour standards in the course of implementing the TPP. If Korean companies do not comply with strengthened labour standards in Vietnam, they will face a pressure from the Vietnamese government as well as the US government. Core reason of this pressure is that many of Vietnam's local production is for re-export purposes. In addition, the EU has concluded an FTA with Vietnam in August 2015, and plans to proceed with the ratification process soon after completing the legal review. Therefore, it is necessary for Korean companies having production facilities in Vietnam to understand the labour standards incorporated into Vietnam's FTA with US and EU and to pay attention to labour-related cooperation issues and prospects that the two sides are promoting with FTA partners. This case does not limit to Korean investments in Vietnam and can be applied to investments of any companies in East Asia. As more countries have FTAs with the US and EU and production networks are intertwined over different countries and regions, it will be more necessary to adapt labour management in overseas production plants in line with international labour standards.

References

Aggarwal, Vinod K. (2013), "US free trade agreements and linkages," *International Negotiation, 18*(1), pp. 89-110.

Aleo, Michael E. (2006), "Comparative Advantage and Economic Reform: Making Labour Provisions Trade Agreements Practical and Effective," *Bepress Legal Series*. Paper No. 958.

Anderson, Kym (1998), "Environmental and Labour Standards: What Role for the WTO," in Anne O. Krueger, ed. *The WTO as an International Organization*, Chicago: The University of Cicago Press.

Anuradha R.V. and Nimisha Singh Dutta (2012), "Trade and Labour under the WTO and FTAs," *Centre for WTO Studies*.

Aidt, Toke and Zafiris Tzannatos (2002), "Unions and collective bargaining: Economic effects in a global environment," *Directions in Development Series*, The World Bank, Washington D.C.

Bae, Yeon-Jae (2014), "Protecting Labour Rights through FTAs: Focusing on Labour Regulations of US FTAs," *Commercial Law, 117*. Ministry of Justice (in Korean).

Bhagwati, Jagdish (2001), Free Trade and Labour, *Financial Times* (August 29).

Burtless, Gary (2001), "Workers' Rights: Labour standards and global trade," Brookings Institute.http://www.brookings.edu/research/articles/2001/09/fall-globaleconomics-burtless (accessed November 7, 2017)

Busse, Matthisas (2002), "Do Labour Standards Affect Comparative Advantage in Developing Countries?" *World Development, 30*(11), pp. 1921-1932.

Chan, Anita and Robert J. S. Ross (2003), "Racing to the Bottom: International Trade without a Soical Clause," *Third World Quarterly, 24*(6), pp. 1011-1028.

Davies, Ronald B. and Krishna Chaitanya Vadlamannati (2013), "A race to the bottom in labour standards? An Empirical Investigation," *Journal of Development Economics, 103* July, pp. 1–14.

Deblock Christian (2005), "Les Etats-Unis et la liberalisation de l'investissement," in Michele Roux ed. *Globalisation et pouvoir des entreprises*, Montreal: Athena Editions.

Ebert, Franz C. and Anne Posthuma (2011), "Labour Provisions in Trade Arrangements: Current Trends and Perspectives," International Labour Organisation.

Elliott, Kimberly Ann (1998), "International Labour and Trade: What Should Be Done?" in Jeffrey J. Schott ed. *Launching New Global Trade Talks: An Action Agenda*, Special Report 12. Peterson Institute for International Economics.

European Commission (2010), *Trade, Growth and World Affairs: Trade Policy as a Core Component of the EU's 2020 Strategy*, COM(2010) 612.

Golub, Stephen S. (1997), "Are International Labour Standards Needed to Prevent Social Dumping?" *Finance & Development*, December pp.20-23.

Häberli, Christian, Marion Jansen and José-Antonio Monteiro (2012), "Regional Trade Agreements and Domestic Labour Market

Regulation," *Employment Working Paper* No. 120, International Labour Organisation.

Han, Chang-hoon (2000), *Trade and International Labour Standards: A Historical and Theoretical Review of New Round Issues*, Korea Labour Institute (in Korean).

Horn, Henrik, Petros C. Mavroidis and André Sapir (2009), "Beyond the WTO? An anatomy of EU and US preferential trade agreements," *Bruegel Blue Print.*

Huh, Jae-Jun (2007), "A Study on the Implementation of the Agreement on the Agreement between the US-Korea FTA and the Labour Agreement", Ministry of Labour (Current Ministry of Employment and Labour), Korea Labour Institute. (in Korean)

International Labour Organisation (2015), *Social Dimensions of Free Trade Agreements.*

International Labour Organisation (2014), "Presentation for EESC Round Table on Labour Rights and Civil Society Participation in TTIP," Brussels (November 12).

Kim, Hong-Ryul (2001), "US Policy Changes on Labour Trade Linkages," *KIEP World Economy*, March 2011, pp. 14-23 (in Korean).

Kim, Mi-young (2012), "The content and interpretation of the labour clause of the Korea-US Free Trade Agreement," *Labour Law, 43.* pp. 97-137 (in Korean).

Kim, Sang Man (2014), "A Study on Labour Agreements in the ILO Core Agreements and FTA Agreements," *Inha University Legal Studies, 17*(2), pp. 219-243 (in Korean).

Kraatz, Susanne (2015), "The Transatlantic Trade and Investment Partnership (TTIP) and Labour," *Briefing*, European Parliament.

Krugman, Paul (1994), "Does Third World Growth Hurt First World Prosperity?" *Harvard Business Review*, July-August, https://hbr. org/1994/07/does-third-world-growth-hurt-first-world-prosperity (accessed November 7, 2015).

Lim Seok-Jun (2013), "Promoting Labour Standards through International Trade. - ILO and Cambodia's 'Better Factory' Case Study," *International Relations Research, 18*(1), pp. 165-198 (in Korean).

Martin, W., Maskus, K. E. (2001), "Core Labour Standards and competitiveness : Implications for global trade policy," *Review of International Economics*, 9(2), pp. 317-328.

Meunier, Sophie (2005), *Trading Voices: The European Union in International Commercial Negotiations*, New Jersey: Princeton University Press.

Ministry of Employment and Labour, *Archives of labour related issues in FTAs*, http://www.moel.go.kr/policyinfo/fta/view.jsp?cate=2&sec=5 (in Korean) (accessed March 10, 2016).

Organisation for Economic Cooperation and Development (1990), *Labour market Policies for the 1990s*.

Panagariya, Arvind (2001), "Labour Standards and Trade Sanctions: Right End Wrong Means," Paper presented at the conference "Towards An Agenda for Research on International Economic Integration and Labour Markets," January 15-16, 2001, East-West Center, Hawaii.

Park, Ji-Eun, Lee, Hye-Yeon, Myung, Jin-Ho, Seo, Eun-Young and Jung, Hye-Sun (2015), "Current FTAs and Prospect for 2015: 20 economic regions and 73 countries," Institute for International Trade, *IIT Trade Focus*, No. 14-3 (in Korean).

Stern, Robert M. and Katherine Terrell (2003), "Labour Standards and the World Trade Organization," Research Seminar in International Economics, Discussion Paper No. 499.

Tsogas, George (1999), "Labour Standards in International Trade Agreements: An Assessment of the Arguments," *The International Journal of Human Resource Management, 10*(2), pp. 351-375.

Turnell, Sean (2002), "Core Labour Standards and the WTO," *The Economic and Labour Relations Review, 13*(1), pp. 105-126.

UNCTAD (1994), *World Investment 1994: Transnational Corporations, Employment and the Workplace* (executive summary).

WTO, http://rtais.wto.org/UI/PublicAllRTAList.aspx (accessed November 20, 2015).

Personal Information Protection and Management: Taiwan's Perspectives

Po-Yu Su

Section Manager, Science & Technology Law Institute,
Institute for Information Industry

I. The principles of personal data protection

Nowadays, when it comes to personal data protection, the following data protection principles should be taken into account:

1. *Fairness*

This principle means data is processed fairly, in other words, it should be transparent to natural persons that personal data concerning them are collected, used, consulted or otherwise processed and to what extent the personal data are or will be processed. Furthermore, the use of data should not beyond the expectation of the data subject.

2. *Transparency*

This principle means that any information and communication relating to the processing of those personal data be easily accessible and easy to understand, and that clear and plain language be used. That principle concerns, in particular, information to the data subjects on the identity of the controller and the purposes of the processing.

3. *Data minimization (Collection limitation)*

This principle limits collection of data by reference to the purposes for which it is collected. The collection of the information should be relevant to such purposes, and proportionality to the fulfillment of such purposes may be a factor in determining what is relevant.

4. Purpose limitation(Use limitation)

This principle means data is collected for specified, explicit and legitimate purposes and not further processed in a manner that is incompatible with those purposes. Application of this principle requires consideration of the nature of the information, the context of collection and the intended use of the information. The fundamental criterion in determining whether a purpose is compatible with or related to the stated purposes is whether the extended usage stems from or is in furtherance of such purposes. The use of personal information for "compatible or related purposes" would extend.

There is one case about the principles in the different situations, how to resolve relevant disputes through the above principles.

Case 1

Multinational companies within a group companies presence may face some other issues related to the data protection laws and principles. For instance, the transfer of personal data of employees employed at some countries entities to global HR databases need to requires the obtaining of employees' specific prior written consent. The same relates to the transfer of any employee data to any third party, including companies belonging to the same group. Needless to say, the maintenance of global HR databases must be compliant with the data localization rules (i.e., GDPR article 3 Territorial scope).

The necessity to obtain an employee's written consent for the transfer of his or her data to a third party may become an issue in the case of the conducting of internal investigations. As a practical solution, it is always recommendable to obtain very full data processing consents at the moment of hiring employees – this would allow proceeding without the necessity to obtain their consent when a conflict situation has emerged.

II. Introduction of Taiwan Personal Information Protection Act

First of all, we're going to introduce Legal System of privacy in Taiwan, and it's a better way for you to know the latest development. "Computer-Processed Personal Data Protection Law" was enacted and carried into effect in Chinese Taipei ever since 1995. However, in order to broaden the scope of personal information protection, advocates of amendment were put forward soon after its enforcement. Therefore, as the beginning of the new millennium, Ministry of Justice commenced to draft the amendment. After a long discussion, the amendment bill was passed by the Legislative Yuan (Congress) and thus renamed as "Personal Information Protection Act (PIPA)" in April, 2010. Compared with the previous law, there are tremendous amendments in the new Act and heavier liabilities are imposed. Breaching of personal data may result in up to NT$200 million compensation in civil liabilities; and that is approximate 6.5 millions in US dollars. The new Act adopted "class litigation" and advocating of class litigation never ends. "Who is going to be the first one?" is highly concerned yet there is still no formal case filed.

Besides, PIPA empowers the central competent authorities of subject industry to enact generated rules. Article 27 requires the non-government agencies should adopt proper security measures to prevent personal information from being stolen, altered, damaged, destroyed or disclosed. Moreover, not merely the enforcement rules of PIPA indicate 11 subsections of technical or organizational measures, but PIPA also empowers the central competent authorities of subject industry to enact regulations of "the plan of security measures for personal information files" for non-government agencies. There are 32 regulations enacted by different authorities, such as MOEA for "Online Retail

Business", Financial Supervisory Commission for "Banking", National Communications Commission for "Telecommunication Industry", etc. .

In order to intensify the protection of privacy, "duty of notification" is necessitated in the new Act. Industries shall fulfill its duty of notification either via direct collection or indirect collection of personal information unless applicable to the exceptions. Including "the purpose of collection", "time period of the use of personal information" and other 4 subsections are required to be told spontaneously.

Due to the reason that the preceding law was not applicable to most of the industries; and thus, industries are inevitably confronted by the increasing of operating cost under the regulation of new Act. For example, the above mentioned "duty of notification" resulted in great influence on "Call Center Marketing", while some enterprises have quitted as a result of inconvenience when performing the duty of notification.

And then, PIPA was amended again on March 15th 2016 to strengthen its effectiveness. The focus of amendments of PIPA in Taiwan are emphasized on Article 6 and 54 which respectively regulate "sensitive data" and "duty of notification, redeeming", and are suspended from being in effect when the Act became effective in October 2012.

III. Introduction of European General Data Protection Regulation

The main reason of amendment of from European Directive 95/46/EC on data protection (Data Protection Directive) to European General Data Protection Regulation(GDPR) is that ensuring a consistent and high level of protection of natural persons and to remove the obstacles to flows of personal data within the Union, the level of protection of the rights and freedoms of natural persons with regard to the processing of such data should be equivalent in all Member States.

Some of the key changes and requirements of GDPR include:

1. Extra-territorial applicability

The GDPR, as it applies to all companies processing the personal data of data subjects residing in the Union, regardless of the company's location.

2. Lawful, fair and transparent processing

Lawful processing means personal data should be processed on the basis of the consent of the data subject concerned or some other legitimate basis, laid down by law, and fair and transparent processing means data subject understand the personal data processed by what purposes.

3. Limitation of purpose, data and storage

Limitation of purpose means the processing of personal data should be allowed only where the processing is compatible with the purposes for which the personal data were initially collected.

4. Data subject rights

The data subject rights includes right to access(the right for data subjects to obtain from the data controller confirmation as to whether or not personal data concerning them is being processed, where and for what purpose.), right to be forgotten(the right for data subject to have the data controller erase his/her personal data, cease further dissemination of the data, and potentially have third parties halt processing of the data.), and data portability(the right for a data subject to receive the personal data concerning them, which they have previously provided in a commonly use and machine readable format and have the right to transmit that data to another controller.), etc.

5. *Consent*

Consent must be clear and distinguishable from other matters and provided in an intelligible and easily accessible form, using clear and plain language, and the data subject is allowed to withdraw his consent at any moment. Prior to giving consent, the data subject shall be informed thereof. It shall be as easy to withdraw as to give consent. Where processing is based on consent, the controller shall be able to demonstrate that the data subject has consented to processing of his or her personal data.

6. *Breach Notification*

Data controllers or processors must notify data subjects of any data breaches which result in a risk for the rights and freedoms of individuals within 72 hours of first having become aware of the breach.

7. *Privacy by Design*

The controller shall, both at the time of the determination of the means for processing and at the time of the processing itself, implement appropriate technical and organizational measures, such as pseudonymizing, which are designed to implement data-protection principles, such as data minimization, in an effective manner and to integrate the necessary safeguards into the processing in order to meet the requirements of this Regulation and protect the rights of data subjects.

8. *Data Protection Impact Assessment*

Where a type of processing in particular using new technologies, and taking into account the nature, scope, context and purposes of the processing, is likely to result in a high risk to the rights and freedoms of natural persons, the controller shall, prior to the processing, carry out an assessment of the impact of the envisaged processing operations on the protection of personal data. A single assessment may address a set of similar processing operations that present similar high risks.

9. Data transfers

Any transfer of personal data which are undergoing processing or are intended for processing after transfer to a third country or to an international organization shall take place only if, subject to the other provisions of GDPR, the conditions laid down in Chapter 5 are complied with by the controller and processor, including for onward transfers of personal data from the third country or an international organization to another third country or to another international organization.

10. Data Protection Officer(DPO)

DPO appointment will be mandatory only for those controllers and processors whose core activities consist of processing operations which require regular and systematic monitoring of data subjects on a large scale or of special categories of data or data relating to criminal convictions and offences. And the DPO would have the responsibility of advising the company about compliance with EU GDPR requirements.

IV. Comparison between GDPR and Taiwanese PIPA

The data protection principles above are enacted in GDPR article 5, and implemented in article 6, article 12, article 13, article 14, article 15, and article 18, etc. In comparison with GDPR, Taiwanese PIPA also implements a number of data protection principles in Article 5, Article 8, Article 9, Article 15, Article 16, Article 19, and Article 20, etc.

1. Article 5 is about the principle of fairness

The rights and interests of the Party should be respected in collecting, processing or using personal information and the information should be handled in accordance with the principle of bona fide. It should not go beyond the purpose of collection and should be reasonable and fair.

2. Article 8 and Article 9 are about the principle of transparency

Some items hould be told precisely to the data subject by a government agency or non-government agency like the name of the agency, purpose of collection, classification of the personal information, etc.

3. Article 15, Article 16, Article 19, and Article 20 are about the principle of data minimization and purpose limitation

The government agency or non-government agency should not collect or process personal information unless there is a specific purpose and should comply with one of the legitimate conditions. The government agency or non-government agency should use the personal information in accordance with the scope of the specific purpose of collection provided.

V. The evidence of accountability principle—TPIPAS

How to clarify the standard and make the requirements clear in order to let industries achieve the demands of personal information protection laws are key issues for major countries and thus bring forth the "Personal Information Management System" (PIMS). PIMS even turns into national standards in some of the countries. For example, Republic of Korea, Japan and the United Kingdom, based on their personal information protection Acts, have designed and published personal information protection standards – KISA PIMS, JIS Q15001 and BS10012, and Dalian City in China has set up a system called "PIPA" referring to JIS Q 15001.

If we review the PIPA and other relevant regulations in Taiwan again, we may find that the Ministry of Justice has indicated 11 subsections of security measures which include technical and organizational measures. And if we examine all those subsections in detail, we may find it an epitome of "Personal Information Management System".

To help enterprises to comply with the domestic privacy laws and the privacy related requirements from APEC and other major international organizations on the one hand, and to establish an environment in which individuals are of confidence with regard to the process and use of their personal information on the other, in October 2010, the Ministry of Economic Affairs (MOEA), R.O.C. launched a project to establish "Taiwan Personal Information Protection and Administration System (TPIPAS)" along with its certification mark, "Data Privacy and Protection Mark (dp.mark)" so as to establish an environment in which individuals are of sense of security with regard to the collect, process and use of their personal information and thus gain consumers' confidence in e-commerce and retail marketing.

The system "TPIPAS" is constructed on the basis of the framework of the law-abiding and requirements under PIPA and the necessities and demands of enterprises as well. In another word, TPIPAS is not only a law-abiding guidance but also a perfect personal information management system. There are four main aspects and essential works under "TPIPAS", and they are "Professionals Training Programs", "Certifying Counseling Institutes", "System Verification" and "Maintenance & Operation for regulations".

And how to establish "TPIPAS" step-by- step, and the process for enterprises to submit application for certification? First of all, understanding of TPIPAS is the fundamental step. And after evaluation, enterprises need to set up an operation crew under inherent departments for TPIPAS. And then we may proceed to determinate of seeking aid of registered counseling institutes or not. And right after "plan drafting", "interior management process"

By the end of March 2018, 20 enterprises including the following industries: E-commerce, Retailers & Wholesalers, Depository & Clearing Corporation, Information Service, Joint Credit Information Center and Biotechnology have been entitled to certificate of "dp.mark" and 1,449 professionals, including internal management specialist, internal auditor and certified verification professional, have been trained for the purpose of improving the ability to build up internal personal information management of enterprises.

These two Acts has or will become effective in Taiwan. However, we're still adjusting our steps and finding the way out. Any implement and enforcement of a new system takes time to make an accommodation. As you can see, in order to assist enterprises, companies and other organizations in abiding the new "PIPA", the impetus and promotion of TPIPAS acquires fundamental achievements. Moreover, TPIPAS gains the confidence & reliance of the citizens! Thus, we hold a positive attitude toward the new Act and believe that it's beneficial to help the protection of personal information of the citizens. Though there are still some problems remain to be amended in order to fit in with the practical operation.

Introduction on Policies to Promote the Development of Social Innovation Enterprises in Taiwan

Shu-Chun Liao

Section Manager, Science & Technology Law Institute,
Institute for Information Industry

I. The emergency of social enterprises

The social enterprise or social innovation enterprise movement has become a hot issue around the world. For example, in 2007, the famous media pundit—David Gergen, mentioned that social entrepreneurship is one of the hottest movements among the youth in USA.[1] This movement not only combines social good and entrepreneurship, but also breaks the boundaries between the nonprofit and for-profit sectors. Therefore, some would like to refer this movement as the "emerging fourth sector".[2] Otherwise, some would like to mention social enterprises as a useful approach to apply private efforts to remedy social ills.[3]

However, the definition of social enterprise or social innovation enterprise is vague since it was first used in 1978[4]. Some defines social enterprises as business that intentionally impact social good or business

---

[1] Thomas Kelley, "Law and Choice of Entity on the Social Enterprise Frontier," *Tulane Law Review* 84 (2009): 337- 338.

[2] Ibid., at 337.

[3] Mystica M. Alexander, "A Comparative Look at International Approaches to Social Enterprise: Public Policy, Investment Structure, and Tax Incentives," *William & Mary Policy Review* 7, no. 2 (2016): 1-2.

[4] Ibid., at 6.

that develop and use value-created strategies or business method to provide services to socially neglected people or to achieve social goals they pursue[5]. Professor Mystica M. Alexander mentioned that the social enterprises could be defined from two-fold focus—mission base and use of surplus[6]. As far as the mission base, the mission of the social enterprise is to provide social value and serve the interest of the public, instead of maximizing profits for their shareholders or owners[7]. That is, social enterprises are driven by their social mission, not by their need to seek profits. As far as the use of surplus, the surplus of the social enterprise will be mainly reinvested in tackling the social or environment issues[8]. In other words, the social enterprise is able to return profits to its shareholders or owners, but the profit is principally used to serve public interests.

The Social Enterprise Alliance (SEA), a national membership organization who supports the growth of social enterprises, defines social enterprises as "organizations that address a basic unmet need or solve a social problem through a market-driven approach" and social entrepreneurs as those who create system change, improve the lives of underserved or marginalized groups by solving critical problems and address basic unmet needs through innovation.[9] Also, SEA distinguishes social enterprises from traditional non-profits organization and business in three dimensions. First, social enterprises focus not only on theirs social mission but also on their financial sustainability. Second, the founders of social enterprises make social mission and financial sustainability as

---

[5] Alina S. Ball, "Social Enterprise Governance," *U. Pa. J. Bus. L.* 18 (2016): 919, 927-929; Robert A. Katz & Antony Page, "The Role of Social Enterprise," *Vt. L. Rev.* 35 (2010): 59.

[6] Mystica M. Alexander, supra note3, at 4.

[7] Ibid., at 3-4.

[8] Ibid., at 5.

[9] https://socialenterprise.us/about/social-enterprise/ (accessed on 21 February 2018).

part of such organizations' DNA. Third, social enterprises integrate social impact into business operation and pursue the fulfillment of social goals over the financial returns, but still maintain the financial sustainability.[10]

Therefore, the social enterprise may be defined as an innovative business with the following three characteristics: (1) its aim is to pursue financial sustainability and some kinds of social missions or social benefits at the meantime, (2) it combines social impact and entrepreneurship together, integrating social mission as part of its DNA, and (3) it develops and takes strategies and business methods to address social or environment issues with its surplus.

Over hundreds of social enterprises were established in the past few years in Taiwan. According to the investigation made by United Marking Research in 2017, less than 30% of social enterprises are registered as non-profit organization and the rest are registered as corporate or business (for profit organization)[11]. And, near 60% of social enterprises are established in 5 years[12]. Otherwise, over 40% of social enterprises are located in northern Taiwan[13]. Second, As far as the social missions they pursue, food and agriculture innovation ranks first (29.8%), service for remote rural areas and vulnerable populations ranks second (29%), and environment protection (22.5%) ranks third[14]. Besides, as far as the target consumers of social enterprises, farmers and those working in agriculture ranks first (17.6%), elders ranks second (14.7%) and the youth and students ranks third (10.6%)[15]. Finally, as far as the way social enterprises earn profits, most of their profits come from the sales of products and the

---

[10] Ibid.

[11] United Marking Research, *2017 Social Enterprises Investigation*, 2 (2017), http://p.udn.com.tw/upf/vision/2017/2017visionstory79004.pdf.

[12] Ibid.

[13] Ibid.

[14] Ibid., at 2-3.

[15] Ibid., at 3.

provision of services (89.8%) and this means most social enterprises in Taiwan have established their own business model.[16]

II. First phase : deployment and implementation of Social Enterprise Action Plan (2014-16)

1. The definition and scopes of social enterprises

In 2014, the Social Enterprise Action Plan was announced to establish a friendly environment to accelerate the development of social enterprises. And, the government defined year 2014 as "the first year of an era for social enterprises"[17]. However, it is undeniable that non-profit organizations have devoted themselves into the social or environment issues and for-profit organizations have allocated their resources to realize their corporation social responsibility for many years[18].

The action plan defines social enterprise from two aspects. Broadly speaking, the social enterprise is a for-profit or non-profit organization that reinvests its surplus to form and apply business models to solve social or environment problems. Such organization pursues social and economic benefits at same time, but more focus on the creation of social impacts. Narrowly speaking, the charter of the social enterprise shall state that the establishment of such enterprise is to solve social problems or provide social care. And, at the end of each financial year, except publishing the social benefit report, the financial report of such enterprise shall be verified by the accountant and filed to the concerned authority. Besides, at least 30% of the surplus of such enterprise shall be reinvested

---

[16] Ibid., at 5.

[17] http://www.seinsights.asia/news/131/2494 (accessed on 12 March 2018).

[18] Ministry of Economic Affairs, *Social Enterprise Action Plan (2014-2016)*, 2 (2014), https://www.ey.gov.tw/Upload/RelFile/26/716149/8d8b6be7-0e21-4a37-9c72-871e28b325d2.pdf.

in the social missions.[19]

i. The vision and three pillars of the action plan

The vision of this action plan is to form a friendly and healthy eco-system to foster the establishment and growth of social enterprises. Under this vision, the action plan contains three pillars, including establishing a friendly environment for social enterprises, developing stronger social enterprises, and shaping the networks and platform of social enterprises.[20]

ii. The four priorities of the action plan

The action plan takes the following strategies to fulfill the vision of this plan, including:[21]

(1) Reviewing and amending regulations: The concerned regulations will be reviewed, including the issues of legal entities, tax incentives, public procurement and so on.

(2) Shaping the platform: Shaping the social enterprise trend, networking social enterprises and other organizations, providing one-stop services to social entrepreneurs, and establishing social enterprise registration mechanism to disclose related information.

(3) Encouraging the investment to the social enterprises: Persuading public funds, private investors, angel funds etc. to invest social enterprises, evaluating the possibilities of social enterprises credit guarantee mechanism and so on.

(4) Incubating social enterprises: Encouraging public incubators and accelerators to incubate social enterprises, teaming up mentors to help social entrepreneurs, using the public space to build a hub for social enterprises and so on.

---

[19] Ibid., at 9.

[20] Ibid., at 10.

[21] Ibid., at 10-14.

iii. The outcomes of the action plan

The action plan intends to arouse the social attention on social enterprises, try to combine social impact with entrepreneurship, and therefore shape the social enterprise movement. According to the data disclosed by Ministry of Economic Affairs, as of 2014, the number of companies that registered their corporate name with "social enterprise" was 47 companies, but as of 2016, the number rose to 111 companies. If not considering the corporate name but only the mission of the company, as of 2014, the number of companies that took social missions as their primary purpose was near to 200 companies, but as of 2016, the number increased near to 400 companies.[22] Otherwise, as of 2016, near to 200 million Taiwan new dollars were invested or loaned to social enterprises. Obviously, social enterprises has gradually become another option for entrepreneurs and recognized by the investors or bankers.

III. Second phase : facilitating social innovation with government procurement (2017-now)

1. Continuously shaping the social enterprise movement

At the second phase, shaping the social enterprise movement is still vital for the concerned authority. For example, Small and Medium Enterprise Administration (SMEA) tries to hold hundreds of social enterprise meetups and various kinds of events around Taiwan to propaganda the concept of social enterprises, discover the potential social entrepreneurs, and at the meantime to network investors, entrepreneurs, incubators, mentors and those who would like to devote themselves into

---

[22] Small and Medium Enterprise Administration, Ministry of Economic Affairs, *Social Enterprise Action Plan* (2016), https://speakerdeck.com/audreyt/2016-dot-10-dot-18-she-hui-qi-ye-xing-dong-fang-an-bao-gao.

the social enterprise movement[23].

Otherwise, in order to encourage social enterprises to solve social problems and create social impacts with their innovative solutions and to form a sustainable ecosystem for the development of social enterprises, and eventually to drive the capability of social innovation in Taiwan, Social Innovation Lab was launched in Oct 2017[24]. The Lab enables social entrepreneurs or enterprises to locate at its actual physical space and access to mentorship, networking and funding that allow them to develop and commercialize their innovations or to make their early-stage enterprises thrive[25].

2. Support social enterprises to realize market opportunities

In addition to provide social enterprises with mentorship, networking and funding etc., several measures are taken to help social enterprises realize market opportunities, especially through the government procurement.

First, if a company has its social mission and would like to solve social or environment issues with its innovations, such company is able to apply for registration as a Social Enterprises. Those companies who meet the eligibility requirements will be listed on the Youth Startup website (https://sme.moeasmea.gov.tw/startup/modules/se/mod_case/) sponsored by SMEA and information regarding their social mission, products and services, and social impacts etc. will be disclosed to the public. However, it shall be noted that SMEA will unregularly organize advisory board

---

[23] https://sme.moeasmea.gov.tw/startup/modules/se/mod_confere/trackdone.php?tid=44 (accessed on 2 March 2018).

[24] http://host02.iiiedu.org.tw/socialinnovationlab/ (accessed on 2 March 2018); http://www.chinatimes.com/newspapers/20171019000170-260210 (accessed on 12 March 2018).

[25] http://host02.iiiedu.org.tw/socialinnovationlab/%E8%BC%94%E5%B0%8E%E6%96%B9%E5%BC%8F/ (accessed on 2 March 2018).

meetings to review the qualifications of applicants[26]. In 2016, there were 12 companies registered as social enterprises and listed on the website, and in 2017, 12 companies registered and listed[27].

Second, as the public sector is one of the biggest buyers in the market, the public sectors are encouraged to purchase services or products from social enterprises listed on the Youth Startup website (here referred as "listed social enterprises") under related government procurement regulations. Since 2017, SMEA holds a competition called "Buying power—social innovative products and services procurement awards event" each year. Government agencies, government-owned companies and private companies or associations, who purchase products and services provided by listed social enterprises, are qualified to participate in this competition. Those whose total amount of procurements counts over 1 million NT dollars will be awarded first prize.[28] In 2017, up to 60 public and private institutions purchased products and services provided by listed social enterprises. Among them, 15 institutions got first prize. In total, the amount of procurements of social innovative products and services counted over 83 million NT dollars.[29]

Finally, based on the article 93 of Government Procurement Act which prescribes that a government agency may execute an inter-entity supply contract with a supplier for the supply of products or services that are commonly needed by government agencies, public schools or government-owned enterprises, SMEA tries to figure out the common needs of the public sector so that it can initiate an inter-entity supply

---

[26] https://sme.moeasmea.gov.tw/startup/modules/se/mod_case/ (accessed on 2 March 2018).

[27] https://sme.moeasmea.gov.tw/startup/modules/se/mod_case/list.php?city=all&solutio n=all&regYear=2017&keyword= (accessed on 5 March 2018).

[28] https://sme.moeasmea.gov.tw/startup/modules/se/mod_bp/ (accessed on 5 March 2018).

[29] http://www.chinatimes.com/newspapers/20171214000152-260210 (accessed on 12 March 2018).

contract to help social enterprises access government market. In 2018, SMEA initiated inter-entity supply contracts with listed social enterprises to offer two kinds of professional learning courses, including social innovation services (ex: care at home, including accompanying to medical appointments, advice and guidance on health care etc.) and multiple experience programs (ex: agriculture experience program, cooking DIY program etc.) that are commonly needed by government agencies, public schools or government-owned enterprises.

IV. Removing the legal barriers and create incentives to social entrepreneurship

As the emergency of social enterprises, many legal issues were concerned and discussed by the scholars, legal experts and those involve in the social enterprises movement. Those discussed legal issues could be separated into two categories-one is how to remove the legal barriers to social entrepreneurship and the other one is how to create incentives to encourage the development of social enterprises. However, the most important or popular debate is how to define the legal definition of the social enterprise and its legal status.

1. *Removing the legal barriers to social entrepreneurship*

As mentioned above, the social enterprise could be a non-for-profit organization or for profit organization, but the choice of legal entity on the social enterprises is not such easy in the real world. The legal definition of social enterprise and its type of legal entity are often discussed and debated under the existing legal framework. In some countries, the social enterprises shall be only formed as a non-for-profit organization, but in some countries it is allowed to be formed as a for-profit organization or a hybrid organization. Otherwise, some countries would introduce regulations exclusively designed for social enterprises via drafting a new law or adjust the existing law to facilitate the development of social enterprises and to satisfy the demand of corporate governance. For example, according to Companies (Audit, Investigations and Community Enterprise) Act 2004 (here referred as Companies Act 2004), social enterprises in UK are able to be formed as a community interest company which derives from the idea of creating a public interest company[30] and is primarily a non-profit-distributing enterprise providing benefit to a community but still subject to the general framework of company law[31]. And, as requested by article 34 of Companies Act 2004, in every financial year a community interest company must prepare a community interest company report which explains its activities during the financial year.

The legal forms of social enterprises in Taiwan have also been discussed in these years.. For example, some members of Legislative Yuan used to introduce "Social Enterprise Development Bill" which is mainly based on the UK model in 2017[32]. The bill defines the social enterprise as a new form of legal entity which meets the following four requirements, including (1) it shall state its social mission in its charter, (2) it shall reinvest at least 50% of its surplus to realize the mission and no more than 30% of its surplus could be redistributed to its shareholders, (3) it shall generate at least 50% of its profit from the provision of its

---

[30] Analysis: The Rise and Rise of Community Interest Companies, Third Sector (June 1, 2015), http://www.thirdsector.co.uk/analysis-rise-rise-community-interest-companies/ governance/article/ 1348096 *quoted in* Michelle Cho, "Benefit Corporations in the United States and Community Interest Companies in the United Kingdom: Does Social Enterprise Actually Work?" *Northwestern Journal of International Law & Business* 37, no. 1 (2017): 149, 161, http://scholarlycommons.law.northwestern.edu/njilb/ vol37/iss1/4.

[31] Explanatory Notes of Companies (Audit, Investigations and Community Enterprise) Act 2004 , n.n. 189-191, http://www.legislation.gov.uk/ukpga/2004/27/notes/ division/5/2.

[32] https://lci.ly.gov.tw/LyLCEW/agenda1/02/pdf/09/03/13/LCEWA01_090313_00019. pdf (accessed on 12 March 2018).

products or services annually, and (4) it shall regularly disclose its social impact evaluation report and financial statements to the public. It shall be noted that the bill excludes political associations registered under Civil Associations Act from the definition of the social enterprise. However, the bill was not approved and did not enter into force.

Some members of Legislative Yuan proposed to amend the existing Company Act, mainly add a new chapter named "Public Interest Company" (here referred as the draft chapter) which was drafted with the reference to benefit corporations in US, to define the social enterprise and regulate its activities in 2016[33]. The draft chapter establishes a new type of company, the public interest company, for use by social enterprises wishing to operate as a company. If a social enterprise would like to register as a public interest company, it has to state its general public interest mission in its charter and such mission must satisfy the requirement that its business or operation has essential positive impact on the whole society or environment. As making business decision, the public interest company shall take the following stakeholders' interests into consideration, including shareholders, employees, contractors, consumers, communities and so on, instead of pursuing shareholders' interests only. At the end of financial year, the public interest company shall make and disclose its public interest report which explains its financial activities and how it realizes its public interest mission and the results. Since the draft charter is part of the Company Act, the public interest company is supposed to be subject to the general legal framework of the Act. However, this proposal was not with most members' support and therefore did not enter into force.

No matter it is to draft a new law or adjust the existing Company Act, the aim of both approaches is to give a definition to social enterprises

---

[33] https://lci.ly.gov.tw/LyLCEW/agenda1/02/pdf/09/02/15/LCEWA01_090215_00022.pdf (accessed on 12 March 2018).

and regulate such enterprise's activities. Both approaches emphasize that the social mission shall be state in the charter of an organization and pursuing shareholders' interests is not the only mission, but try to identify that a specific percentage of the surplus shall be reinvested in the implementation of its social mission or other stakeholders' interests shall be taken into account as making decisions. Also, both approaches take the same method to reach the goal of corporate governance, mainly by the way of disclosing the financial statement and actives or measures used to fulfill the planned social mission.

However, at the end of 2017, the Executive Yuan sent the Company (Amendment) Bill to Legislative Yuan[34]. Now the Company (Amendment) Bill is under discussion in Legislative Yuan. The Company Act was amended to create a friendly environment for innovation and startups, to improve the framework of corporate governance, to enhance the protection of stockholders' rights and so on, but it does not address too much on the issues of social enterprises. The Company (Amendment) Bill neither establishes a new type of company for use by social enterprises nor introduces a new chapter to regulate the activities of social enterprises. Otherwise, it does not define the social enterprises. It only mentions "as a company operates its business, it shall comply with regulations and codes of ethics, and are able to take measures to facilitate public interests to realize its social responsibility" in the article 1. Precisely speaking, it does not intend to response to the issues of social enterprises, but to state clearly that a company is encouraged to realize its social responsibility. However, some would prefer to state this article means to promote the development of social enterprises.

As mentioned in the explanation note of the article 1[35], it is a

---

[34] https://www.ey.gov.tw/news_Content2.aspx?n=F8BAEBE9491FC830&sms=99606A C2FCD53A3A&s=066DC33C5ABD6020 (accessed on 12 March 2018).
[35] Ibid.

prevalent view in many countries that being a member of this society, except perusing for profits, a company shall take the corporate social responsibility. The so-called corporate social responsibility means that a company shall comply with regulations; take ethic factors into consideration and therefore take good practices to do business; and make reasonable donations for the sake of public interests, humanism and charitable purposes. Also, Regulations Governing Information to be Published in Annual Reports of Public Companies prescribes a public company shall include the corporate governance report into its annual report, and the corporate governance report shall detail the state of the company's performance of corporate social responsibilities, including measures or practices regarding environment protection, community participation, contribution and services to the society, social and public interests, consumer protection, human rights, safety and health, and other corporate social responsibilities and activities, and the execution of these measures or practices. As a whole, companies in Taiwan have taken action to fulfill corporate social responsibilities. Therefore, the Company (Amendment) Bill includes the ideology that a company shall fulfill its social responsibilities.

However, it is doubted that a social enterprise is able to be registered as a company under the current Company Act or the Company (Amendment) Bill because article 1 of the Act and the bill both state that a company is "a corporate juristic person organized and incorporated in accordance with this Act for the purpose of profit making". And, as mentioned above, a social enterprise combines social good and entrepreneurship and tries to fulfill its social mission and at the meantime keep the financial sustainability. That is, the mission or purpose of the social enterprise is not only for profit making. However, it may be contrary to the rule set by the current Company Act or the Company (Amendment) Bill that requires the responsible person of a company to do his best to maximize shareholders' benefits and distribute the surplus to shareholders[36]. Prof. Ming Jye Huang mentioned that the Company Law is a purpose-neutral law. This means that the Company Law aims to provide various types of companies and therefore regulates those companies' activities, rather than their purpose. Therefore, Prof. Ming Jye Huang proposed the article 1 of Company Act which states profit-making is the purpose of the company shall be amended or deleted to allow a corporate juristic person to be organized and incorporated under this Act for other purposes.[37]

Though neither the framework of existing Company Act or the Company (Amendment) Bill proposed by Executive Yuan defines the social enterprises and regulates its activities, a social enterprise is able to be formed as a foundation which is a juristic person with the purpose for public interests under the Civil Code[38]. Otherwise, a social enterprise is able to be formed as a non-for-profit organization under the Civil Code and Civil Associations Act in Taiwan. Per the Civil Associations Act, there are three kinds of associations, including occupational associations, social associations, and political associations. A social enterprise is able to be formed as a social association which is "composed of individuals and (or) associations for the purpose of promoting culture, academic research,

---

[36] Sherry Y. Chen, "Legal structures for social enterprises- a study on the legislation of social enterprises in the United States," *Chung Cheng Financila and Economic Law Review* 14(2017): 1, 5-6; Per the first paragraph of article 23 of Company Act, the responsible person of a company shall have the loyalty and shall exercise the due care of a good administrator in conducting the business operation of the company; and if he/she has acted contrary to this provision, shall be liable for the damages to be sustained by the company there-from.

[37] Ming-Jye Huang, "Analysis on important issues of the newly-amended company act: focusing on company registration, affiliated enterprises and social enterprises," *The Taiwan Law Review* 268(2017): 30, 41.

[38] Per the article 59 of the Civil Code, a foundation shall get the permission from the authority concerned before registration. And, per the article 60 of the Civil Code, those who would like to establish a foundation shall draw up an act of endowment which shall detail the purpose of the foundation and the assets endowed to it.

medicine, health, religion, charity, sports, fellowship, social service, or other public welfare"[39], but it shall be noted that a social association is not a juristic person unless it is registered as a charitable corporation under the Civil Code[40].

2. Creating incentives to encourage the development of social enterprises

For the way social enterprises do business has positive impacts on the solving of social or environment issues and thus is able to inspire the social good and improve the quality of citizens' life, the development of social enterprises is worth encouraging. As mentioned above, many measures are taken to inspire the prevalence of social entrepreneurship and help the establishment and sustainable development of social enterprises. However, some measures will function better or result to more effective outcomes with mandatory regulations. Otherwise, the regulation could demonstrate the determination of the government to promote social enterprises.

For example, the Social Enterprise Promotion Act got into force in 2007 in South Korea. This Act aims to support for the establishment and operation of social enterprises and the promotion of social enterprises because of the contribution made by social enterprises, including creating new jobs and providing social services that are originally offered by few suppliers or not offered in the market to tackle social or environment problems[41]. This act also claims measures Korea government could take, including establishing a basic plan for promotion of social enterprise[42],

---

[39] Civil Associations Act §39.

[40] Civil Code §46; Per the article 45 and 46 of the Civil Code, there are two types of corporation, one is the business corporation whose purpose is for profit-making, and the other one is the charitable corporation whose purpose is for public interests.

[41] Social Enterprise Promotion Act §1 (Korea).

[42] Ibid., at 5.

granting certification of social enterprises[43], providing support etc. Such supports to social enterprises are in many forms, including (1) provision of professional advice and information[44], (2) education and training to cultivate the professional capabilities and abilities needed for the establishment and operation of social enterprises[45], (3) subsidies or loans for land purchase expenses, facility expenses and so on[46], (4) financial support, such as for labor costs, operating expenses, consultation expenses and so on[47], (5) promotion of the preferential purchase of the goods and services produced by social enterprise[48]...etc.

In Taiwan, SMEA is considering amending the Act for Development of Small and Medium Enterprises to deal with the impacts from the rapid change of the business environment on small and medium enterprises and the needs of startups and social enterprises. As mentioned above, the social entrepreneurship was inspired and hundreds of social enterprises were established. How to help social enterprises realize their market opportunities to satisfy the needs of financial sustainability and fulfill their social missions at the same time is essential vital. Therefore, the priority procurement of services or products provided by social innovation enterprises is proposed to help such enterprises scale their business.

According to the draft article, the follow subjects shall preferentially purchase the services or products provided by social innovation enterprises certificated by the concerned authority under a reasonable price and lower than a certain budget amount, but such budget amount

---

[43] Ibid., at 7.

[44] Ibid., at 10.

[45] Ibid., at 10-2.

[46] Ibid., at 11.

[47] Ibid., at 14.

[48] Ibid., at 12.

is not limited if the procurement is processed in form of an inter-entity supply contract.

i.   Public agencies
ii. Public schools
iii. Public business agencies
iv. Institutions, associations, and private schools that receive subsides or grants from public agencies

This measure allows certificated social innovation enterprises to access government customers more easily and the achievement that their products or services are adopted by the government could be a reference case as they would like to access other domestic or abroad customers. In other words, government's purchase may make their products or services more persuasive. Thus, certificated social innovation enterprises are more easily to scale and replicate their business.

However, it is no doubt that further rules or regulations are needed in the near future in order to implement this article. And, some issues are needed to be clarified in advance. For example, a reasonable price and a certain budget amount are needed to be specified. Most important of all, the definition of social innovate enterprises must be given and the requirements or qualifications which an enterprise needs to meet in order to get certification from the concerned authority shall be established.

V. Conclusion : Future Challenges

It has been many years since the first social enterprise action plan was proposed and implemented. Many measures have been taken in the past few years. And, those legal issues that would hobble or foster the development of social enterprises were discussed and amendments are proposed. It is found that policies and measures have aroused the attention to the social enterprises. Hundreds of social enterprises were established and millions of dollars were invested or loaned to social enterprises. Obviously, the concept of social enterprises is gradually accepted by entrepreneurs, investors, bankers and so on.

As the concept of social enterprises is more understood by the public and more people would like to devote themselves into establishing and operation a social enterprise, how to efficiently integrate the resources from public and private sectors to help social enterprises scale and replicate their business and establish a successful social entrepreneurship model to attract more young people to the social enterprises movement deserves to be given attention. Otherwise, bills that aim to encourage the establishment of social enterprise and help them scale up were proposed, but are still not approved by the Legislative Yuan. Therefore, in the near future, it may be a concern for the government to persuade the public and members of Legislative Yuan to support those bills. Also, as those bills are reviewed by the public and the Legislative Yuan, more details are needed to be clarified as mentioned above and tasks of drafting enforcement rules or regulations may be needed to be processed in the same time in order to meet the public's expectation and interest.

Nachhaltige Entwicklung und Grüne Wirtschaft : Entwicklung und Ergebnisse im Bereich des Energiesektor

Wilson Hong

Project Manager, Science & Technology Law Institute,
Institute for Information Industry

I. Einleitung

Die EU hat 2014 eine Richtlinie zur Erweiterung der Berichterstattung von großen kapitalmarktorientierten Unternehmen, Kreditinstituten, Finanzdienstleistungsinstituten und Versicherungsunternehmen verabschiedet (sog. CSR-Richtlinie). Ziel der Richtlinie ist es, die Transparenz über ökologische und soziale Aspekte von Unternehmen in der EU zu erhöhen. Dabei geht es um Informationen zu Umwelt-, Sozial- und Arbeitnehmerbelange sowie die Achtung der Menschenrechte und die Bekämpfung von Korruption und Bestechung. Deutschland hat deshalb 2017 die Richtlinie in nationales Recht umgesetzt (CSR-Richtlinie-Umsetzungsgesetz), welches ab dem Geschäftsjahr 2017 anwendbar ist.[1] Entsprechend müssen alle betroffene Unternehmen 2018 sämtliche relevanten Daten und Kennzahlen für das Jahr 2017 veröffentlichen. Außerdem hat die Europäischen Kommission ihre Leitlinien für die Offenlegung nichtfinanzieller Informationen veröffentlicht, um betroffenen Unternehmen eine unverbindliche Hilfestellung für die

---

[1] Neue CSR-Berichtspflicht für Unternehmen ab 2017, Bundesministerium Für Arbeit Und Soziales[BMAS], http://www.csr-in-deutschland.de/DE/Politik/CSR-national/ Aktivitaeten-der-Bundesregierung/CSR-Berichtspflichten/csr-berichtspflichten.html (Letzter Abruf: 30/04/2018).

Berichterstattung zu bieten.[2] Der wichtigste Teil der CSR-Berichtspflicht von Unternehmen ist die Äußerung der Umweltbelange, z.B. die Angaben zu Treibhausgasemissionen, zum Wasserverbrauch, zur Luftverschmutzung, zur Nutzung von erneuerbaren und nicht erneuerbaren Energien oder zum Schutz der biologischen Vielfalt. Wird die Berichtspflicht von den Unternehmen erfüllt, trägt dies zu einer nachhaltigen Entwicklung als auch zum Ziel der Energiewende bei.

Aus politischer Sicht hat sich die deutsche Energiepolitik rasend entwickelt und die Regierung sich frühzeitig um die Energiewende bemüht. Hierbei standen drei Themenschwerpunkte im Vordergrund: raus aus den konventionellen, rein in die erneuerbaren Energien und mehr Energieeffizienz.[3] Eben dieser grundlegende Wandel ist der Kern der Energiewende. Die Energieversorgung in Deutschland soll umweltverträglich und weitgehend klimaneutral werden. Auf welche Weise Unternehmen zu diesen Zielen beitragen, spielt in die Zukunft ein groß Rolle. Einige der daraus resultierenden Themen werde ich im Folgenden ansprechen. Darüber hinaus sollen in diesem Aufsatz ebenfalls die Energiewende in Taiwan und wie Unternehmen ihre Verantwortung für nachhaltige Entwicklung in die Praxis umsetzen, diskutiert werden.

Unternehmen, die unter die Berichtspflicht fallen, müssen sich zu folgenden Themen äußern: Umweltbelange[4], Arbeitnehmerbelange[5],

---

[2] Communication from the Commission—Guidelines on non-financial reporting (methodology for reporting non-financial information, C/2017/4234), O.J. (2017 215), p. 1-20.

[3] P. Ulrich & U. Lehr, Erneuerbar beschäftigt in den Bundesländern, Bundesministerium Für Wirtschaft Und Energie[BMWi], 29. März 2018, https://www.bundesregierung.de/Content/Infomaterial/BMWI/erneuerbar-beschaeftigt-in-den-bundeslaendern_687590.html?view=trackDownload (Letzter Abruf: 30/04/2018).

[4] z.B. Angaben zu Treibhausgasemissionen, zum Wasserverbrauch, zur Luftverschmutzung, zur Nutzung von erneuerbaren und nicht erneuerbaren Energien oder zum Schutz der biologischen Vielfalt.

[5] z.B. Angaben zu Maßnahmen, die zur Gewährleistung der Geschlechtergleichstellung ergriffen wurden, zu Arbeitsbedingungen, zur Achtung der Rechte der

Sozialbelange[6], Menschenrechte[7], die Bekämpfung von Korruption und Bestechung.

II. CSR und Energiewende in Deutschland

1. Energiewende in Deutschland

Wie bereits Eingangs erwähnt, hat Deutschland seine Energiepolitik zügig in die Wege geleitet und sich im Vergleich zu anderen Industrienationen vorzeitig um die „Energiewende" bemüht. Mittlerweile stammt fast ein Drittel des Stroms aus Wind, Sonne, Wasser oder Biomasse, womit erneuerbare Energien mittlerweile eine sehr wichtige Stromquelle in Deutschland darstellen.

Der Begriff Energiewende bezeichnet den Umstieg der Energieversorgung von fossilen und Kernbrennstoffen auf erneuerbare Energien. Hauptziel der Energiewende ist die Realisierung einer nachhaltigen Energieversorgung in den drei Sektoren Strom, Wärme und Mobilität. Mit der Implementierung des Nachhaltigkeitsgedankens soll somit eine Verbesserung im Nachhaltigkeits-Dreieck Ökonomie – Gesellschaft – Ökologie hergestellt werden und zugleich eine globale und Generationen übergreifende Solidarität erreicht werden.[8] Dabei geht es auch um den Begriff Nachhaltigkeit, da Lösungen für die dringlich gewordenen Umweltprobleme gefunden werden müssen. Hiermit geht auch die Forderung nach einem Umdenken in der Wirtschaft einher.

Arbeitnehmerinnen und Arbeitnehmer sowie der Gewerkschaften, zum Gesundheitsschutz oder zur Sicherheit am Arbeitsplatz.

[6] z.B. Angaben zum Dialog auf kommunaler oder regionaler Ebene oder zur Sicherstellung des Schutzes und der Entwicklung lokaler Gemeinschaften ergriffenen Maßnahmen.

[7] z.B. Angaben zur Verhinderung von Menschenrechtsverletzungen.

[8] Valentin Crastan: Elektrische Energieversorgung 2, 2012, S. 20.

Die deutsche Regierung hat sich das Ziel der Energiewende bis zum Jahr 2050 gesetzt. Bis zu diesem Zeitpunkt soll die Energie hauptsächlich aus regenerativen Quellen, wie Wind- und Wasserkraft, Sonnenenergie, Geothermie oder nachwachsenden Rohstoffen bezogen werden. Es kann somit von grüner Energie gesprochen werden.die politischen Ziele bilden den Rahmen für den Umbau der Energieversorgung. Sie umfassen:[9]

- die Klimaziele, einschließlich einer Senkung der Treibhausgasemissionen um 40 Prozent bis zum Jahr 2020,
- den Ausstieg aus der Nutzung der Kernenergie zur Stromerzeugung bis zum Jahr 2022 sowie
- die Sicherstellung von Wettbewerbsfähigkeit und Versorgungssicherheit.

Erneuerbare Energie ist eine der wichtigsten Stromquellen in Deutschland und ihr Ausbau eine zentrale Säule der Energiewende. Die Stromversorgung in Deutschland wird Jahr für Jahr „grüner" - der Beitrag der erneuerbaren Energien wächst beständig. Im Jahr 2016 haben die erneuerbaren Energiequellen bereits 29 Prozent zur Bruttostromerzeugung (insgesamt in Deutschland erzeugte Strommenge) beigetragen. Die wachsende Bedeutung von erneuerbaren Energien im Strombereich ist im Wesentlichen auf das Erneuerbare-Energien-Gesetz (EEG) zurückzuführen. Seit der Einführung des EEG ist der Anteil der erneuerbaren Energien am Bruttostromverbrauch (insgesamt in Deutschland verbrauchte elektrische Energie) von rund sechs Prozent im Jahr 2000 auf 31,5 Prozent im Jahr 2016 gestiegen. Bis zum Jahr 2025 sollen 40 bis 45 Prozent des in Deutschland verbrauchten Stroms aus erneuerbaren Energien stammen.[10]

---

[9] BMWi, Fünfter Monitoring-Bericht zur Energiewende, 2015, S. 8, https://www.bmwi.de/Redaktion/DE/Publikationen/Energie/fuenfter-monitoring-bericht-energie-der-zukunft.pdf?__blob=publicationFile&v=19 (Letzter Abruf: 30/04/2018).

[10] Erneuerbare Energien, BMWi, https://www.bmwi.de/Redaktion/DE/Dossier/

Deutschlands Energie wird nicht nur immer grüner, man verbraucht sie auch immer sparsamer. Der Schwerpunkt „Zweites Instrument" der Energiewende ist die Verringerung des Energieverbrauchs durch eine sparsame und effiziente Nutzung der Energie.[11] Bis zum Jahr 2020 soll der Primärenergieverbrauch in Deutschland gegenüber dem Jahr 2008 um 20 Prozent sinken. Um hier notwendige Fortschritte zu erzielen, hat die Bundesregierung 2014 den Nationalen Aktionsplan Energieeffizienz (NAPE)[12] zur weiteren Steigerung der Energieeffizienz beschlossen. Die Grundsätze des NAPE sind „Informieren, fördern, fordern".[13] Damit will Deutschland alle gesellschaftlichen Akteure dazu motivieren, Energie sparsamer zu nutzen. Denn die Energieeffizienz ist eine gesamtgesellschaftliche Aufgabe. Doch: Nur wenn Bürgerinnen und Bürger, Unternehmen und Kommunen wissen, wo ihre Einsparpotentiale konkret liegen, können sie sich energieeffizient verhalten. Mit dem NAPE wird daher einen Fokus auf den Ausbau des Informations- und Beratungsangebots gelegt. Einen weiteren Schwerpunkt bildet die gezielte und innovative Förderung von Effizienzinvestitionen: So umfasst der NAPE neben einer Aufstockung und Erweiterung des erfolgreichen CO_2-Gebäudesanierungsprogrammes, beispielsweise ein neuartiges wettbewerbliches Ausschreibungsmodell für Stromeffizienz und ein Förderprogramm zur Abwärmevermeidung und Abwärmenutzung. Der dritte Grundsatz des NAPE lautet "Fordern": Der Aktionsplan verpflichtet große Unternehmen zu Energieaudits und etabliert Standards für Neuanlagen und Neubauten. Unternehmen sollen zudem

---

erneuerbare-energien.html (Letzter Abruf: 30/04/2018).

[11] Deutschland macht's effizient, https://www.bmwi.de/Redaktion/DE/Dossier/energieeffizienz.html (Letzter Abruf: 30/04/2018)

[12] Der Nationale Aktionsplan Energieeffizienz (NAPE), BMWi, 2014, https://www.bmwi.de/Redaktion/DE/Downloads/M-O/nationaler-aktionsplan-energieeffizienz-nape.pdf?__blob=publicationFile&v=4 (Letzter Abruf: 30/04/2018).

[13] aaO.

eigenverantwortlich in bis zu 500 Energieeffizienznetzwerken gemeinsame Effizienzziele definieren und diese in der Gruppe umsetzen.

2. Energiewende in Unternehmen

Die Steigerung der Energieeffizienz ist eines der wichtigsten und damit für den Erfolg kritischen Handlungsfelder der Energiewende. Für Unternehmen ist die Energieeffizienz ein wichtiger Wettbewerbsfaktor. Durch den Einsatz von Energieeffizienztechnologien lassen sich im beträchtlichen Ausmaß Einsparungen beim Energieverbrauch, bei den CO_2-Emissionen und bei den Energiekosten erzielen. Deutschland fördert zum einen konkrete Effizienzmaßnahmen in Unternehmen, zum anderen unterstützt es durch die Förderung von Energieberatungsangeboten in Form von Energiediagnosen oder regt den Erfahrungsaustausch zwischen Unternehmen durch die Förderung überbetrieblicher Energieeffizienztische an. Die Vorteile von Effizienztechnologien sind immer noch zu wenig bekannt und die vorhandenen Einsparpotentiale werden oftmals unterschätzt. Aus diesem Grund unterstützt das Bundesministerium für Wirtschaft und Energie (BMWi) Unternehmen dabei, ihre Energiebilanz zu verbessern - unter anderem über verschiedene Förderprogramme zur individuellen Energieberatung.[14]

Speziell an Unternehmen richten sich Projekte wie die Klimaschutzpartnerschaft mit Industrie- und Handelskammern und das Rationalisierungs- und Innovationszentrum der Deutschen Wirtschaft. Gesetzliche Auflagen sollen die Bemühungen zu mehr Energieeffizienz in der Wirtschaft flankieren.[15] Die Klimaschutzpartnerschaft mit

---

[14] Energieeffizienz in Unternehmen, BMWi, https://www.bmwi.de/Redaktion/DE/Publikationen/Energie/energieeffizienz-in-unternehmen.pdf?__blob=publicationFile&v=8 (Letzter Abruf: 30/04/2018).

[15] Energieeffizienz und Energiesparen, Bundesregierung, https://www.bundesregierung.de/Content/DE/StatischeSeiten/Breg/Energiekonzept/Fragen-Antworten/4_

Industrie- und Handelskammern hat es sich zum Ziel gesetzt, diese gerade auch in mittelständischen Unternehmen breit vorhandenen, kostengünstigen Potenziale für Klimaschutz und Energieeffizienz stärker zu erschließen. Innovative Technologien sollen in der betrieblichen Praxis engagiert vorangetrieben werden. Im Rahmen der Initiative Energieeffizienz Mittelstand erhalten Betriebe Zuschüsse zu einer Erst- oder Detailberatung in Höhe von 80 beziehungsweise 60 Prozent der Kosten.

Seit dem 1. Oktober 2012 fördert die Bundesregierung darüber hinaus Investitionen, die den Einsatz hocheffizienter Querschnitttechnologien in kleinen und mittleren Unternehmen als Ersatz für veraltete Technik zum Inhalt haben. Die Zuschüsse betragen bis zu 30 Prozent des förderfähigen Investitionsvolumens.

Im Sommer 2012 hat die Bundesregierung einen Gesetzentwurf im Steuerrecht verabschiedet. Mit der Neuregelung des so genannten Spitzenausgleichs bei der Strom- und Energiesteuer erhalten Unternehmen diesen Ausgleich nur noch dann, wenn sie Energie- oder Umweltmanagement-Systeme einführen.

Mit der Novelle des Kraft-Wärme-Kopplungsgesetzes hat die Bundesregierung 2012 die Abwärmenutzung der Nutzung von KWK-Wärme gleichgestellt. Im Marktanreizprogramm sind seit August 2012 auch Wärmenetze, die Abwärme nutzen, förderfähig. Damit sollen die großen vorhandenen Potenziale zur Energieeinsparung durch Abwärmenutzung effizienter ausgeschöftwerden.

Deutschlandweit haben sich 136 Energieeffizienz-Netzwerke (Stand: Oktober 2017) gegründet. Über 1.300 Unternehmen in diesen Netzwerken profitieren vom Knowhow, dem Erfahrungsaustausch und von neuen Impulsen für technische Innovationen. Gemeinsam mit einem

Energiesparen-Energieeffizienz/4-Energiesparen-Energieeffizienz.html (Letzter Abruf: 30/04/2018).

Energieberater spüren sie Einsparpotenziale im Betrieb auf und setzen wirtschaftlich lohnende Effizienzmaßnahmen gezielt um. Sie steigern ihre Energieeffizienz, senken zudem ihre Energiekosten, verbessern dadurch die Wettbewerbsfähigkeit und leisten einen wichtigen Beitrag zum Klimaschutz. Die Initiative Energieeffizienz-Netzwerke ist eine Maßnahme des Nationalen Aktionsplans Energieeffizienz (NAPE) der Bundesregierung und startete im Dezember 2014. Das Ziel der von den 22 Wirtschaftsverbänden gemeinsam mit dem Bundeswirtschafts- und Bundesumweltministerium getragenen Initiative ist, dass sich 500 Effizienz-Netzwerke etablieren und der CO_2-Ausstoß insgesamt um fünf Millionen Tonnen reduziert wird. Auswertungen von Energieeffizienz-Netzwerken zeigen: Netzwerkpartner erhöhen ihre Energieeffizienz im Schnitt doppelt so schnell wie vergleichbare Unternehmen. Drei von vier Teilnehmern sind mit den Ergebnissen der Netzwerkarbeit sehr zufrieden. Davon würden 94 Prozent auch anderen Unternehmen die Teilnahme an einem Netzwerk aktiv weiterempfehlen.[16]

Durch die Energiewende verändert sich die Struktur der Energieversorgung. Der Anteil der volatilen erneuerbaren Energie an der Stromerzeugung, insbesondere Windkraft und Photovoltaik, steigt zunehmend. Dafür muss das gesamte Energiesystem flexibler werden. Deshalb werden z.B. ausreichend flexible Kraftwerke benötigt, die dann Strom produzieren, wenn der Wind nicht in ausreichendem Maße weht oder die Sonne nicht scheint. Darüber hinaus kann die Flexibilisierung der Stromnachfrage über das sogenannte Demand-Side-Management (DSM) einen Beitrag leisten. Hier wird die Stromnachfrage auf Zeiten verschoben, in denen ausreichend Strom aus erneuerbaren Energien zur Verfügung steht. Nach bisherigen Erkenntnissen kann vor allem das Demand-Side-Management von Unternehmen einen relevanten Beitrag zur Flexibilisierung des Stromsystems leisten. Mit Unterstützung durch

---

[16] aaO.

das Bundesministerium für Wirtschaft und Energie hat die Deutsche Energie-Agentur (dena) ein Pilotprojekt zur Erschließung von DSM-Potentialen in baden-württembergischen Unternehmen initiiert. Ziel des Projekts ist es, die existierenden DSM-Potentiale in den Unternehmen zu analysieren und einen Beitrag zu deren Nutzbarmachung zu leisten.

3. Unternehmen und CSR-Berichtpflicht

Der Umbau des Energiesystems, das vorrangig auf den erneuerbaren Energien basiert, bedeutet eine große Umstellung für die Unternehmen. Dieser Umbau kann nur gelingen, wenn die Unternehmen bei der Ausgestaltung der Energiewende einerseits mitgenommen werden und sich andererseits auch aktiv einbringen.[17] Infolgedessen will die Regierung Unternehmen ganz gezielt bei der Entwicklung neuer Geschäftsmodelle oder beim Energiesparen unterstützen. Dies geschieht zum einen durch Förderprogramme, als auch durch Informationsaustausch und Öffentlichkeitsarbeit. Dies soll die Unternehmen selbst befähigen, eine proaktive Rolle einzunehmen und letztlich auch von der Energiewende zu profitieren.

III. CSR und Energiewende in Taiwan

1. Hintergrund

Taiwan hat seine Energiewende gestartet. Im Jahren 2016 hat die Regierung beschlossen den Übergang zu einer nuklearfreien Heimat zu vollziehen und den umweltfreundlichen Energiesektor zu fördern. Entsprechend wurde bis zum Jahr 2025 das Ziel gesetzt, 20 Prozent der Elektrizität des Landes mit erneuerbaren Energiequellen zu erzeugen

---

[17] Untersteller F. (2016) CSR und Energiewirtschaft aus baden-württembergischer Perspektive. In: Hildebrandt A., Landhäußer W. (eds) CSR und Energiewirtschaft. Management-Reihe Corporate Social Responsibility.

und dadurch die hohen Energieimporte zu senken. Dafür investiert die Regierung über 34,37 Milliarden Euro in den Ausbau der Solarenergie. Zunächst wird vor allem die Kapazität der Solarenergie erweitert. Insgesamt soll der Ausbau in den nächsten neun Jahren die installierte Solarenergieleistung auf 20 Gigawatt (GW) steigern. Gemessen an der aktuellen erneuerbaren Kraftwerksleistung ist dieser Wert enorm: Im Jahr 2014 betrug die gesamte Leistung aller Kraftwerke etwas mehr als 41,100 GW. Davon entfiel mit knapp 2,1 GW nur etwas über fünf Prozent auf erneuerbare Energien.[18]

Am 27. Oktober 2016 hat die Regierung von Taiwan das Industrielle Innovationsprogramm für grüne Energietechnologien vorgelegt, um Taiwans Energiestruktur zu transformieren und das zuvor angesprochene Ziel bis zum Jahr 2025 zu erreichen.[19] Ein weiteres Ziel des Programms für erneuerbare Energie besteht darin, Taiwans Selbstversorgungsrate anzuheben, die derzeit bei lediglich 3 Prozent liegt.

Das Programm wird umweltfreundliche Energietechnologien fördern und Taiwans Energiewende und wirtschaftliche Entwicklung vorantreiben. Das Programm konzentriert sich auf Energieerzeugung, Energiespeicherung, Energieeinsparung und Systemintegration. Dafür räumte man verschiedenen Initiativen Priorität ein, darunter ein Zweijahresplan zur Förderung der Sonnenenergie, ein Vierjahresplan zur Förderung der Windenergie, ein Projekt für Photovoltaik-Dachfläche, ein Pilotprogramm für Smart-Meter, und ein Testfeld für die Green Energy Science City „Shalun", welche derzeit entwickelt wird. Insgesamt zielt das Programm darauf ab, Binnennachfrage nach Strom zu decken, wichtige Marktnischen zu eröffnen, umfangreiche Investitionen, in- und

---

[18] KUO, Taiwan strebt 20 Prozent erneuerbare Energie an, 14.10.2016, https://taiwanheute.tw/news.php?unit=117,118&post=104125 (Letzter Abruf: 30/04/2018)

[19] Executive Yuan(R.O.C), Energy transformation: Industrial innovation for green energy technologies, https://english.ey.gov.tw/News_Hot_Topic.aspx?n=59DEADADC8768 A6B&sms=BC2B3196A2DFE029 (Letzter Abruf: 30/04/2018).

ausländischen Investoren anzuziehen und hochwertige Arbeitsplätze für 32.000 Menschen zu schaffen.

2. *Änderung des Elektrizitätsgesetzes und Beseitigung regulatorischer und institutioneller Hindernisse*

Die Entwicklung grüner Energiequellen und die Umgestaltung des bestehenden Energiemodells Taiwans sind derzeit die wichtigsten politischen Prioritäten, um das grundlegende Umweltrecht vollständig umzusetzen. Das bedeutet, dass Taiwan schrittweise ein Atomenergie freies Land wird und die im Gesetz zur Reduzierung und zum Management von Treibhausgasen festgelegten Ziele erreicht werden, indem die Treibhausgasemission bis zum Jahr 2050 auf 50 Prozent des Niveaus von 2005 gesenkt wird.

Um einer passenden Umgebung für die Erzeugung von Strom aus grünen Quellen zu schaffen, hat das Wirtschaftsministerium im Jahr 2017 einen zweistufigen Plan zur Änderung des Elektrizitätsgesetzes vorgelegt. Änderungen der ersten Stufe fördern die Liberalisierung des grünen Energiemarkts und den offenen Zugang zu den Stromübertragungs- und Stromverteilungsnetzen. Nachdem die Systeme und Mechanismen der ersten Stufe gut funktionieren, werden die Änderungen der zweiten Stufe folgen. Die schrittweise vonstattengehende Reform der Energieindustrie und die Transformation des inländischen Energiemodells soll zu einer vollständigen Liberalisierung der Energieindustrie und gleichzeitig zur Entwicklung der grünen Industrien in Taiwan führen.

Außerdem wurde das „National Renewable Energy Certification Center" am 12. Juni 2017 eröffnet, um einen vertrauenswürdigen Standard zur Zertifizierung von erneuerbaren Energien zu etablieren. Darüber hinaus wurde bereits ein großer Fortschritt im Bereich erneuerbare Energien erzielt: Der Exekutiv-Yuan hat am 11. Januar 2018 einen Änderungsentwurf zum Erneuerbare-Energien-Entwicklungsgesetz verabschiedet. Hierbei wurde das Ziel die erneuerbaren Energien auf 20

Prozent zu steigern zusätzlich in einem Gesetzeswerk zusammengefasst und die Verantwortlichkeiten der großen Stromverbraucher für saubere Energie definiert.

Grüne Energietechnologien sind der neue Motor für Taiwans Energiewende und wirtschaftliche Entwicklung. Die Regierung wird weiterhin die industrielle Innovation und das Wachstum für grüne Energietechnologie und verwandte Industrien fördern, während sie ausländische Investoren anzieht und neue Arbeitsplätze für lokale Gemeinschaften schafft. Taiwan wird auch seine Energiestruktur so umgestalten, dass es seine Ziele für Energiesicherheit, ökologische Nachhaltigkeit und eine grüne Wirtschaft fördert.

3. *"Taiwan Renewable Energy Certificate"*

Das erste "Taiwan Renewable Energy Certificate" (T-REC) wurde durch das Bureau of Standards, Metrology and Inspection, Ministry of Economic Affairs (MOEA) ausgegeben und markierte den Beginn einer neuen Ära für die erneuerbaren Energien mit einer festen Finanzierung.

Um nachzuweisen, dass der verwendete Strom aus erneuerbaren Energiequellen stammt, wurde der "Taiwan Renewable Energy Certificate" Mechanismus von der Regierung entwickelt. T-REC kann somit als Identifikationskarte für erneuerbare Energien verwendet werden. Eine weitere Verwendungsweise ist die Verfolgung und Verwaltung der Nutzung oder des Kaufs von Strom aus erneuerbaren Energien. Die Herausgabe des ersten T-REC durch das „Bureau of Standards, Metrology and Inspection (BSMI) MOEA" wurde am 19. Mai 2017 veranlasst. Jedes T-REC repräsentiert 1000 kWh erneuerbarer Elektrizität. Bis zum 28. Feb. 2018 wurden insgesamt 19.625 T-REC verliehen. Damit wird Taiwan in die neue Ära der Nutzung erneuerbarer Energien eintreten. Um die Transformation der Energiestruktur zu erreichen, hat die Regierung dem BSMI beauftragt, den Zertifizierungsmechanismus für erneuerbare Energien als Reaktion auf die Bedürfnisse der Industrie zu entwickeln.

Am 12. Juni 2017 öffnete das Nationale Zertifizierungszentrum für erneuerbare Energien (T-REC Center). Abgesehen von dem zuvor erwähnten Elektrizitätsgesetz, spielt der Einrichtung des T-REC Center bei der Energiewende Taiwans eine übergeordnete Rolle. T-REC Center hat nicht nur den zuvor aufgeführten Mechanismus eingerichtet, sonder auch aus den Erfahrung von Europa, den Vereinigten Staaten, Japan und anderen Ländern gelernt, um den T-REC-Mechanismus zu vervollständigen. Inzwischen hat das T-REC Center Kontakt mit der Industrie aufgenommen, um Meinungen, Anerkennungen und Bereitschaft zur Teilnahme zu erhalten. Außerdem wurde ein strenger Überprüfungsmechanismus eingerichtet. Die Erneuerbare-Energien-Anlagen müssen ein strenges Verfahren zur Überprüfung der Ausrüstung durchlaufen, um die tatsächliche Stromerzeugungsmenge zu bestätigen. Erst hierdurch wird die Glaubwürdigkeit des T-RECs geschaffen. Das BSMI weist darauf hin, dass viele taiwanesische Unternehmen und lokale Regierungen auf die Anwendung von T-REC mit Begeistert reagiert haben. Kommunale Regierung, wie Pingtung, Yunlin und Changhua haben in ihre alle möglichen Gebiete, die für die Entwicklung Erneuerbare-Energien geeignet sind, inventarisiert. Andere Unternehmen, wie Apple und Cathay Financial Holdings sind an Teilnahme am T-REC-Programm für Corporate Social Responsibility (CSR) interessiert, um Teil der internationalen grünen Lieferkette zu werden. Als Reaktion auf den weltweiten Trend zur Entwicklung erneuerbarer Energien haben sich Unternehmen verpflichtet, erneuerbare Energien zu nutzen. Diese Thematik stellt für die Regierungen ein wichtiges Thema für die nachhaltige Entwicklung der Erde dar. Daher soll durch konzertierte Bemühungen aller Sektoren ein glaubwürdiger Zertifizierungsmechanismus für erneuerbare Energien etabliert werden.

4. *Änderung des Erneuerbare-Energien-Entwicklungsgesetz*

Das Kabinett hat am 11. Jan. 2018 Gesetzesentwürfe zum Erneuerbare-Energien-Entwicklungsgesetz verabschiedet. Der Entwurf wird nun dem Legislativ-Yuan zum Diskutieren und Abstimmen vorgelegt. Die Regierung will die Förderung aller damit verbundenen Politik und Mechanismen aktiv vorantreiben, um den Anteil der erneuerbaren Energien an Taiwans Stromversorgung bis 2025 auf 20% zu erhöhen. Die Überarbeitung des Erneuerbare-Energien-Entwicklungsgesetzes wurden so gestaltet, dass drei Hauptziele erreicht werden: Erschließung neuer Quellen erneuerbarer Energie, Diversifizierung des Marktes und Vereinfachung der damit verbundenen Arbeit. Zu den notwendigen Maßnahmen gehören die Steuerung des Angebots und die Erhöhung der Anzahl erneuerbarer Energieanlagen, die Erweiterung des Geltungsbereichs erneuerbarer Energien und der Schutz der vielfältigen Nutzung von Ökostrom sowie die Vereinfachung der Antragsverfahren, die Erhöhung der Flexibilität bei Netzanschlüssen und die Bereitstellung von Lösungen für das Problem Überkapazitäten an den Zubringerleitungen von Taipower.

IV. Fazit

Deutschland hat beschlossen, die Energiewende konsequent umzusetzen und seine Politik stärker am Prinzip der Nachhaltigkeit auszurichten. Hierfür war ein schrittweises Vorgehen von Bedeutung. Die deutsche Regierung hat sich das Ziel der Energiewende gesetzt und das EEG eingeführt. Dies führte dazu, dass der Anteil der erneuerbaren Energien am Bruttostromverbrauch von rund sechs Prozent im Jahr 2000 auf 31,5 Prozent im Jahr 2016 gestiegen ist. Außerdem ist die Steigerung der Energieeffizienz eines der wichtigsten und damit für den allgemeinen Erfolg kritischen Handlungsfelder der Energiewende. Mit Einführung der Effizienztechnologie werden die Unternehmen selbst befähigt, eine proaktive Rolle einzunehmen und letztlich von der Energiewende zu profitieren. Die Unternehmen sind in der Lage ihre Corporate Social Responsibility durchzuführen. Letztendlich werden die Unternehmen durch diese Maßnahmen nachhaltiger und die Energie wird grüner.

Taiwan treibt inzwischen ebenfalls die Energiewende voran. Auch hier können die Unternehmen daran teilnehmen und davon profitieren. Mit der Änderung des Elektrizitätsgesetzes und des Erneuerbare-Energien-Entwicklungsgesetz erhalten die Unternehmen die Chance gemeinsam mit der Regierung die Energiewende aktiv mitzugestalten.